NEW SACRED ARCHITECTURE

For Memère

Published in 2004 by
Laurence King Publishing Ltd
71 Great Russell Street
London WC1B 3BP
T +44 (0)20 7430 8850
F +44 (0)20 7430 8880
E enquiries@laurenceking.co.uk
www.laurenceking.co.uk

Copyright © 2004

Text © 2004 Phyllis Richardson

All rights reserved. No part of this publication may be reproduced or transmitted in any form or by any means, electronic or mechanical, including photocopy, recording or any information retrieval system, without permission in writing from the publisher.

A catalogue record for this book is available from the British Library.

ISBN 1 85669 384 8

Printed in China

Designed by Mark Vernon-Jones

NEW SACRED ARCHITECTURE

Phyllis Richardson

Laurence King Publishing

CONTENTS

INTRODUCTION A LEGACY OF INSPIRED INNOVATION 6

1 NEW TRADITIONS EXPERIMENTING WITH FORM 16

01 CHAPEL OF ST IGNATIUS 18
Seattle, Washington, USA, Steven Holl Architects, 1997

02 CALTEX TERMINAL MOSQUE 22
Karachi, Pakistan, Mirza Abdelkader Baig, 1998

03 KOREAN PRESBYTERIAN CHURCH OF NEW YORK 26
Long Island City, New York, USA, Garofalo, Lynn, McInturf Architects, 1998

04 JUBILEE CHURCH 30
Rome, Italy, Richard Meier & Partners, 2004

05 JEWISH CULTURAL CENTRE AND SYNAGOGUE 34
Duisburg, Germany, Zvi Hecker Architekt, 1999

06 PRIVATE CHAPEL 38
Valleacerón, Spain, Estudio Sancho-Madridejos, 2001

07 GLASS TEMPLE 44
Kyoto, Japan, Takashi Yamaguchi & Associates, 2000

08 CHAPEL OF ST MARY OF THE ANGELS 48
Rotterdam, The Netherlands, Mecanoo Architecten, 2000

09 NEW SYNAGOGUE 52
Chemnitz, Germany, Alfred Jacoby, 2002

10 MOSQUE DESIGN 58
Strasbourg, France, Zaha Hadid, project 2000

2 INTERVENTIONS FITTING INTO THE BUILT LANDSCAPE 62

   01 OUR LADY OF THE ARK OF THE COVENANT CHURCH 64
Paris, France, Architecture Studio, 1998

   02 JAMAT KHANA 70
University of Natal, Durban-Natal, South Africa,
Architects' Collaborative, 1995

   03 INTERFAITH SPIRITUAL CENTER 74
Northeastern University, Boston, Massachusetts, USA,
Office d'A, 1999

   04 CHAPEL OF RECONCILIATION 78
Berlin, Germany, Reitermann/Sassenroth Architekten, 2000

   05 KOL AMI SYNAGOGUE 82
Hollywood, California, USA, Schweitzer BIM, 2002

   06 ISMAILI CENTRE 86
Lisbon, Portugal, Raj Rewal Associates, 2002

   07 SACRED HEART CATHOLIC CHURCH AND PARISH CENTRE 92
Völklingen, Germany, Lamott Architekten, 2001

   08 CHRIST CHURCH 98
Donau City, Vienna, Austria, Heinz Tesar, 2000

   09 KASSELL SYNAGOGUE 102
Kassell, Germany, Alfred Jacoby, 2000

   10 KOMYO-JI TEMPLE 106
Saijo, Japan, Tadao Ando Architect & Associates, 2000

3 RETREATS RURAL SANCTUARIES 112

   01 MEDITATION CENTRE 114
Fréjus, France, Bernard Desmoulin, 1997

   02 FAITH HOUSE 118
Holton Lee, Dorset, UK, Tony Fretton Architects, 2002

   03 SHINGON-SHU BUDDHIST TEMPLE AND OSSUARY 122
Kagoshima, Japan, Thomas Heatherwick Studio, in progress

   04 CENTER OF GRAVITY HALL 124
New Mexico, USA, Predock_Frane Architects, 2003

   05 MONASTERY OF NOVÝ DVUR 130
Plzen, Czech Republic, John Pawson, 2004

   06 NIGHT PILGRIMAGE CHAPEL 134
Locherboden, Austria, Gerold Wiederin, 1997

   07 WHITE TEMPLE 138
Kyoto, Japan, Takashi Yamaguchi & Associates, 2000

   08 SANTO OVIDIO ESTATE CHAPEL 142
Douro, Portugal, Álvaro Siza, 2001

4 GRAND ICONS PRAYER AND WORSHIP ON A LARGE SCALE 146

   01 CHURCH OF THE SACRED HEART 148
Munich, Germany, Allmann Sattler Wappner, 2000

   02 IMAM MOHAMED IBN SAUD MOSQUE 152
Riyadh, Saudi Arabia, Abdelhalim I. Abdelhalim, 1998

   03 ISLAMIC CULTURAL CENTRE 156
Dublin, Ireland, Michael Collins Associates, 1996

   04 CATHEDRAL CHURCH OF OUR LADY OF THE ANGELS 162
Los Angeles, California, USA, Rafael Moneo, 2002

   05 CHURCH OF SAN GIOVANNI ROTONDO 170
Foggia, Italy, Renzo Piano Building Workshop, 2004

   06 NEW SYNAGOGUE 176
Dresden, Germany, Wandel, Hoefer, Lorch + Hirsch, 2001

   07 LOS NOGALES SCHOOL CHAPEL 180
Bogotá, Colombia, Daniel Bonilla Arquitectos, 2002

5 MODEST MAGNIFICENCE HIGH IDEALS AND HUMBLE MATERIALS 186

   01 YANCEY CHAPEL 188
Sawyerville, Alabama, USA, Rural Studio, 1996

   02 CHURCH AND COMMUNITY CENTRE 192
Urubo, Bolivia, Jae Cha, 2000

   03 CHURCH 196
Mortensrud, Oslo, Norway, Jensen & Skodvin, 2002

   04 PAPER CHURCH 202
Kobe, Japan, Shigeru Ban Architect, 1995

   05 ANTIOCH BAPTIST CHURCH 206
Perry County, Alabama, USA, Samuel Mockbee and Rural Studio, 2002

   06 JESUIT RETREAT CHAPEL 210
Navas del Marqués, Ávila, Spain, Ruíz Barbarín Arquitectos, 2000

Notes 214

Glossary 215

Bibliography 216

Project credits 217

Index 222

Credits and acknowledgements 224

INTRODUCTION A LEGACY OF INSPIRED INNOVATION

1 Chapel of Notre-Dame-du-Haut, Ronchamp, France, Le Corbusier, 1955

'I wanted to create a place of silence, of prayer, of peace and of internal joy.'
Le Corbusier on the chapel of Notre-Dame-du-Haut

Architecture is asked to deliver many things to many people – shelter, comfort and perhaps beauty, expanding to more specialized programmatic or formalistic requirements. The demands of religious structures may include all of these, but it is the extra thing that they must provide or at least facilitate – spirituality – that sets them apart from secular buildings. This is a quality that contributes greatly to their cultural value since they are meant to inspire something beyond the physical satisfactions of space and, in many cases, say something about the community that they serve. Their inherent transcendent aspect is what makes them more curious to lay people and what has made them a proving ground for talent through the ages. However, what this book seeks to explore is not the inherent 'differentness' of religious buildings, though that is part of their appeal, but the way in which these buildings become an alembic for ideas, for innovation: though some would dismiss modern religious buildings as unlikely harbingers of cutting-edge design, the projects included here will show that they are just that.

The reasons for the decision to include buildings from different religions and to group them thematically, rather than according to denomination, were the same that drove the decision to make the book in the first place: the buildings have inherent value as significant works of architecture with or without their religious affiliations. The focus in these pages is on how contemporary practice and formal invention have been brought to bear on sacred buildings, and on how these elements make technological, formal, environmental and material contributions to the art of building.

This is not a new phenomenon, merely a continuation of a practice that has been going on for centuries – the patronage of new architecture by religious bodies. St Peter's in Rome was groundbreaking in its day not only for its size and succession of lead architects, but for its modified Greek-cross plan, its chamfered piers creating wider spaces, its sumptuous decoration helping to achieve the aim of Pope Julius II to outshine the ancient monuments of Rome. Creating the largest dome since the construction of the Pantheon also helped to seal this triumph. It deviated from Leon Battista Alberti's guidelines for a religious building, which he laid down in his fifteenth-century treatise on architecture, the most prevalent being the adherence to pure form (a circle or a shape derived from a circle, such as a square, hexagon, etc.) and total harmony.[1] However, then, as now, there were people willing to see beyond what was expected to what was possible.

Following is a brief and very general overview of the traditional requirements of the kinds of religious buildings included in the book. This is not a definitive study, but it helps to give an idea of what the architects are working with and how they have departed from or adhered to tradition. The forms for synagogue and mosque have been much less prescribed than their Christian counterparts. However, both require certain elements which share some similarities with those in Christian churches. A synagogue should have a bimah, a table on a raised platform from which the Torah is read. The ark is another important feature, as it and the Torah scrolls which are kept inside it are considered 'the holiest features in the synagogue'.[2] Though it was once meant to be a portable furnishing, the ark is now largely a significant fixed element – often elaborately decorated – that, along with the bimah, helps focus the prayer space of the synagogue. The ark, bimah and sometimes a pulpit can be placed in an apse-like space in the eastern side of the room, but the more traditional, Orthodox method is to keep them toward the centre.[3] Like mosques, synagogues usually have space for worshippers to wash before attending prayers. Traditionally, too, men and women are seated separately, with women either on another level or behind a curtain, though in the Reformed movement there is no such separation.

The mosque accommodates prayers that could as easily be said out of doors, and often are. Prayer rugs are important and laid out in courtyard spaces and then taken up again when prayers are finished. Muslims pray facing Mecca, and the orientation of a mosque or indoor prayer space is denoted by the location of the qibla wall which contains the mihrab, a niche of elaborate decoration, pointing to the exact location of the holy shrine, with the minbar, or pulpit, set nearby.[4] Architects in far-flung parts of the world will spend a great deal of time and effort ensuring that the orientation is exactly right. Michael Collins Architects consulted several experts, including an airline pilot, to help calculate and then confirm the direction of Mecca for their Islamic Cultural Centre in Dublin. In their gridded layout, all of the rooms face the qibla so that people can orient themselves for prayer within any space. Most Islamic prayer facilities include a space for ablutions, which, at least in projects here, are not mere public washrooms, but are designed to signal the transition to the prayer space.

Inside, the main prayer space in a mosque usually has room for rows of men to face the qibla wall shoulder-to-shoulder[5] in a hypostyle hall articulated with a series of columns and horseshoe arches, which are used to great rhythmic effect in some of the most celebrated Islamic buildings, such as the Alhambra in Granada. Men and women pray separately, and if a mosque accommodates women they usually sit in a mezzanine space overlooking the main prayer space and are separated by carved wooden screens. Though there are no strict rules governing the look or shape of a mosque, many traditionalists favour the use of at least one dome over the main prayer space, and minarets to distinguish the building.[6] Furthermore, the use of geometric patterning, elaborate carving and other traditional craftwork has come to signify the mosque building, which can be a simple enclosed prayer space or a complex masjid-i jami. The masjid-i jami, or congregational mosque, often includes facilities such as classrooms, a library, residential accommodation and other community services.

The temples shown here are all Buddhist facilities and all are either located in or derived from Japan, where early temples and monasteries adhered to definite guidelines. However, as the projects shown here demonstrate, Buddhist communities today embrace a wide range of variation in temple design. Orientation can still be prescribed, with the Buddha facing south or east and the entrance facing south. Usually the shrine is located against one wall in the butsuden, or main hall. But here again the adherence to rule varies greatly.

It goes without saying that a non-denominational space has no traditional requirements except for that necessary sense of sanctuary. However, spaces that are meant to accommodate more than one faith (as opposed to no particular faith) must present themselves as flexible at the very least, and welcoming to all in the ideal scenario. One project in the book contains elements for four separate faiths (see p.114), while another can be easily transformed from one congregation to another (see p.74), and a third offers contemplation space for all (see p.118).

2 Beth Shalom Synagogue, Elkins Park, Pennsylvania, USA, Frank Lloyd Wright, 1959

3 Crystal Cathedral, Garden Grove, California, USA, Philip Johnson, 1980

4 Cathedral, Brasilia, Brazil, Oscar Niemeyer, 1970

5 Dar al-Islam Foundation Mosque, Abiquiu, New Mexico, USA, Hassan Fathy, 1981

6 Masjid-i Tooba, Karachi, Pakistan, Babar Hameed, 1969

7 King Faisal Foundation Mosque, Riyadh, Saudi Arabia, Kenzo Tange, 1982

8 King Saud Mosque, Jeddah, Saudi Arabia, Abdel Wahed El-Wakil, 1989

The majority of the projects in this book are devoted to Christian worship, a consequence of the availability and proliferation of new projects. To the Western reader, the form will be very familiar. And, even if Alberti had lost reigning influence by the time Rome's best minds were arguing over the form of St Peter's, the basic layout of the Christian church, with its origins in the Latin basilica, has remained largely intact – a cruciform shape with seating in the nave, altar above the transepts, and the whole structure facing east. There have of course been many other elements and variations through the centuries, and the form continues to inspire alternatives – as in a number of projects here.

Though there are projects from 18 countries there are some points of geographic concentration that were not deliberate, but arose from the proliferation of such buildings in those areas. Most of the churches in the book are located in western Europe or the USA. Three of the four synagogues included in these chapters are located in Germany, which again is a consequence of the abundance of building work that has been taking place. In post-war, post-reunification Germany, many Jewish and Christian communities are building (and rebuilding) houses of worship, many destroyed in the Holocaust and the aftermath of the Second World War. Such weighty precedents have given some architects a deep motivation to produce buildings that are somehow both distinctive and sobering, forward-looking and mindful of the past.

For any study of innovation in religious buildings it is helpful to look at some hallmark developments. As in the past (but without the vast coffers of patronage of previous centuries) well-known modern architects have been solicited to produce works for religious communities, and those buildings continue to influence projects both secular and divine. Le Corbusier's chapel of Notre-Dame-du-Haut, Ronchamp, has become a modern icon. Strangely enough, as it was designed as a piece of one-off craftsmanship and is a distinct departure from the rational forms with which the architect is generally associated, its use of sprayed-on concrete and organic shapes brought the Catholic Church firmly into the world of modern architecture. (Perhaps it is a telling sign of a renewed reverence for both the architect and spiritual buildings that Corbusier's Saint-Pierre Church in Firminy, France, is now due for completion, 30 years after it was abandoned, unfinished.) Frank Lloyd Wright's design for the Beth Shalom Synagogue in Elkins Park, Pennsylvania (largely influenced by his designs for a steel cathedral which was sadly never built), and his various other churches and chapels, helped bring his particular style of craftsmanship married with modular design to the wider public. Philip Johnson's Crystal Cathedral in California, recently enhanced by a partner building designed by Richard Meier, remains one of the great achievements of twentieth-century architecture. (Johnson's Cathedral of Hope for Dallas, Texas, was completed in 2004). The sweeping grace of Oscar Niemeyer's cathedral for Brasilia, and his other buildings for the capital, still reign as some of the twentieth century's most forward-looking works of architecture.

Twentieth-century landmarks in mosque design can be seen in the work of Babar Hameed, whose Masjid-i Tooba in Karachi, built in 1969, is a Modernist statement of white concrete shells and sculptural arches, not so far removed from Niemeyer's futuristic forms. Hassan Fathy may be the mosque architect most known to Westerners, having achieved a reputation for his designs that integrate mosques within the larger context of a planned community, as in New Gourna, Egypt, and the Dar al-Islam community of Abiquiu, New Mexico. Once a student of Hassan Fathy, Abdel Wahed El-Wakil has moved on to become one of the foremost architects of mosque buildings in the Middle East. Though he has never set out to directly challenge traditional precedent, in the words of James Steele, Wahid's 'eclecticism continues to redefine traditional architectural perceptions.'[7] The King Saud Mosque (1989), modelled on the fourteenth-century Sultan Hasan Mosque in Cairo, demonstrates his ability to translate history with a modern sense of subtlety. More adventurous is Kenzo Tange's Al-Khairia complex and mosque in Riyadh, which is an unusual example of an architect imposing largely non-Islamic forms, as the design reduces the geometric patterning to essential shapes expressed in separate built elements.

While there are numerous architects undertaking new religious projects every day, there are some whose work consistently stands recognition. Tadao Ando has created some of the world's most mellifluous religious buildings. Both his churches, such as the Ibaraki Church of the Light, and his temples like the Komyo-ji (see p.106), use the naturally ethereal qualities of light and shadow, and demonstrate that the architect can work as deftly with wood as with concrete. His contribution to the development of truly inspirational buildings is without question.

So too are the light-infused spaces of Finland's Juha Leiviskä, who manages to achieve a sense of delicate refinement using brick and steel. The interiors of such buildings as the Myyrmäki Church abound in carefully orchestrated details that exist in quiet, serene harmony – which even Alberti might approve of E Fay Jones, who apprenticed with Frank Lloyd Wright, seeks to evoke more drama in his soaring, cross-membered spaces. Jones's Thorncrown Chapel in Eureka Springs, Arkansas (1981) has achieved its own place in the iconography of American religious architecture. Similarly, Peter Zumthor's wood shingle chapel of Sogn Benedetg in Sumvitg, Switzerland (1988) helped many architects and enthusiasts to rediscover the possibilities of spiritual building at the end of the twentieth century.

While this book does not undertake to represent every religion, it does try to show some of the best and most recent examples of innovation linked with spiritual intent. Five chapters present the buildings along the lines of form, context and size. But across those groupings it is possible to see shared interests and lines of experimentation. It is also possible to compare, for example, the elements that a mosque, synagogue and Christian church have in common, and how contemporary architects have responded to them. The most obvious advance is in computer technology, and while Greg Lynn, Douglas Garofalo and Michael McInturf lead the way with their groundbreaking design for the Korean Presbyterian Church in New York, others are using technology to achieve forms that are perhaps less complex, but no less indicative of the potential of computer programming as the architects' tool.

Religious buildings seem ripe for ecologically conscious design, and architects Hadrian Predock and John Frane have made the Buddhist centre in the desert of New Mexico a showpiece for renewable resources. Sustainably harvested Brazilian hardwood and TimberStrand gave the architects great flexibility in design as well as eco-cred, and rammed-earth walls combined with underground geothermal activity greatly improved energy efficiency.

Shigeru Ban's church made largely of cardboard tubes has become widely known and is included here both for its ecological ingenuity and for its aesthetic appeal. The same could be said for Jae Cha's Bolivian church/meeting house and for both projects that appear under the name of Rural Studio, whose houses and community projects for the rural poor in southern Alabama are perhaps now forever associated with the grandiloquent image of the rubber-tyre and salvaged-metal form of the Yancey Chapel (see p.188). Less overt, but no less interesting, touches of green architecture appear in a sculptural synagogue and community centre in Germany by Zvi Hecker and in the small but poetic Faith House by Tony Fretton in Dorset, England.

Materials, especially in smaller structures, achieve a great poignancy in religious buildings and many architects explore the ability of materials to communicate spiritual ideals.

9 Church of the Light, Osaka, Japan, Tadao Ando, 1989

10 Myyrmäki Church, Juha Leiviskä, Vantaa, Finland, 1984

11 Thorncrown Chapel, Eureka Springs, Arkansas, USA, E Fay Jones, 1981

12 Sogn Benedetg chapel, Sumvitg, Switzerland, Peter Zumthor, 1988

Heinz Tesar's perforated metal-clad box of a church – lined in amber-hued birch plywood and Canadian maple – achieves both urban integration and inner sanctuary, while Lamott Architects use prerusted steel to refer to a town's industrial heritage and to its new community. Wandel, Hoefer, Lorch and Hirsch created the new synagogue in Dresden with a deliquescent metal curtain inside that enshrines and irradiates the interior, and a specially reformed concrete that could take the massive weight of the building twisting off its axis. Though the first impression of Architecture Studio's Paris church is of the extruded stainless-steel grid structure, a closer look reveals the words of prayer etched into the exterior surface, itself a remarkable achievement in recycled paper strengthened with resin. The glass-box enclosure of the Church of the Sacred Heart in Munich features technologically advanced glass panels that aid thermal efficiency. Like Predock and Frane in New Mexico, Reitermann and Sassenroth have made use of 'loam', or rammed earth, in their Chapel of Reconciliation in Berlin for both ecological and symbolic purposes.

Though the first chapter concentrates on form, most of the buildings included in the book experiment with form in some way. From Abdelkader Mirza Baig's Bedouin tent-shaped mosque to the computer-generated organic volumes achieved by Garofalo, Lynn and McInturf, to the perfect cube presented by Paris's Architecture Studio – and the many folding, soaring, twisting, elliptical, monumental and intimate spaces in between – we see the spiritual journey as it is envisioned by thousands of worshippers and translated through numerous planners, committee members and draughtspeople to 39 architectural offices around the world whose aim is to put a modern, inventive built form to the ideal.

Throughout history, that form has had a close relationship with light. Light features prominently in the liturgy and symbolism of most religions, and continues to be a key element in sacred buildings. Steven Holl's Jesuit chapel in Seattle, Heinz Tesar's seemingly solid box of a chapel and Alfred Jacoby's synagogues all focus and manipulate light. Richard Meier's Jubilee Church, Sancho-Madridejos' private chapel and Jae Cha's simple enclosure use light as a discreet element of design. Elsewhere light is consciously screened, diverted, shadowed and embraced to exploit its ethereal ambience.

The projects include two unbuilt schemes and three that are in progress. Though Thomas Heatherwick's design for a Buddhist sect in Japan has yet to go into construction at the time of writing, its unique form and methodology can be appreciated in the model stage presented here. Like the calligraphy-inspired curves of Zaha Hadid's wonderfully original design for a mosque in Strasbourg, even as an unbuilt work it holds the promise of great things to come. The buildings by Richard Meier, John Pawson and Renzo Piano are all long-anticipated projects that have garnered well-deserved interest from their inception. Though they are not yet finished buildings as this book goes to press, their completion dates are imminent, as is their success.

As a final note on the impetus and value behind a book of this nature, architect Bernard Desmoulin, whose meditation centre in Fréjus, France, is presented in Chapter 3, makes perhaps the most compelling argument. He explains that 'because of its metaphysical value, religious architecture frees itself from a strict adherence to utility to achieve a mystical and poetic dimension. In this regard it corresponds generally to a real demand of architecture.' For centuries people have demanded something far beyond utility in architecture. Today, those capable of bringing that further dimension to modern building hold the distinct hope of contributing something of lasting cultural and aesthetic value to the built environment.

1 NEW TRADITIONS EXPERIMENTING WITH FORM

Mosque design, Strasbourg

While nearly all of the buildings included here experiment with form in one way or another, whether from programmatic or site constraints, or from the architects' wish to engage more with metaphysical sensibilities, the projects in this chapter show the remarkable degree to which religious buildings are being re-shaped. Here are forms that will challenge any notion that ecclesiastical architecture is moribund or prescribed. There are representatives from three major religious faiths in seven countries, demonstrating that innovative design crosses beliefs and cultures.

With religious architecture that is meant to address the spiritual and therefore demands to be considered beyond its physical shape, architects have both a duty and an opportunity to look past practical requirements to create something that exhorts visitors to do the same. Mirza Abdelkader Baig, architect of the small Karachi mosque on the site of the Caltex petroleum complex, was inspired by the shape of Bedouin tents and 'the interlocking segments of the space station'. He describes his solution as 'a divine blessing' in his search to achieve something new.

Using symbol as form is something that goes back to the first cruciform churches, but in the third millennium architects continue to find ways to experiment. Alfred Jacoby's design for a synagogue in Chemnitz, Germany, is, he explains, 'an elliptical exposed concrete crown growing towards heaven'. Its form mirrors the shape of a library, which extrudes from the other side of the complex, emphasizing the identity of Jews as 'the people of the book'. A similar theme is the basis for Zvi Hecker's new Jewish cultural centre, which simulates the pages of a book.

The manipulation of light, itself a potent symbol in many religious rites, was the motive behind Steven Holl's St Ignatius Chapel in Seattle, which takes its shape from the concept of 'vessels of light'. Takashi Yamaguchi's partially submerged Glass Temple is a container for pure, white light, while Sancho-Madridejos' 'folded' concrete chapel has, they say, 'a naked design' in which 'light takes on the role of a second material'.

However formally revolutionary these buildings may be, they are produced by architects who take historical precedent seriously, even if they do not seek to emulate past designs. In some cases, architects acknowledge traditional elements through other means and highly innovative forms result, as in Mecanoo's vivid little Chapel of St Mary of the Angels in Rotterdam whose curving outline and bright colours confound common associations with modern churches. But the spaces it delineates and the hues it presents so unabashedly are easily located in the tradition of Byzantine or Baroque churches. Richard Meier produced an arrangement of graduated shells that are like a modern pictogram of Gothic form. Here too, light drove important features of the church that celebrates the Pope's jubilee in 2004.

In terms of formal innovation, the Korean Presbyterian Church in Long Island City, New York, by Douglas Garofalo, Greg Lynn and Michael McInturf is one of the most progressive buildings presented here. As one of the first buildings whose form was entirely generated through computer-modelling and -animation techniques, it represents a watershed in building design. The architects used the digital technologies to build around an existing building, bringing computer design hard up against the urban landscape and enveloping it in a new, highly complex skin. As a religious building it offers a vast congregational space that almost hums with dynamism.

1 The shaved curves of the chapel articulate individual spaces and allow for large window openings to flood the interior with light.

2, 3 The elevations show the arrangement of curves, which arc away from each other, and the simple shapes of the tilt-up concrete slabs used for cladding.

CHAPEL OF ST IGNATIUS

SEATTLE, WASHINGTON, USA

STEVEN HOLL ARCHITECTS

1997

St Ignatius of Loyola founded the Society of Jesus, later called the Jesuits, in the early sixteenth century. Educating the young and the poor was a part of the Jesuits' vocation, as was the promise to embark on missions for the Pope. Light is a powerful metaphor for teaching, as it is for the soul, and for the idea of God in many religions. Steven Holl designed his chapel for the Seattle University campus with deliberate focus on the manipulation and containment of light. Light here is not just the metaphor, it is the modus operandi; not a playful experiment, but the determining factor in a deliberate plan of spaces that have specific referential value. In this 'gathering of different lights,' the architect explains, 'each light volume corresponds to a part of the programme of Jesuit Catholic worship'.

To this end, Holl devised the concept of 'seven bottles of light in a stone box', individually shaped structures distinguished by light filtered through a coloured glass 'lens' that is then reflected off a baffle of the complementary colour. 'The south-facing light corresponds to the procession, a funda-

mental part of the Mass,' Holl says, and is filled with natural sunlight. 'The Chapel of the Blessed Sacrament corresponds to the mission of outreach to the community'. The light here is filtered first through a purple lens and reflected off an orange 'field'. Running east–west, the main area of worship – encompassing the nave and altar – catches the strongest light, and is distinguished by a yellow field and blue lens in the east and a blue field with a yellow lens in the west. The north-lit choir is illuminated through a red lens reflected off a green field. By manipulating colour as well as the degree and shape of the light, Holl has imbued each space with a separate atmosphere and sense of purpose without the overt use of ornament. He has also ensured that at night, 'the light volumes are like coloured beacons shining in all directions out across the campus'.

The articulation of the spaces is readily visible from the exterior shape of the building, which is made up of a series of curved volumes cut off at their crest. This is a shape Holl has used before, perhaps most dramatically in

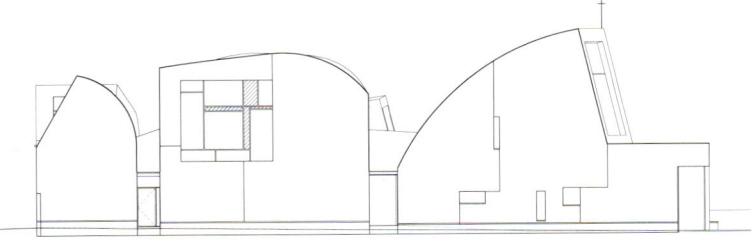

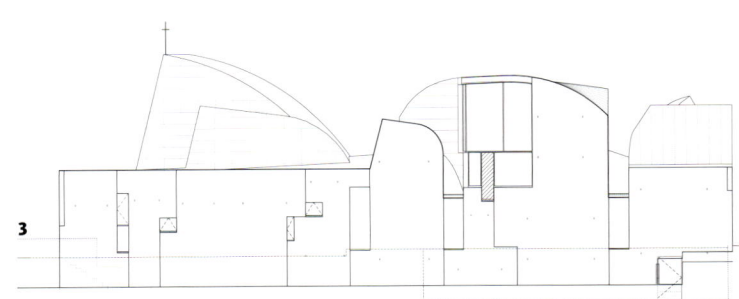

4 Holl's rendering of the concept of 'seven bottles of light' shows the differences in form and colour he sought to create.

5 A slender, sculptural campanile seen across a rectangular pond adds drama to a small chapel on a plain site.

6 The entrance façade demonstrates both the simplicity of the orthogonal concrete base and the intriguing arrangment of projecting light boxes.

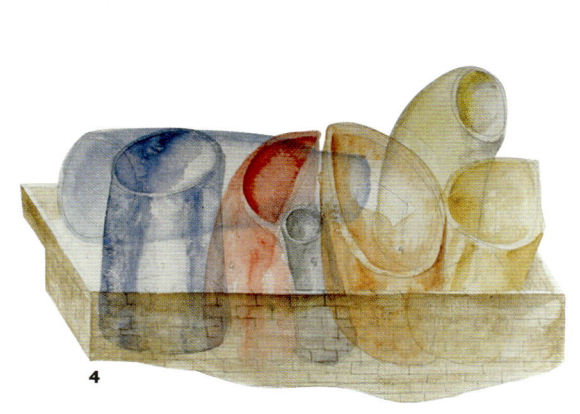

7 The plan shows the unconventional entrance from the south (1), at a right angle to the altar (2).

8 The textured plaster walls of the nave help to contain and reflect the different hues of light reflected into the interior, an effect enhanced by a blue baffle on the left and a yellow lens in the ceiling on the right.

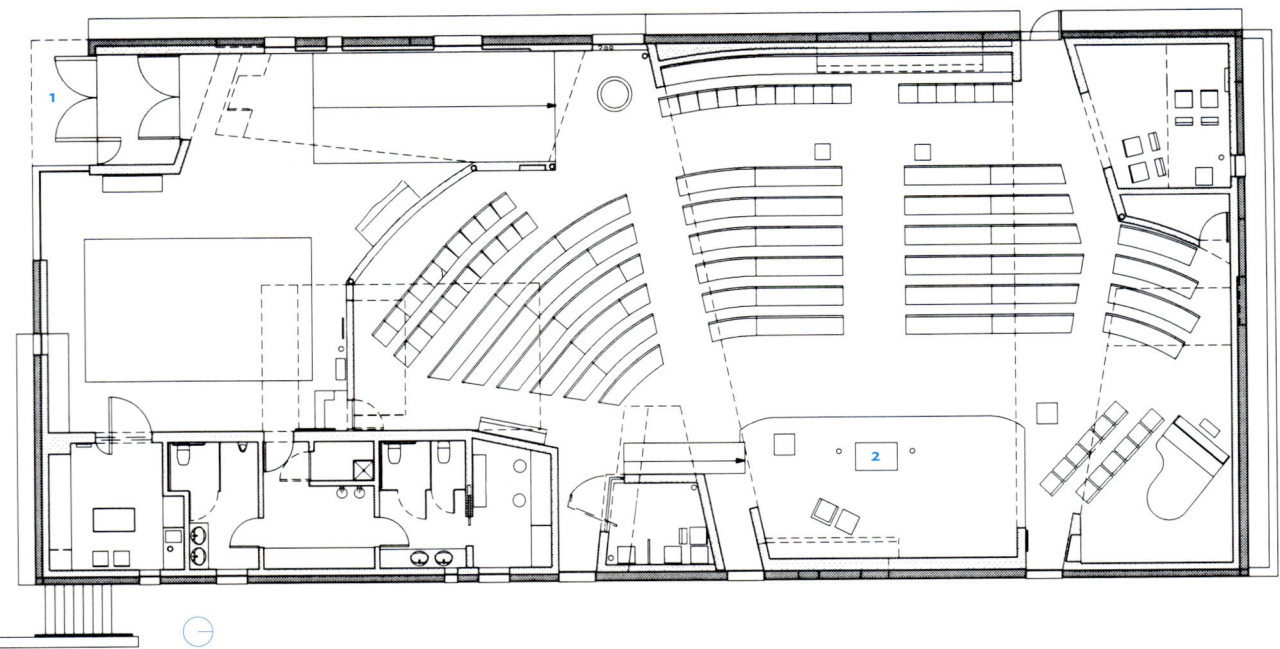

9 The south entrance corridor shows how the interior spaces become 'bottles' of light.

10 The axonometric shows the articulated volumes suggested by the rendering in built form.

his design for the Museum of Contemporary Art in Helsinki. The curved profile in the museum is one giant, sweeping gesture, whereas in the St Ignatius Chapel a series of curves provides the different spatial opportunities for numinous effects. The use of complementary colours in each window opening is explained by the architect as representative of 'the two-fold merging of concept and phenomena', something parishioners may not immediately appreciate, though they cannot help but find the results affecting – more dramatic than stained glass, more nuanced than single-coloured windows.

Holl's desire to express spiritual and philosophical meaning does not preclude him from very practical applications. The exterior walls and made of tilt-up concrete slabs that were cast on site in precise, interlocking shapes that allowed for window openings. These panels were then craned into place over two days and rendered with an amber-hued penetrating stain. Inside, polished, coloured concrete flooring and natural ash furnishings are elegant minimal foils for the luminescent effects, as are the spare, whitewashed plaster walls. The organization of the spaces is slightly irregular. Entering from the south, visitors continue past the baptistery to find themselves in the nave with the altar to their right. It is a nice concession to the narrowness of the site that allows the entrance to be treated separately from the nave. It all makes for a journey, perhaps not in the rugged tradition of the Jesuit missionaries, but suggestive of the many paths to enlightenment.

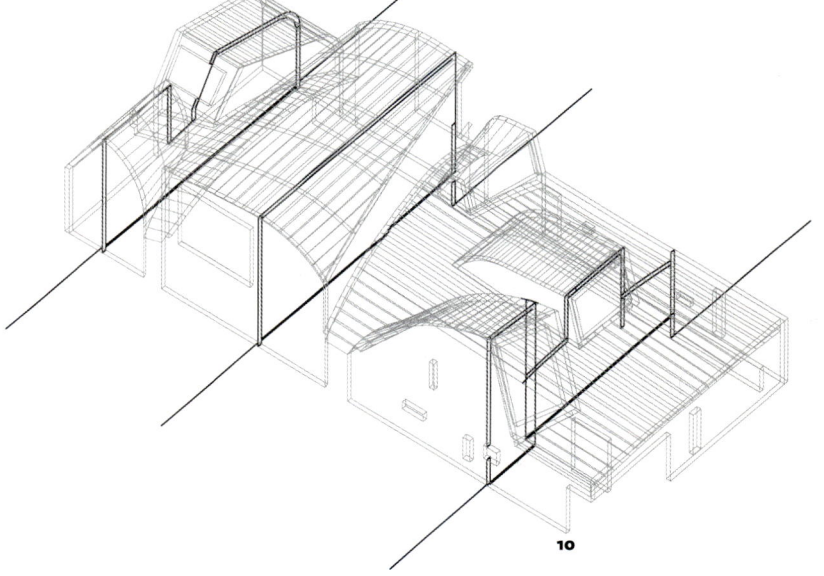

CALTEX TERMINAL MOSQUE

KARACHI, PAKISTAN

MIRZA ABDELKADER BAIG

1998

Prayer spaces constructed as part of larger complexes have their own constraints, but a modest budget and a desire to remain true to the religious intent would seem to doom most projects to be mediocre cut-outs of traditional building types. However, architect Mirza Abdelkader Baig also wanted to make something 'symbolic and different', so he took the small site donated by the Caltex petroleum company and created, in his words, 'a modern version of the traditional tent': a wholly new structure in mosque design even if its origins, the Bedouin tent structure, go back millennia. The angles, irregular planes and rectangular window openings are not from any textbook structure, and yet Baig was not trying to defy or break with tradition or type. He sees the design as 'an answer to my attempt in seeking a different view of what a mosque could look like and feel like as space'.

With its smooth, unadorned walls and angular shape, the Caltex Mosque is striking not only as a mosque but as a public building. However, it is the architect's knowledge of archetypal buildings and a thorough understanding of the architecture of the great mosques married with his appreciation for innovation that has produced such an unusual structure. What it does have in common with more traditional buildings is the aim of separating the space for prayer from everyday concerns. 'Within the small-scale space I could feel the transition from the material world into the spiritual conscious', Baig explains, and he used various elements to achieve this. Everything, from the high walls to the pebble walkway leading to the entrance, is designed to 'cut off the mundane as one enters the mosque'. This in turn, he believes, 'is like leaving behind whatever you had been tied to, like a sense of spiritual freedom'.

Especially in such a context (that of an industrial zone), the building does have the sense of a retreat, a haven of calm, but in addition to its aesthetic achievement it has symbolic strength. At the entrance, instead of a towering, stand-alone minaret, a vertical wedge-shaped corner that is peaked at the top signals the location of the mosque. The dome is small, in keeping with the scale of the building, but recognizable against the white, sharp-cornered form and made of translucent, green-tinted fibreglass, which casts a mellow coloured light inside the mihrab. The interior is plain, and

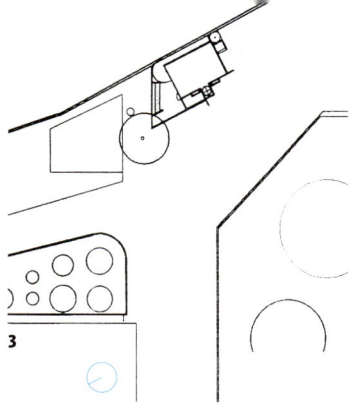

1, 2 & 4 The form of this small mosque departs from the traditional use of arches and domes, being inspired by a 'space-age version' of a Bedouin tent with sharp, sloping corners rendered in smooth concrete. The whitewashed exterior contrasts with the dome, which is green fibreglass, green being a popular colour in mosque decoration. The pebbled entrance is meant to signal the transition to the meditative space.

3 The site plan shows the confined footprint of the mosque on the Caltex compound.

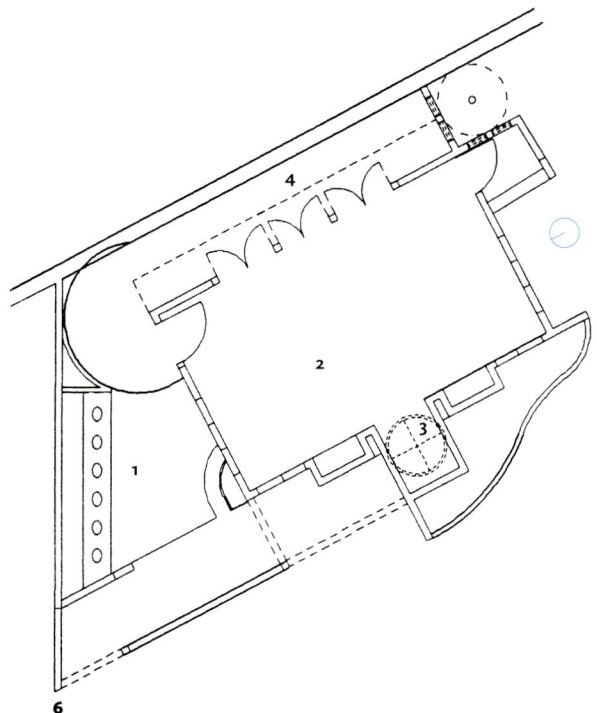

5 The entrance to the ablutions area of the mosque building features more use of colour.

6 The plan shows the ablutions area at left, the main prayer space with the dome in an enclosure that forms the qibla wall and houses the mihrab, and another courtyard area behind the main space. 1. ablutions, 2. main prayer space, 3. dome, 4. courtyard

7, 8 The interior is cast in a greenish glow from the dome and is also lit by rectangular windows. Small, and located high along the wall, they let in light while protecting the private sanctuary of the space. Storage niches on either side of the mihrab area are also bathed in green light.

well-lit from the small, clerestory-style windows and from the oblique light wells that the architect created inside the shelving niches used to house the Koran. Within the tent-style geometry that encloses a mere 93 square metres (1,000 square feet) Baig has even managed to fit in space for courtyards, including one with a tiled wall that is used for ablutions.

It is often in the face of huge constraints that huge creativity emerges. Here in a small, whitewashed cottage of a prayer space the imaginative powers of an architect deeply concerned both with the intentions of a traditional structure – to create a spiritual experience towards the offering of Salaa' ('prayers') – and with the ability of modern architecture to enhance such a structure, have come to bold fruition. The Caltex Mosque may look like the work of someone out to challenge a historical building type (and indeed, in addition to the Bedouin tent, Baig admits 'the interlocking segments of space stations' were a possible influence). However, this building was not an act of rebellion but one of necessity, of meeting certain demands on a restricted budget. That the architect came up with something altogether unique and surprising is itself a triumph of spirit.

1 The reoriented entrance of the new building retains elements of its industrial heritage.

2, 5 The metal-clad protrusions of the north, parking lot façade contain the large outdoor fire stair with entrances to each floor. This structure was intended as a secondary exit but it provides a major circulation path for the thousands of visitors to the building. The spaces between the shells also allow for the flow of air and light between spaces.

3 The balcony-level plan shows how the articulation of the ceiling in the worship space echoes the form of the building.

4 The new main sanctuary takes up most of the top-floor plan with access to the space on three sides.

1.03

KOREAN PRESBYTERIAN CHURCH OF NEW YORK

LONG ISLAND CITY, NEW YORK, USA

GAROFALO, LYNN, MCINTURF ARCHITECTS

1998

Greg Lynn, Douglas Garofalo and Michael McInturf have separate architectural practices in Los Angeles, Chicago and Cincinnati, respectively, but they share a keen interest in, and talent for, using digital technology. They have each produced structures using computer animation software and have experimented individually with the innovative and replicative potential of digital design. This project for the Korean Presbyterian community of Long Island City in New York was a collaboration between the three and presented yet another participatory element in the form of the existing Knickerbocker Laundry. This industrial laundering facility of 8,400 square metres (90,000 square feet) was to form the basis of the complex, which would include classrooms, cafeteria, library, daycare centre, offices and meeting rooms in addition to the main church (which was to hold 2,500 people) and a wedding chapel for 600.

As all three architects are known for their highly original and technologically advanced approaches, it was clear that this was not going to be a mere ad hoc addition. Neither was it going to be an effort to reproduce an existing form. This is a case of the old building being swallowed – literally – by the new, with the rooftop of the former providing the space necessary for the large prayer space. A digitally formulated curved shell encloses the old building within the new, bigger structure. As is often the case in digital design, the application, if one is using conventional materials, is something of a compromise between the pure described shape and the potential of steel, concrete or metal sheeting, etc., to approximate to it. Here, the digitally inspired building has been honed by the imaginative and practicality-driven architects into something achievable in wood, metal and glass, and is significant as one of the first wholly digitally formed structures to be built.

The undulating metal roofline is joined by a series of graduated shells that are attached to the side of the building. These wood-formed, metal-clad open shapes intersect at various levels with the original building and, being open rather than rounded out as perfect curves, allow light into the grand structure. The walls of each segment supply divisions for the various rooms and separate functions. The main prayer space that is now sited on top of the old roof space is also covered over in a series of curved structural elements, but these form one continuous, though continuously changing, whole, with spanning arches that could be read as morphed Gothic vaults. Interior and exterior walls undulate so that the building is alive with three-dimensional surfaces.

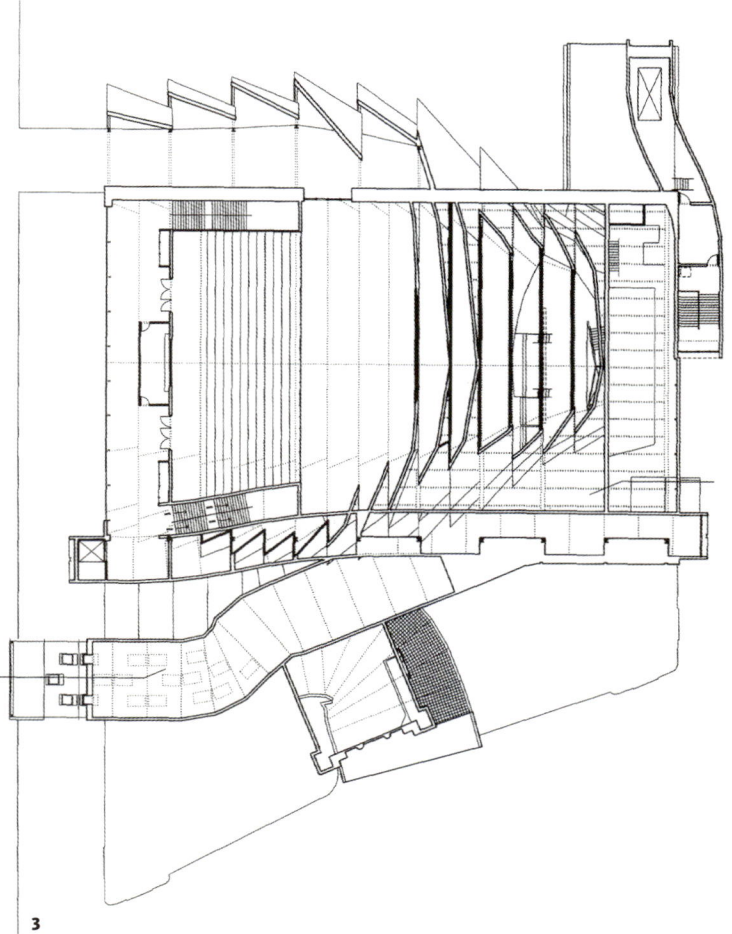
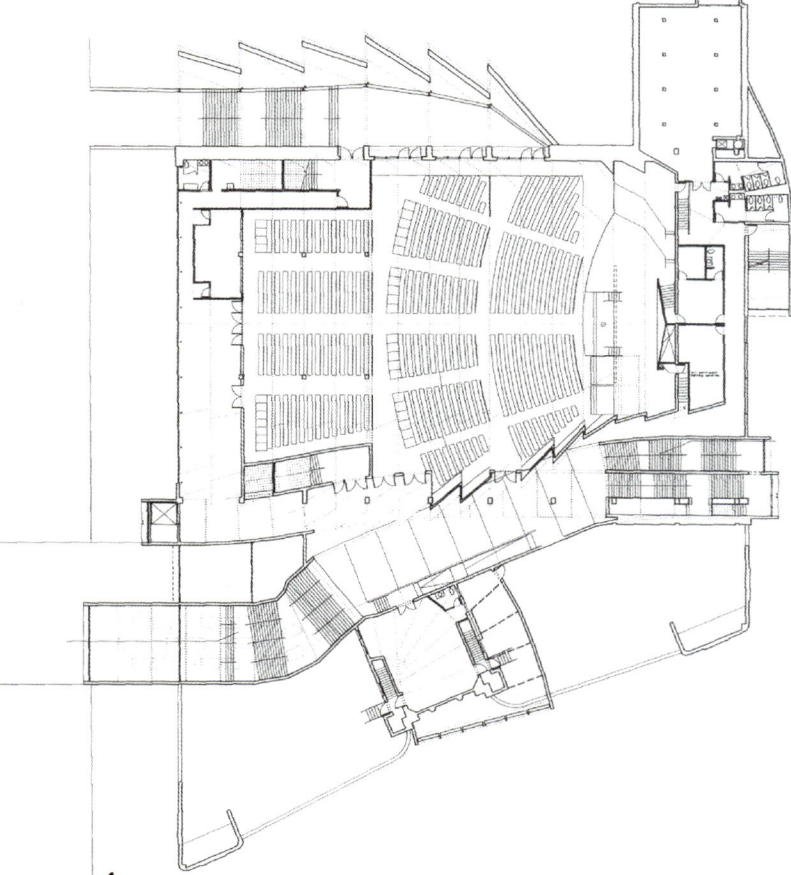

6–9 Computer models show how the shape evolved from an early idea of form (6) to the highly controlled final shape (9) that maximizes the use of the existing building and adds the required space – all within a limited budget. This is achieved as the architects manipulate all dimensions at once, pulling, squeezing or inflating a shape to exact specifications.

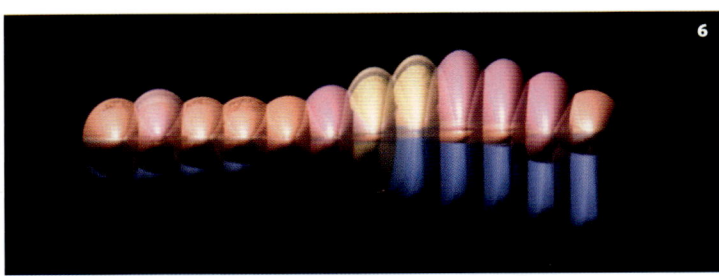

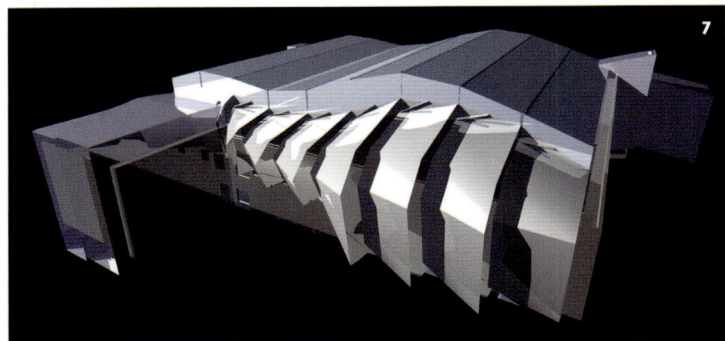

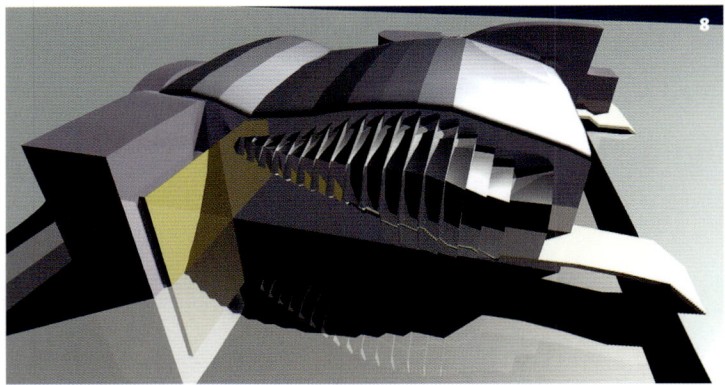

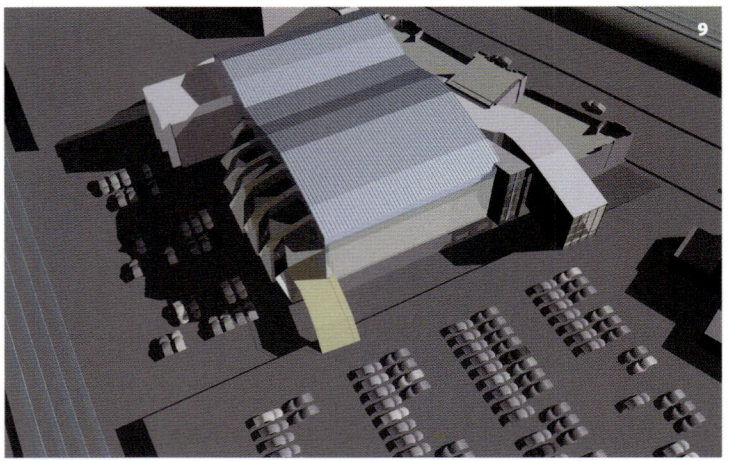

Little remains visible of the 1932 Art Deco-style laundry, but preservation was never the aim. The need to accommodate such a large, multi-use facility on a limited budget meant that completely tearing down and rebuilding was probably not an option. Adaptive reuse were the watchwords, with an enthusiastic response to both elements of that concept. But it was the application of cutting-edge technology that produced a groundbreaking new structure of such great flexibility. The main church space is vast, and some might say impersonal, but it defies the empty ring of spaces designed for thousands, without relying on weighty symbolic references. Hundreds of pinpoint spotlights and recessed lighting give depth and dimension to the undulating ceiling soffits. These are matched by the curve of the red-upholstered metal benches, so that the room flows from side to side and from top to bottom with light, form and colour. The design is a hugely bold gesture for a huge facility. Something grand was required and the architects say they achieved it by joining forces, as none of them could have handled such a large project on their own. The result is a testament to the huge possibilities of digital technology and to the spirit of creative collaboration.

10 The interior of the main sanctuary: the 2,500-capacity worship space was added to the top of the existing building but is an independent structural entity. The undulating ceiling has an acoustic effect but also creates a sense of dynamism and texture in a vast interior. An asymmetric design adds to the unique appeal of the large auditorium.

11 The longitudinal section through the sanctuary shows how a series of nesting curves helps articulate and encourage the flow of the space within.

12 Transverse section through the sanctuary.

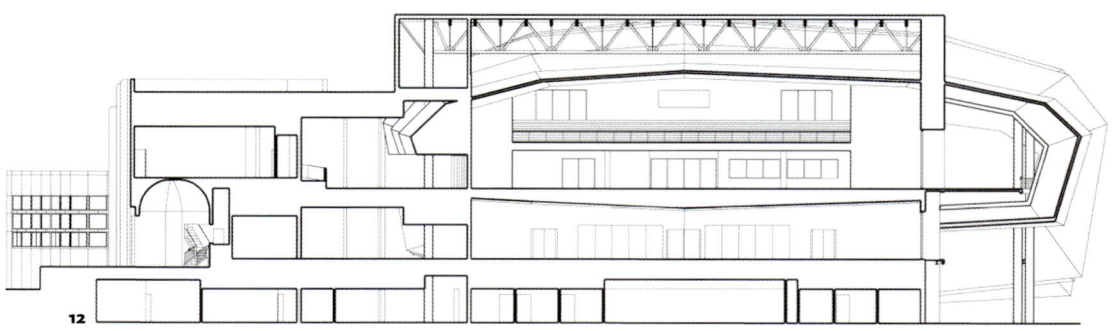

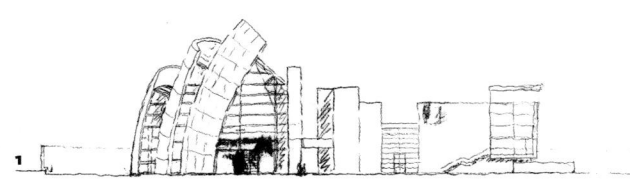

1 The architect's rendering shows the arcing shells of the church reaching toward the block containing the community centre.

2 The grid patterns cast skewed crosses along the interior wall, making the white space a spectacle of light and shadow. Light enters from the top and through the cut-outs in the shell forms at the left.

1.04

JUBILEE CHURCH

ROME, ITALY

RICHARD MEIER & PARTNERS

2004

It was to be the Church of the Year 2000 and started one of the most high-profile competitions of the architecture world. Such internationally known builders as Santiago Calatrava, Frank Gehry, Tadao Ando, Peter Eisenman and Günter Behnisch approached the directive from the Vicarate of Rome for a church built to celebrate the two-thousandth anniversary of Christ's birth with projects that must have at least confirmed the prelates' faith in the transcendence of the human imagination.

This competition to build a new church and community centre in the Tor Tre Teste area of the city was part of a larger scheme of the Church in Rome to reach out to deprived areas and create 'places of welcome'. Now renamed the Jubilee Church and scheduled for opening in 2004, the design completed by Richard Meier is faithful to the competition-winning entry, which combines secular public facilities with a new church in a disadvantaged neighbourhood on the site of an empty lot. The scheme expresses ideas both familiar to his oeuvre and wholly innovative. His name has become almost synonymous with great white buildings – the Getty Center in southern California, the Barcelona Museum of Contemporary Art and the City Hall in the Hague, to name but a few – so perhaps it is not surprising that even for this sacred commission he has chosen white as his starting point. For here it really is a base from which many elements emerge.

From Meier's white drawing board springs a scheme, which he describes as 'based on a series of squares and four circles'. It combines a series of shell-shaped walls that define the church itself and are met by a glass atrium that provides the transition to the L-shaped community centre, an altogether more regular form. It is easy to see from a distance how Meier has saved his most poetic turn for the church itself. The three walls, formed on 'three circles of equal radius' are graduated in height, with the tallest located at the innermost point. This approach addresses a few traditional elements at once. While, as Meier points out, 'the three shells imply the Holy Trinity', the focus of height at the centre approximates the effect of a dome or steeple. As the space between the walls is covered in glass, it refers to the clerestory. The vertical reach and curve of the walls is reminiscent of the Gothic arch, with the smaller walls even capable of being read as flying buttresses. Since the inner two walls are cut out at room height, the light coming through the glass roofs, the zenithal sidelights and the light from the vertical glass walls that join the concrete structures flows into the main space. At the same time, these separate wall structures create the aisles, here only on the south side, inherent in the early basilica form. The campanile is a 20 metre tall (65 foot) rectangular tower that anchors one end of the community centre and joins the two halves of the project together.

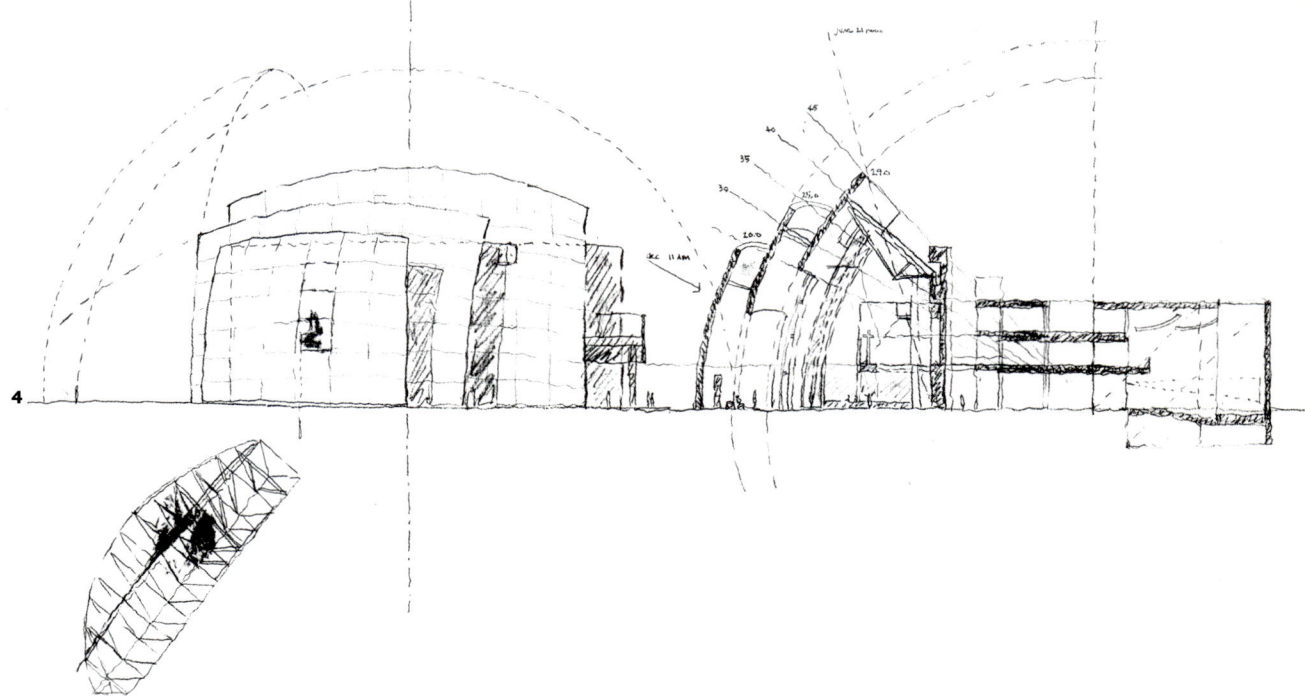

3 The computer rendering shows the completed form of the church with the spine wall that defines the nave at centre right and the campanile at far right. The glazed infilled walls gradually increase in area, bringing the largest amount of light to the central space.

4 The rendering of the south elevation and longitudinal section shows the form of the three circles of equal radius that Meier used to create the arcing walls.

5 The glazed skylights suspended between the shells are lit by zenithal sidelights which creates the changing pattern of light inside.

6 The shell walls are made up of individual precast concrete units with steel reinforcement that are held together by post-tensioned cables both in the vertical and horizontal directions.

7, 8 The elevation (7) and section (8) show how the grid system in the concrete panels is mirrored by the glazing grid. The concrete-block forms rise to a height that is within reach of the highest shell which seems to bring the rest of the building into a protective embrace.

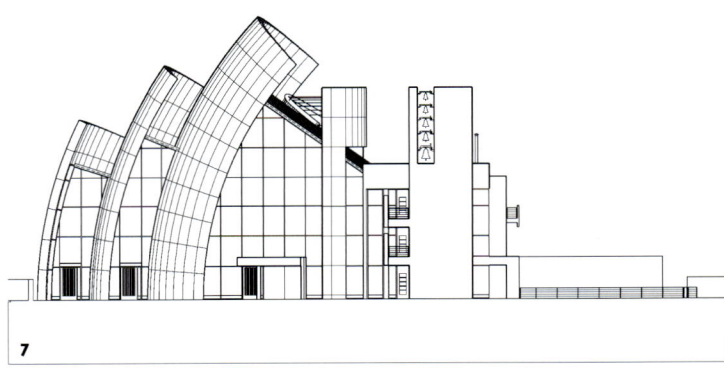

The interior of the church is much more intimate than all this language of concrete and glass would suggest, being relatively small – suitable for a congregation of no more than 266. Meier has taken the opportunity offered by pure white surfaces to get the maximum effect from light and shadow entering from the walls and roofs, which are glazed panels and so project a skewed grid shape or a multitude of crosses along the interior walls and floor. The slender cross behind the altar mimics the lines of the grid, emphasizing this association with the shadows.

As a place of welcome, the project does not stop at the threshold but incorporates walkways, a reflecting pool, courtyard, parking and planting on a triangular site that is overlooked by 10-storey apartment buildings. The architect created a paved sagrato leading from the eastern entrance, which, he says, 'extends it into the heart of the housing complex and provides an open plaza for public assembly'. The reflecting pool provides both a reference to baptismal rites and a quiet outdoor meditative space. Even the signature white is seen by the architect as 'referencing the fabric of the adjacent residential area', ensuring that however world-renowned a project, it remains grounded in the community, with an upward gaze.

9 The balcony continues the play of lines and cut-out orthogonal shapes and is lit from behind and above.

10 The western façade of the unfinished structure shows the sculptural concrete community centre building. The graduated shells (the tallest is 26.66 metres/87½ feet) create a vaulting effect.

11 The site plan shows how the architect worked to the triangular site, orienting the entrance and footpath toward the existing apartment buildings to the east. A reflecting pool is in the south-west corner. Paving and planting in outdoor areas help integrate the church and community centre with the existing neighbourhood. The community centre is in the northern section of the complex, with the sacred realm to the south of the spine wall.

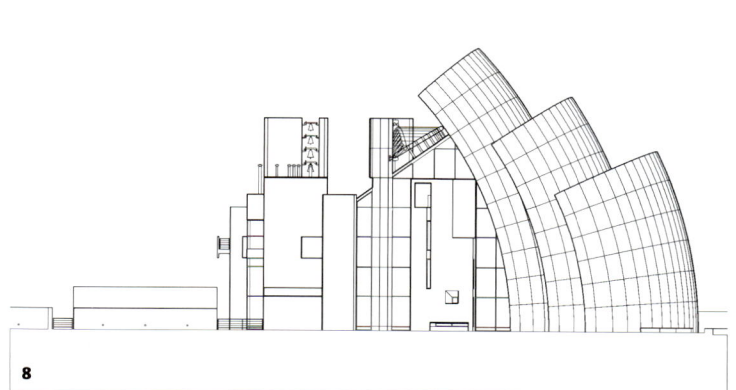

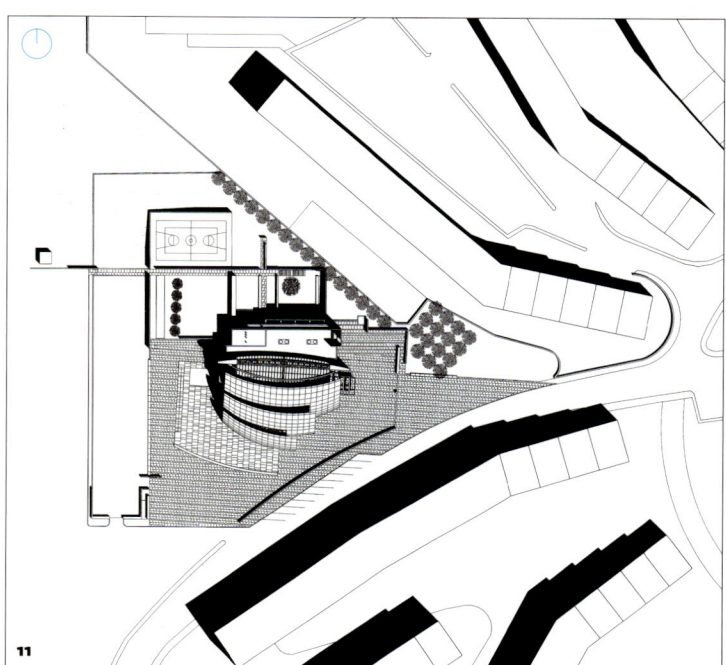

1 Sculptural segments fan out from the core of the building like the pages of a book, with the glazed central atrium providing access to each area.

2 The north-east side of the building, with the black form of the synagogue's misrach wall pointing east.

1.05

JEWISH CULTURAL CENTRE & SYNAGOGUE

DUISBURG, GERMANY

ZVI HECKER ARCHITEKT

1999

Zvi Hecker has written that architecture is 'above all an act of magic' because of the fact that 'it hides more than it reveals. What we look at, what we see, is only a reflected image of what we cannot see: the architecture's soul.' He has also made buildings that address the human soul. For the Jewish Cultural Centre in Duisburg the architect referred to the book. 'Jewish culture and Jewish identity thrived mainly through writing,' he says. 'It was the Book that bound together, by the universality of Jewish tradition and customs, the scattered communities in diaspora. In Jewish history text replaced territory, the Book a kingdom.' The book is a literal interpretation as well as a figurative one, with the building resembling five separate 'pages' in white plastered masonry radiating out from a central building. The 'pages' are narrow sculptural projections, rectilinear arches that span beyond the building mass in the direction of the harbour. Each is inflected at the harbour end with open rectangular constructions that look like sculptural or symbolic portals. One of the page segments is breached by the triangular form of the synagogue, which twists eastwards, oriented toward Jerusalem. Approaching the building from the east, one encounters the solid, vertical black-slate box of the synagogue's eastern wall in

3 The eastern façade demonstrates a more regular orthogonal assemblage.

4, 6 The sketch and axonometric show the synagogue building pointing like a turned arrow away from the direction of the wings.

5 Hecker's rectilinear arches contain artful elements that draw attention and meaning beyond the functional structure.

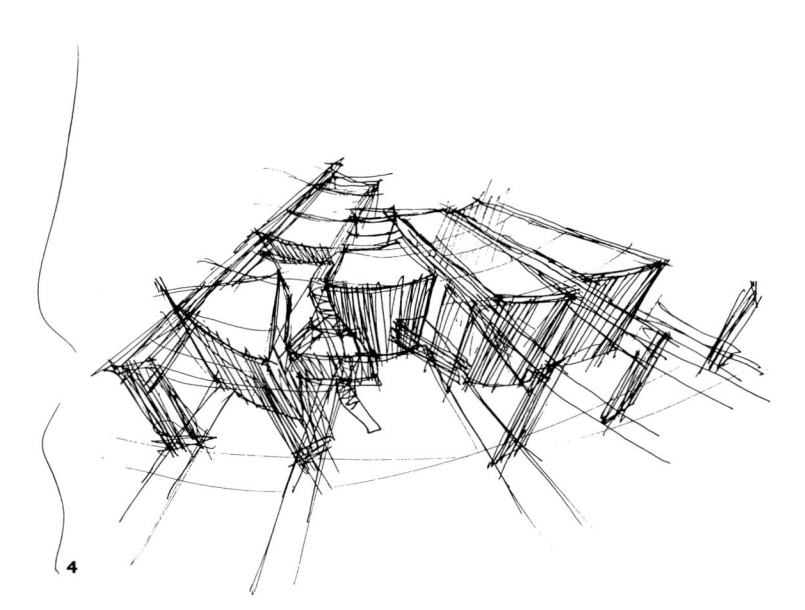

stark contrast to the open, white arms pointing north-west. So, while the harbour seems to draw the building one way, the synagogue turns to its own point of reference.

The brief included specific areas, from a multi-purpose room to a kosher kitchen, classrooms, administrative rooms and accommodation for the rabbi and janitor. However, the building's complexity does not derive from multiplicity of function. Zvi Hecker has expressed in previous projects, such as the apartment house in Ramat-Gan, Israel, or his design for a Jewish primary school in Berlin, an affinity for spiralling or integrated sections. Here, the notion of the book has brought about another thematically bound collection of forms. These 'pages of history', as he has designated them, correspond, he explains, to specific events and traditions: 'the arrival of Jews to the city in the twelfth century; the act of assembling a minyan (gathering of ten adults necessary for a prayer) in 1793; the first permanent location of prayer in the old city; the construction of the first synagogue in 1875 and its destruction during Kristallnacht in 1938; the construction of the new synagogue and community centre.' All of these refer-

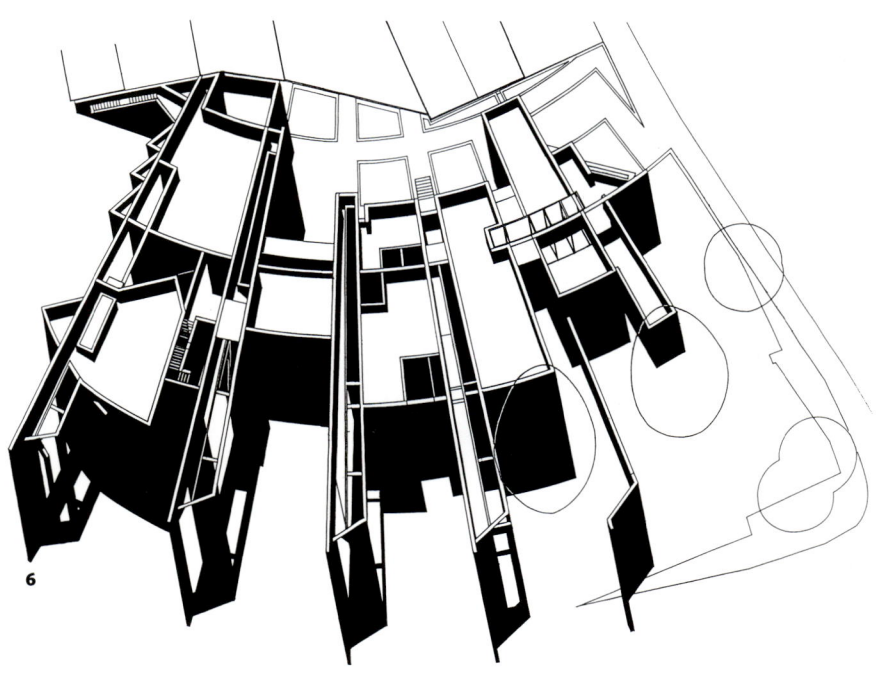

7 The plan shows the wings that radiate northwards toward the river. The arrow shape of the synagogue can be seen at left.

8 The entry on the south side of the building.

9 The projecting wing furthest from the synagogue building is angled to urge the view in that direction.

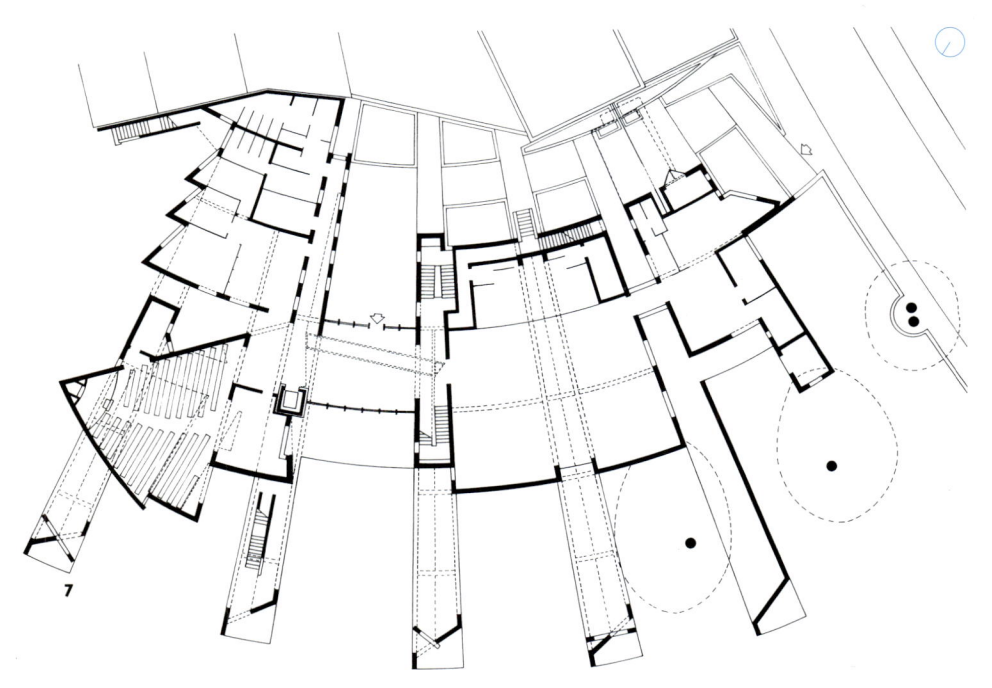

ences are symbolic except for the page referring to the destroyed synagogue, which is actually laid out on axis in the direction of the former building, and the synagogue's crossing of the projecting segments, which forms the Hebrew letter for divinity.

The worship space is spare and serene, with Jerusalem stone flooring and natural wood details and furnishings providing the minimal ornament. A skylit roof strip brings more light to the bright, white heart of the complex. While the exterior forms of the building are graceful and articulate, they beg to be understood, or even explained in some way, and yet the synagogue worship space is refreshingly simple, leaving the mind free to contemplate other things.

Zvi Hecker is determined to invest form with meaning beyond the bounds of necessity. Even for those who will never enter the synagogue the building is affecting in its act of reaching out of itself. Passers-by will perhaps associate it with the sculpture park that has been erected in the green space opposite on the harbourside. And they will perhaps note the black arrow of the synagogue stretching toward a different, elusive objective. Others will 'read' its many meanings while understanding in the open frames of the arches that what fills in the pages is the potential of the human spirit, which must be the source of the architecture's soul.

10 The synagogue interior adheres to the arrow shape of the roofline. Jerusalem stone lines the Torah shrine and balcony.

11 Natural light, pale wood and white walls contrast with the black
solidity of the misrach wall exterior.

1 A long, narrow window in the southeast elevation shows how the architects have reinterpreted traditional stained glass windows.

2 The entrance to the chapel, set within a right triangle, provides both a standard rectangular opening and angular windows in keeping with the overall geometry.

1.06

PRIVATE CHAPEL

VALLEACERÓN, SPAIN

ESTUDIO SANCHO-MADRIDEJOS

2001

The chapel at Valleacerón is part of a larger project undertaken by the Madrid-based architecture team of Sol Madridejos Fernández and Juan Carlos Sancho Osinaga. This commission also designated the construction of a main house, hunting pavilion and guard's residence, all set across a stark, mountainous landscape. The architects' wish to respond to the natural setting with their trademark planar forms resulted in a design that cuts planes, or seemingly folds them, into sharp triangular surfaces that are like sculptural projections on the horizon. The residence, not shown here, is more representative of their trademark rectilinear forms with stepped elements and extruding surfaces. However, it too is the product of the architects' experiments with folding, being – as they call it – a 'fold-wrapper' in heavy stone.

Here, in the chapel, Sancho-Madridejos have eschewed any rigidity in favour of a form that allows the planar surfaces to act as walls, roof, ornament and fenestration. Or, as they say, they used 'a focally tensed box-fold'. It feels as if any surface could act as another, but their genius is in deciding how to use each in a subtle play of angles that tricks the eye into seeing single surfaces in many and vice versa. The interior is lit by both the glazed over-door and long, narrow side windows that suggest traditional stained glass but are modern transformations. There is no artificial light, and only a simple Cross and single image used as a focal point. The chapel is a centre for light and for the trapping of natural light as well as shadows and other dramatic elements of the open sky. The form seems to wrap itself around the streaming sun, acting as a light collector in a handkerchief fashion.

If, when looking at the 'folded' concrete chapel, Le Corbusier springs to mind, it is no accident. The architects admit inspiration from both the pilgrimage chapel of Notre-Dame-du-Haut, in Ronchamp, and the Corbusian 'boîte', which suggested the single material of 'golden concrete'. Like Corbusier's church, Sancho-Madridejos' chapel reflects an artistic, one-off approach. Whereas the architects have in the past shown their affinity for the International Style in their rectilinear forms and fully glazed façades, their method for the chapel is singular, the light, instead of being drawn in in great waves, is artfully framed and focused.

According to Sancho and Madridejos, this is not purely for atmosphere. They explain that the 'trapped direct light' is an inherent part of the design, functioning as 'an additional plane' and taking on 'the role of a second material', a material, they add, 'that contrasts with the concrete, being fragile, changing, mobile, unstable; dominating or vanishing'. While many

2

3 The sketch shows the chapel's relationship to the residential complex in the centre.

4 On the western façade, a ground-level window breaks up the folded mass.

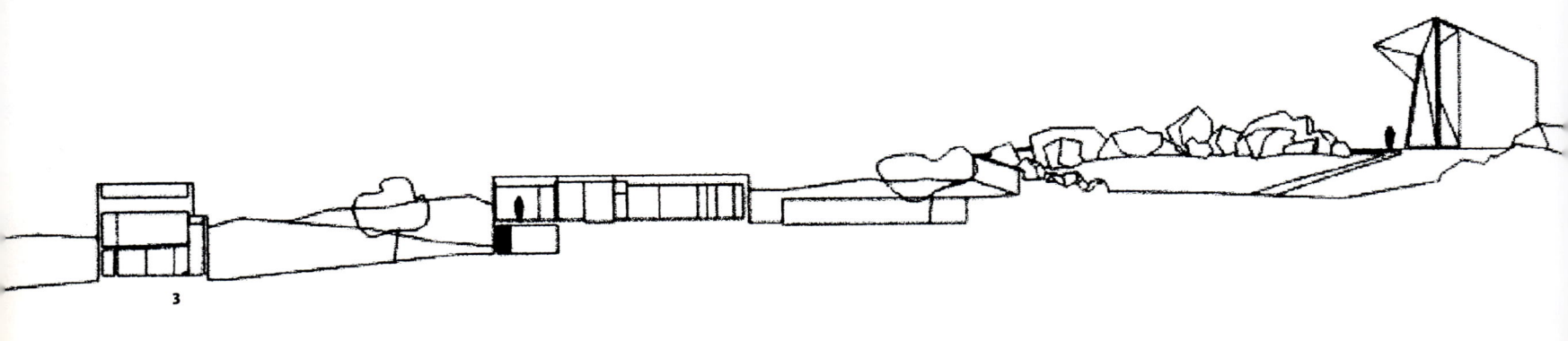

5 The sections of concrete are aligned around corners to emphasize the 'folded' shape.

6, 7 The south elevation (6) and section (7) show how the angular shapes become layered and grow in complexity.

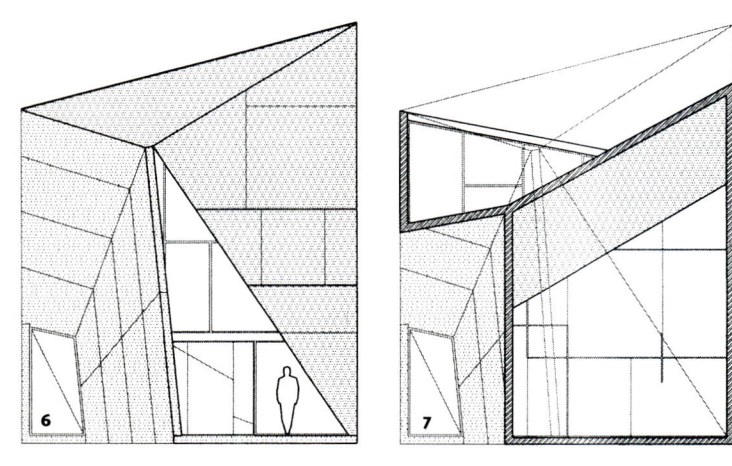

spiritual structures have a special relationship with light, this determination of the natural element as intrinsic to the structure also demonstrates the architects' desire to connect with the natural environment, especially as atmospheric changes are so readily perceptible on the hillside setting.

The interior of the chapel is bare concrete interrupted only by the glazing and the shifting wedge-shaped panes of light that cut across every surface. These provide an unexpected dynamism in the otherwise unadorned space. Not even furniture mars the purity of the interchange between surface and light. It is not hard to imagine how the clients find the space peaceful and inspiring at the same time. The chapel is private, a place meant for Roman Catholic worship, but clearly the clients have been able to exchange the trappings of ceremony and tradition in favour of a reverence for light and earth.

8 The interior is left bare with only the play of light and shadow for ornament.

9 The geometry of folded and cut angles is highlighted by the panelled window openings that frame a spectacular view and create a highly atmospheric and changeable interior light.

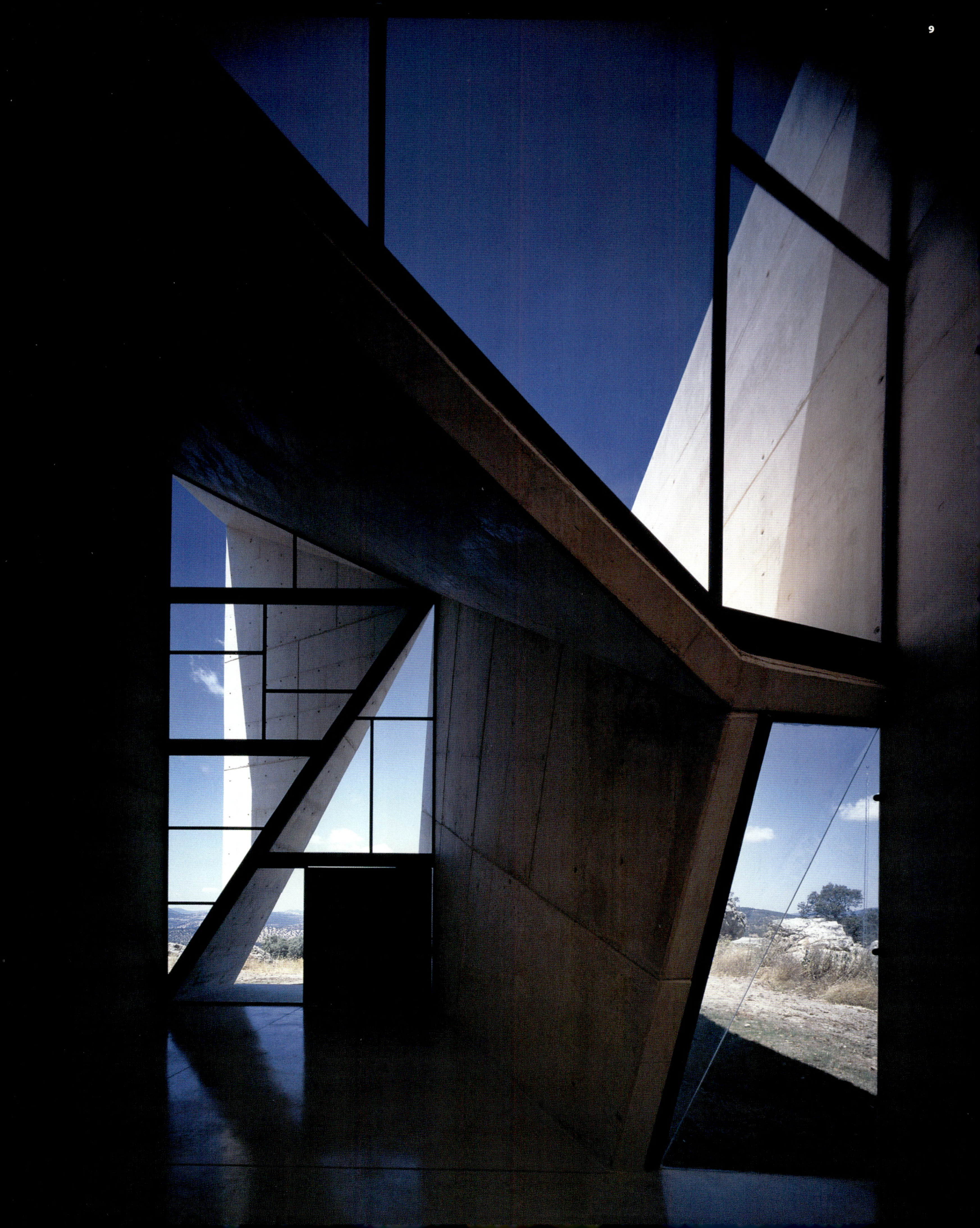

1 From a distance the glow of the submerged chamber serves as a ground lantern for the historic complex.

2–4 The plans (from bottom: lower, upper and roof levels) show the simple form of the temple with the vertical light box and entrance block (seen at the bottom of the plans).

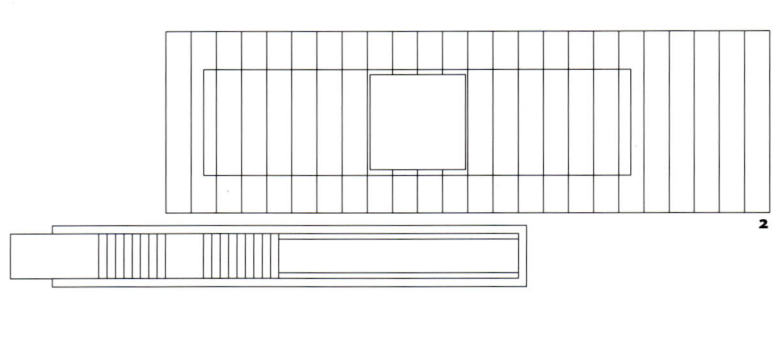

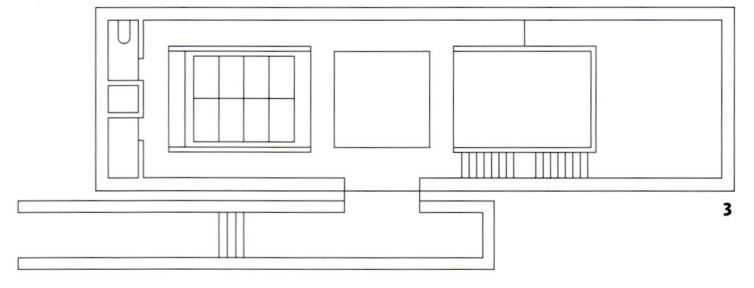

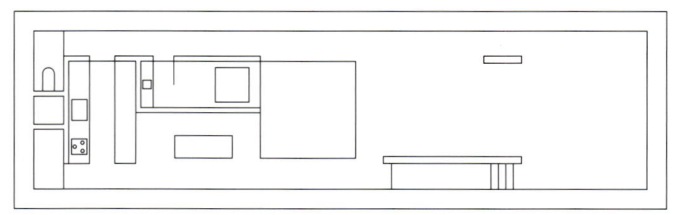

1.07

GLASS TEMPLE

KYOTO, JAPAN

TAKASHI YAMAGUCHI & ASSOCIATES

2000

Takashi Yamaguchi likes to build simple white temples, but they are not mere temples to minimalism. Yamaguchi is the quintessence of light-obsessed. His 'Windy Temple' is partly dug into a hillside and visitors must pass through a dark corridor before reaching a skylit 'plaza'. His 'Underground Temple' is a series of tunnels opening into natural light at both ends and punctured with light sources behind frosted glass along the dark interior corridor. His Water Temple and Memorial Space are both set in a reflecting pond. His Light Temple is composed of a single-storey glass box that sits above ground, on top of a much larger underground interior filled with light from the glass lantern structure. It is not the white box he is after but the supremely illuminated white box, not the bare surfaces but the reflection off the bare surfaces. His two built projects, both near the city of Kyoto, are also temples in the real, spiritual sense, one used for cinerary urns (the White Temple, see p.138) and one, the Glass Temple, used for a gallery and visitors' space at a sacred site.

For the latter, Yamaguchi has taken the form of the single-storey glass lantern and lowered it into the ground so as not to intrude on the presence of the sacred surrounding structures. These structures include the

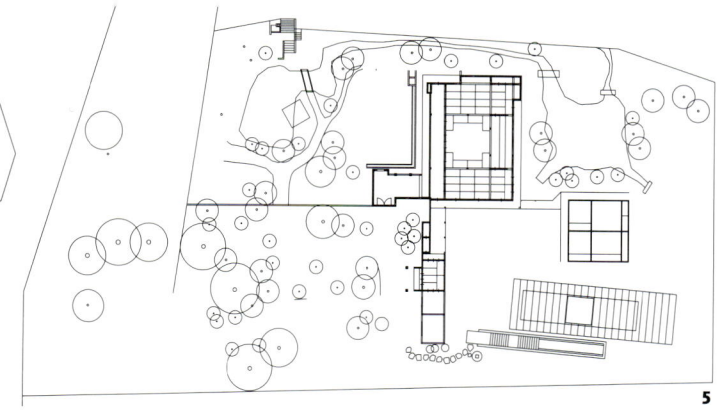

5 The site plan shows the relationship between the temple (bottom) and the original sacred buldings (centre right).

6 Setting the temple in the existing 'maple garden', the architect was inspired by an ancient tree on the site. Being below ground, the new structure has as little impact as possible on the natural and built landscape.

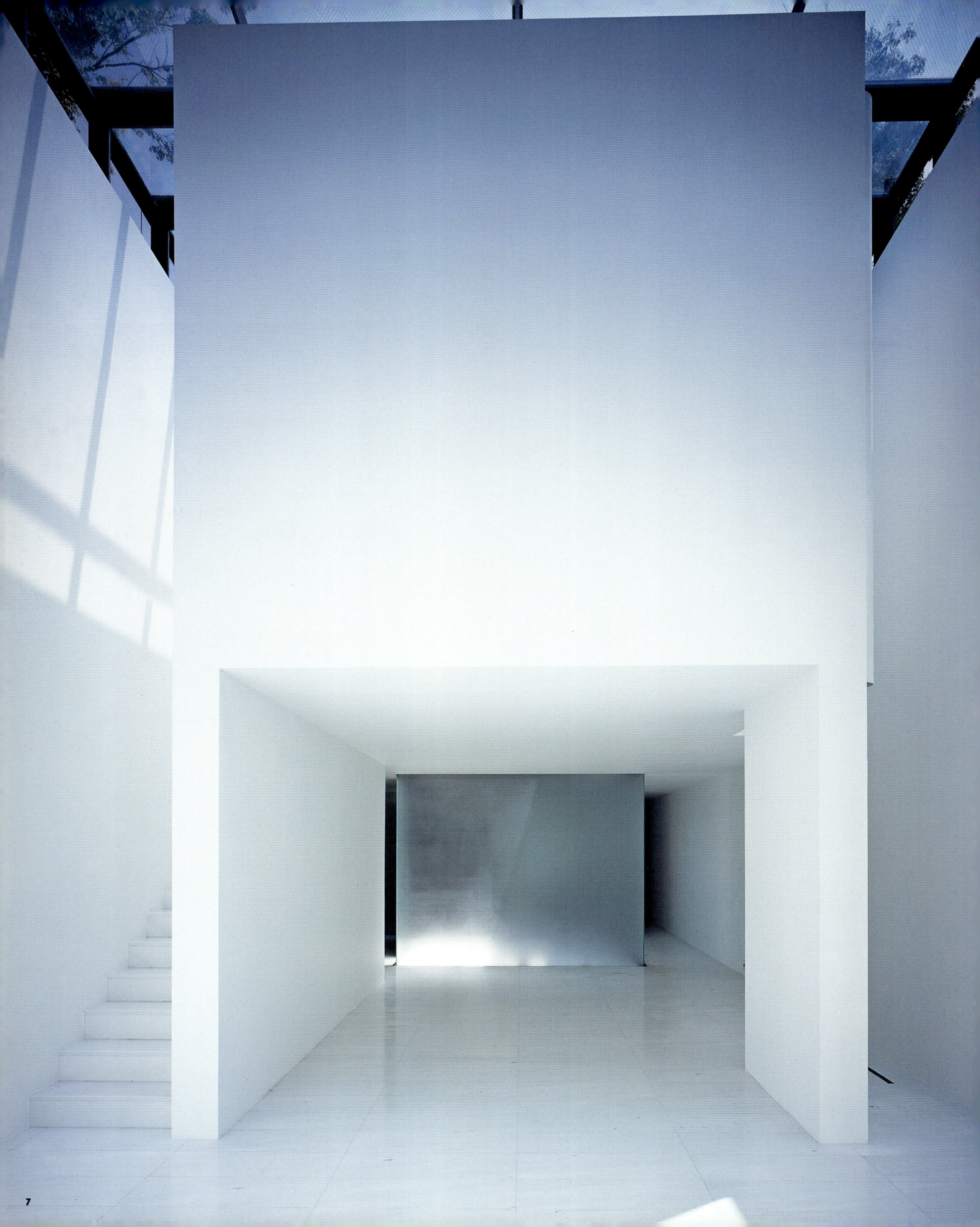

7 The white block partially encloses the entrance stairs and provides an interior focal point, while framing the view of the frosted glass 'light court'.

8, 9 Long section (8) and end section (9).

10 The view of the open sky through the light court.

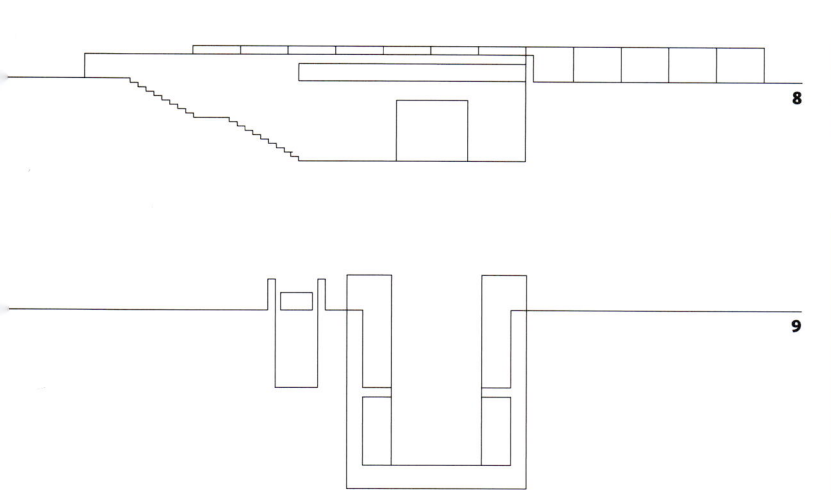

Reigenko-ji, built by the emperor Gomizuno-o in 1638 to honour the priest Isshibunshu. 'Today,' the architect says, 'Reigenko-ji remains a temple for rites of imperial prayer. ... I felt that my mission would be to respect its long and dignified history and, at the same time, to convey to the future the transparent teachings and pure white spirit of the priest Isshibunshu.' As a starting point, Yamaguchi first considered the main hall (butsuden), which, he felt, 'with its slightly convex roofline and light upswing of its eaves, presented a graceful figure'. Such a task of 'intervening in this place of our ancestors and addressing history' was daunting indeed and was one reason that the architect chose to build underground rather than upset the ancient context. Choosing the 'architecturalization of the garden' was part of what he perceived as the 'necessary courtesy' of 'working within the flow of time' and attempting to 'overlay our own time on the past in a way that would render it distinct'.

The new temple is both subtle and distinct. From outside, it looks like a low-profile glass lantern, perhaps an illuminated sculpture on the ground. It is only on closer inspection that the depth of the volume is discernible. In the existing landscape of four gardens – a cherry garden, maple garden, rock garden and pond garden – the architect decided to position the new building in the maple garden. A maple tree that had been 'growing on the site since ancient times and was as conspicuous in its presence as the main hall' was, for him a reference point. The interior of the structure measures 15 x 3.6 metres (50 x 12 feet) in plan and is six metres (20 feet) high, so the feeling inside is anything but the close, claustrophobic quality of most underground enclosures. In a gesture that further dissolves physical boundaries, a 'light court' of frosted glass, a vertical box that negotiates the exterior and interior light, has been inserted in the volume. The soft light filtered through it permeates the rest of the space, while a more direct light enters from the roof above. All the light entering the building, says the architect, 'is amplified in the space of the white interior, so that it erases all form and contour'. The emphasis then becomes what one perceives in the white and in the light, and in the striking contrast of blue sky which becomes, within this frame, the most colourful object one could imagine.

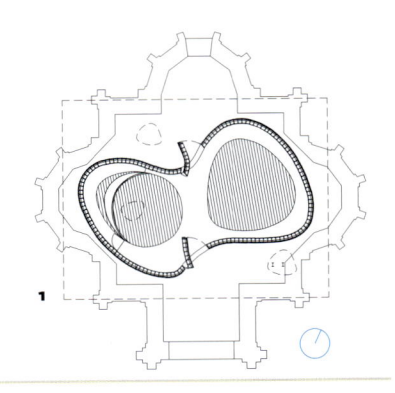

1 In the plan, the soft, organic form of the chapel is shown sitting within the outline of the old church.

2 The sinuous wall is set above the ground with the intervening space filled in with glass, so that the building appears to float.

1.08

CHAPEL OF ST MARY OF THE ANGELS

ROTTERDAM, THE NETHERLANDS

MECANOO ARCHITECTEN

2000

At first, the curving galvanized copper cladding and 'floating' gold-tinted roof seem to have little to do with traditional chapel architecture. There is a self-conscious modernity, even futuristic sense about this little cemetery chapel that denies tradition. And yet, in many ways, its design is about preserving the past. As Francine Houben of Mecanoo relates, the Roman Catholic cemetery founded in 1680 was moved to this spot in 1865 when H J van den Brink designed it as a campo santo, or 'field of the dead'. He also designed the Neo-Gothic chapel of St Lawrence, whose foundations gave way to subsidence so that the church had to be demolished. A new chapel was built in 1963 on the same spot, 'a building shaped like a large Indian tent', and suffered the same indignity of unsteady ground. In November of 1998, a local priest, Father Joost de Lange, asked Houben if she could design a chapel for completion in 2000. What she came up with was a paean to the chapel's history that sets its own story at the same time.

To avoid problems with subsidence, which claimed the previous structure, Houben placed the new chapel on an elevated 'gravel plateau' the shape of which follows the footprint of the nineteenth-century building, keeping the historical reference even in the context of the very new. The plateau is held up on plinths that will ensure a solid foundation for many years to come. Like a colourful sculptural folly, the new chapel of St Mary of the Angels sits amid the greenery of the old cemetery, hovering, quite literally as many elements have been designed specifically to create that effect. In addition to its elevated site, its sinuous, flowing wall lifts the building further, being some 70 centimetres (two feet) off the ground with the intervening space filled in by glass. The wall encloses a space that Houben insisted be 'intimate, whether it is for ten or a hundred people'. That intimacy is achieved by the curve of the encircling wall and by its striking deep blue colour, the colour of a medieval Madonna's robe or a Byzantine cathedral interior.

Though some will see these features as inarguably modern, perhaps a bit too art-piece for the sombre grounds of the cemetery, much, like the colour, can be read as religious iconography: the form is sympathetic to the natural landscape and was intended to aid the flow into the chapel and out to the cemetery during funeral services. The copper roof is a reference to the previous structure, in material if not in form. The ovoid shape actually softens the appearance of the building, which is not higher than the mature trees. The roof's wave has the tilted curves of a nun's habit and, when the

3
The clerestory beneath the wave of the roof lets in natural light in the day, and produces a halo effect at night, when the roof appears to float above the structure.

4 Due to problems of subsidence, which destroyed previous structures on this site, the present building sits on an elevated plateau of new gravel.

5, 6 The galvanized copper cladding and the deep blue and strong gold-yellow colour scheme recall elements of Byzantine decoration in the otherwise thoroughly modern structure.

7 The sectional drawing shows the retaining walls of the new gravel foundation and the gentle inward slant of the roofline.

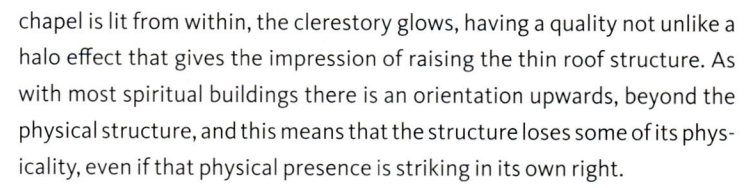

chapel is lit from within, the clerestory glows, having a quality not unlike a halo effect that gives the impression of raising the thin roof structure. As with most spiritual buildings there is an orientation upwards, beyond the physical structure, and this means that the structure loses some of its physicality, even if that physical presence is striking in its own right.

Inside, the blue wall is not just a colourful ribbon but a narrative piece, and is covered with texts from the Requiem Mass. The roof is punctured to allow a column of natural light that is enhanced by the smoke of burning incense. The traditional place of nave and apse have been articulated using the curves of the walls and with demarcated flooring: the seating area for the congregation and the altar space sit on patterned wood decking that is also heated and distinct from the concrete flooring elsewhere. With a conscientious look at the past (Houben prepared for this commission by looking at chapels and churches in Venice), the architects have challenged themselves to create a new, invigorating atmosphere for the place of communion and ceremony.

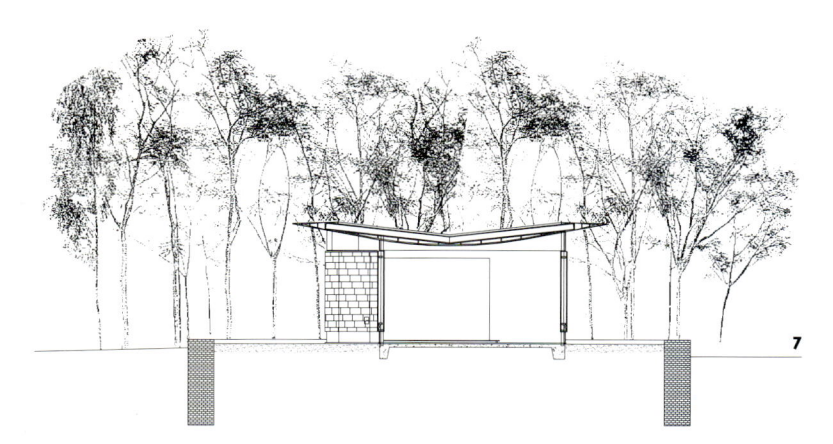

1.09

NEW SYNAGOGUE

CHEMNITZ, GERMANY

ALFRED JACOBY

2002

The latest design by an architect who has built so many synagogues that they were the subject of a travelling exhibition in the United States (1998–2001) is another striking contribution to the genre. It is part of a community centre project that sets the sacred structure firmly at the focal point of a handsome assemblage of wings clad in green granite and joined by a metal-and-glass atrium. The administration and meeting rooms occupy the rectilinear volumes while the synagogue and fan-shaped library, both in exposed concrete, jut out on either side of the length of the rectangle.

Architect Alfred Jacoby developed this arrangement in response to the 'amorphous' inner-city neighbourhood, he says, 'whose building structure has no clear order'. However, the overall shape of the community centre and synagogue is rational, with additional elements that emphasize thinking beyond strictly reasoned boundaries. The site is roughly rectangular and is oriented in an orderly fashion parallel to the street, though on a raised, landscaped level. The rise gives the building prominence and allows all of the elements to be viewed as a whole. However, the syna-

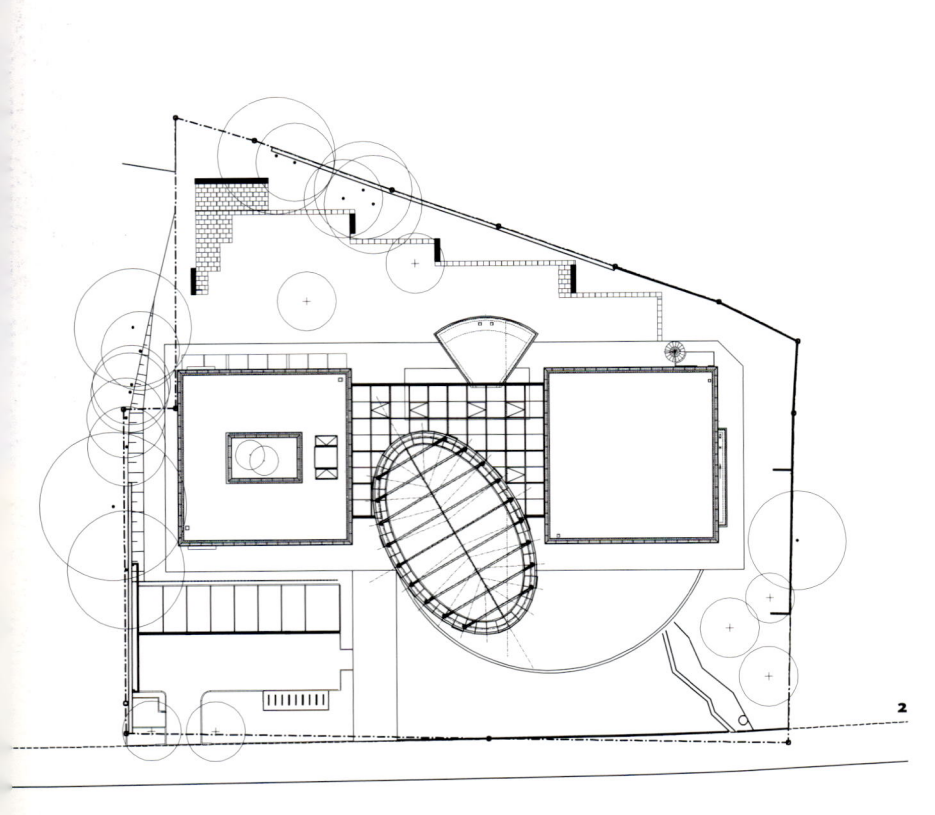

1 The wood-clad projecting window provides a hint of the rich interior. The curving pool is meant as a symbolic gateway to the spiritual realm.

2 The plan shows the architect's predilection for assembling contrasting geometric shapes.

3 The section shows the comparative volumes of the different areas of the complex, with the worship space (on the left) dominating the site.

4 The eight metre (26¼ foot) high window highlights the eastern orientation of the building. The grid of the glass clerestory and the window panes creates harmony among the different shapes and materials.

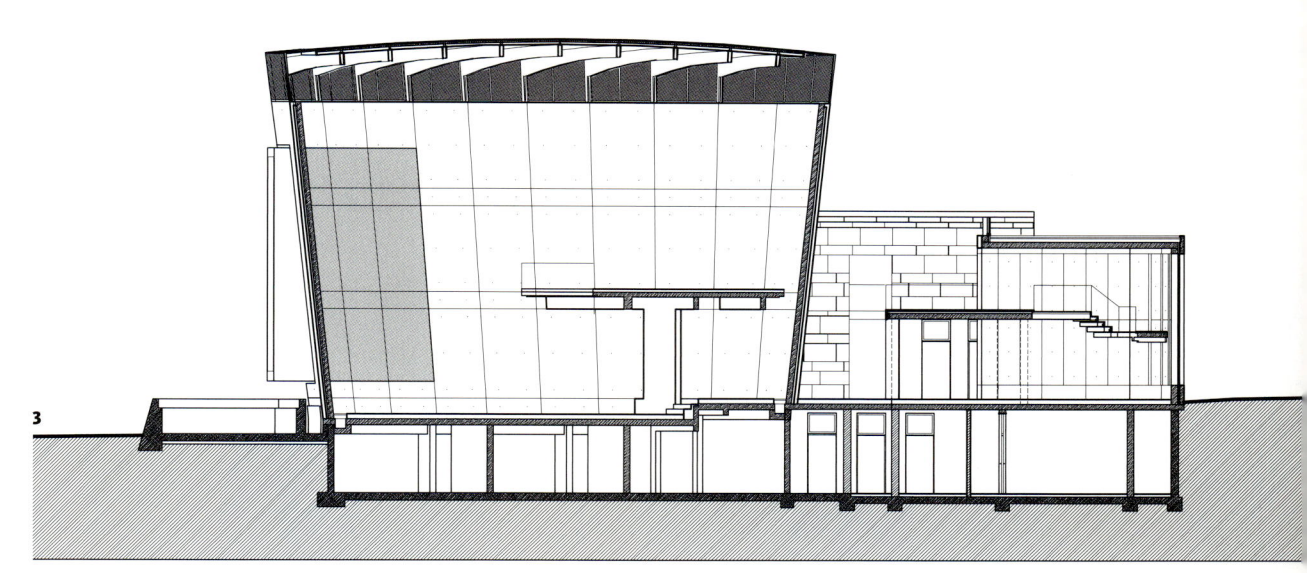

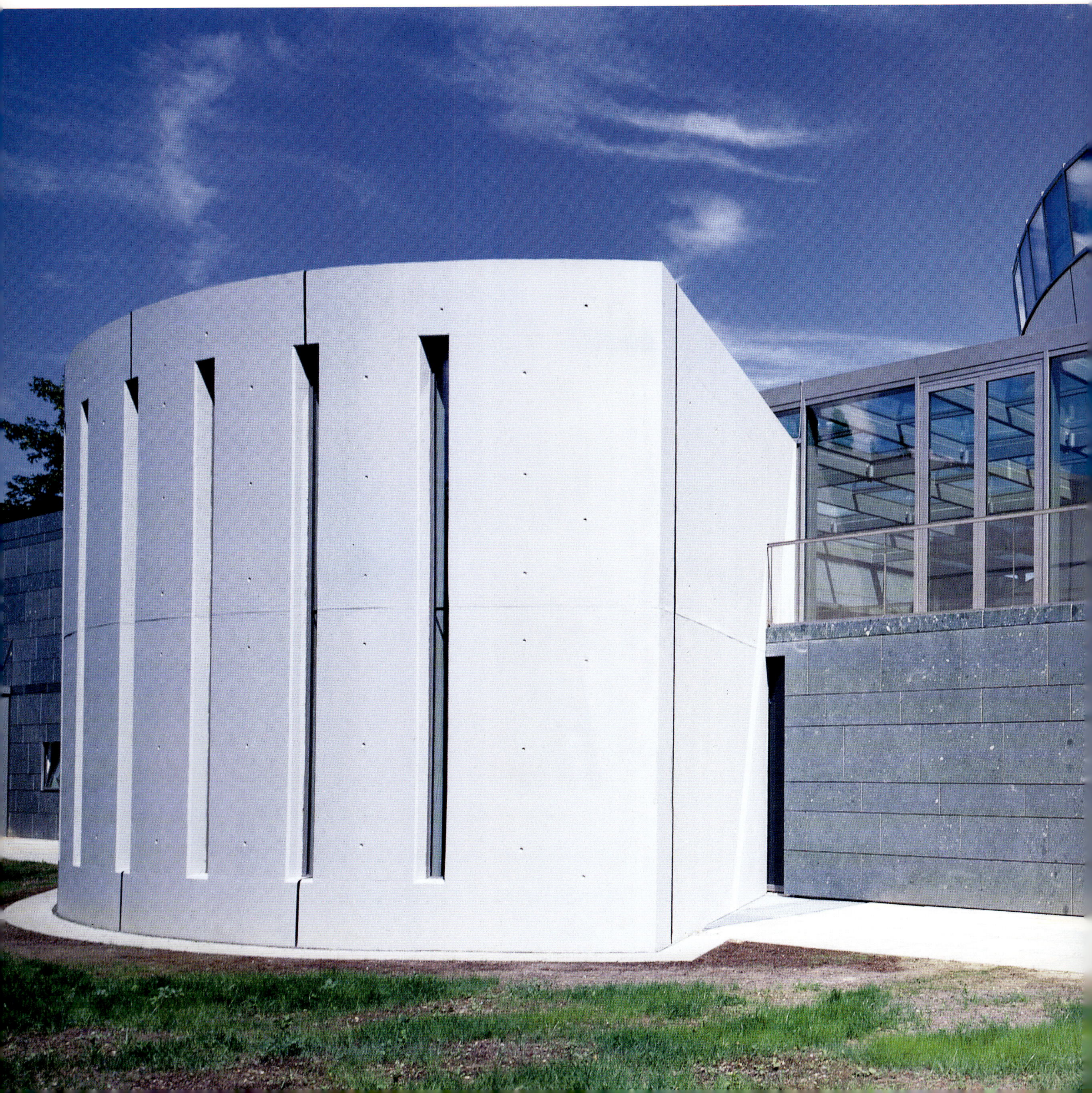

5 The wedge-shaped library wing echoes the synagogue structure in form and material, while the glass atrium of the interior allows the synagogue to remain the visible focus of the complex. The blocks are clad in green granite Verde de Salvan from Switzerland.

6 The plan shows the arrangement of administrative offices at left, with the library and synagogue at centre and a large meeting room at right.

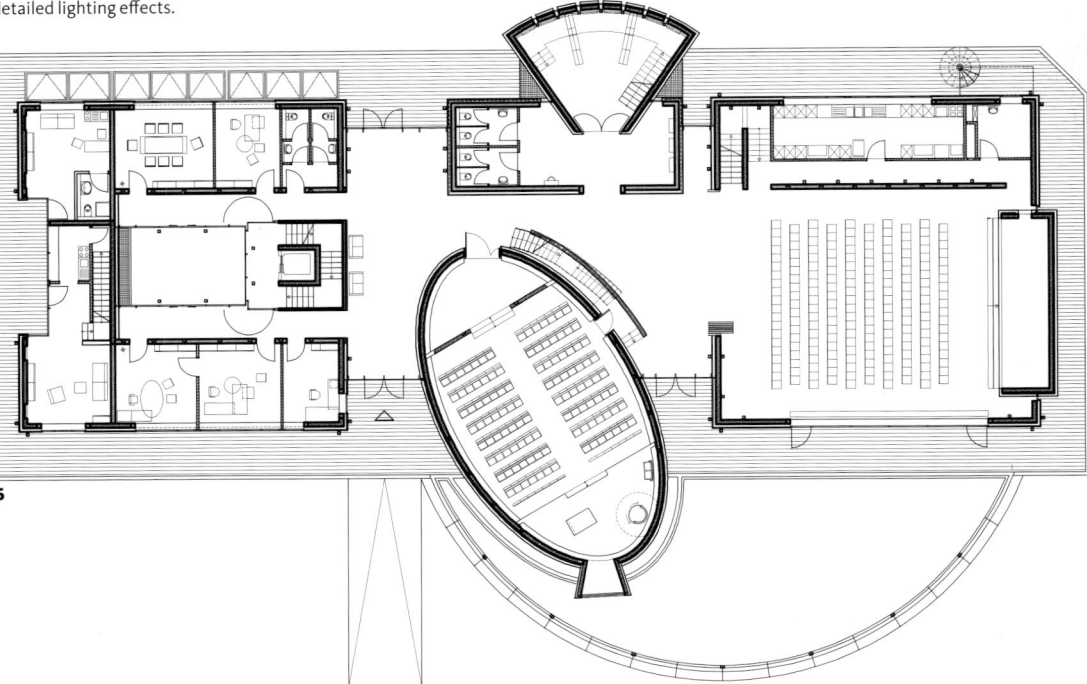

7 Colour and texture make a highly atmospheric interior that features the traditional Jewish colours of blue and white in coloured glass and textiles, dark wood and detailed lighting effects.

gogue's height, shape and contrasting surface material make it quite obviously the centre of attention. The shape, as Jacoby describes it, is 'an elliptical exposed concrete crown growing towards heaven with a glazed rim'. The glass rim and the eight metre (26 foot) high stained-glass window, which is framed in a cedar box that extrudes beyond the surface of the concrete, are the only elements that make reference to the other buildings: the colour and shape of the rectangular glazed panels show harmony with the wing structures of the community centre and with the atrium spaces that connect the complex. A narrow, semicircular 'water basin' forms a symbolic barrier, or threshold, between the narrow slope of lawn bordering the street and the synagogue entrance.

The brilliance of the synagogue interior, which makes vibrant use of the traditional Jewish colours of blue and white, could not be more opposed to the stark concrete exterior. It maintains the elliptical shape of the building and is suffused with an ethereal blue light that filters through the coloured rooflights and the blue stained-glass window set in the eastern wall. The floor and the (oak) benches are warm wood, as is the cedar cladding of the curved wall at the eastern end. The Torah shrine is covered in a deep blue cloth that pulls in the blue panels of the window and the blue-tinted ceiling lights. Clear glass panels, alternating with blue in the ceiling, cast precise squares of white light along the walls like astral beacons. Two glowing Stars of David are depended from the ceiling trusses, and connect with the diffuse white glow of the lighted pulpit with its interior menorah shape.

Amid such bright and bold effects, feelings of joy and wonder pervade the interior. It is not a space that puts one entirely at ease, more in pleasant anticipation. The architect deliberately set the traditional ceremonial elements off-centre of the elliptical axis, in order 'to leave the centre empty … In this way a balance between worldly meditation and religious prayer is brought into this space.' It is a fine balance within a space where the atmospheric lighting and luxurious tones of the wood create an undeniably physical beauty, while the purpose is to worship and honour God. However, it is a beauty that does seem to be pointed somewhere: forward through the prow of the structure, upwards through the skylit roofline and beyond the confines of enclosed earthly space.

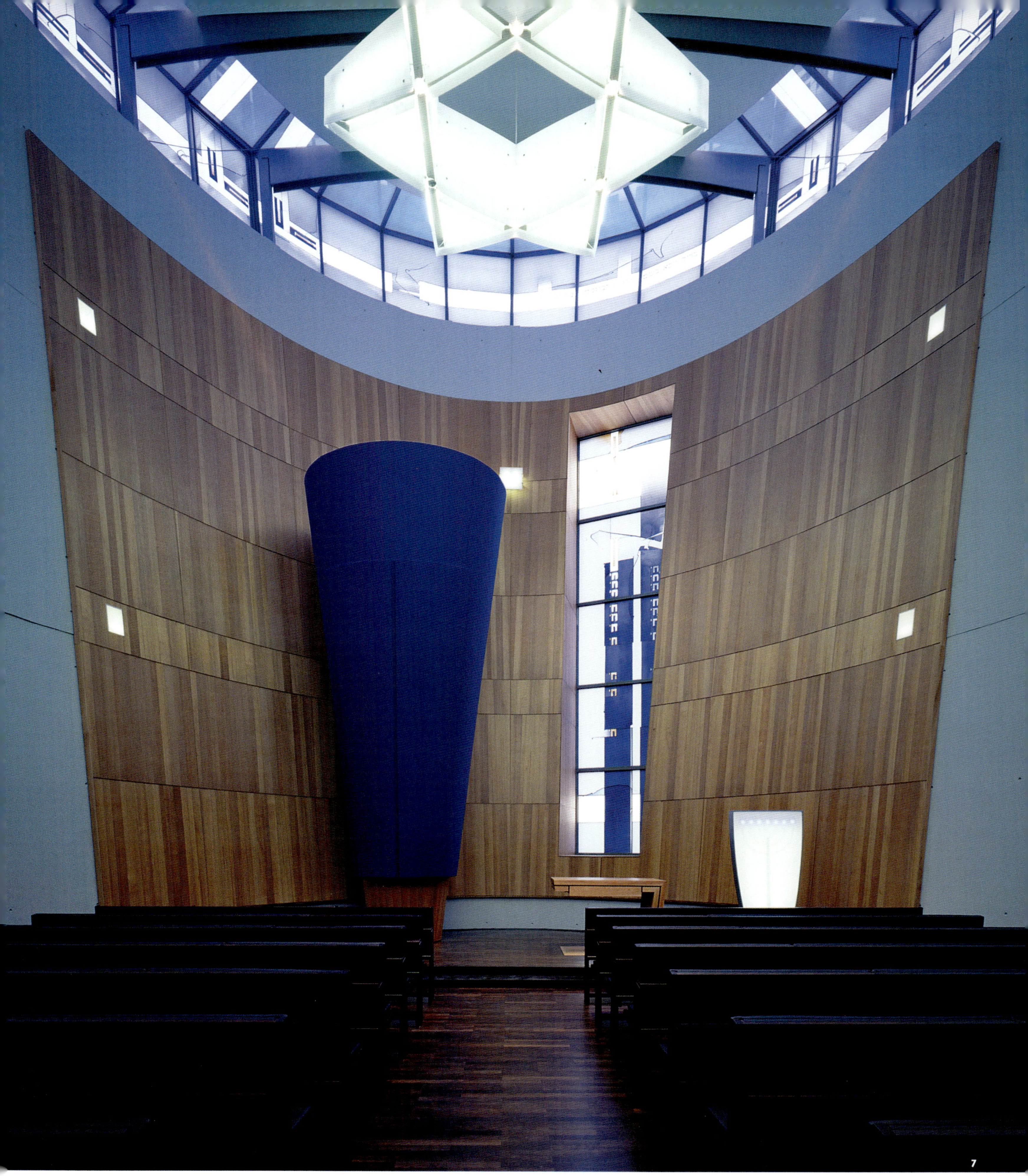
7

1 The internal 'skin' of the prayer halls features Koranic verses in classic script executed by hand by a traditional master calligrapher.

MOSQUE DESIGN

STRASBOURG, FRANCE

ZAHA HADID

PROJECT 2000

'The form of the mosque itself is derived from sound patterns, reverberations and the play of daylight,' says Zaha Hadid in her description of a competition scheme for a complex in Strasbourg. Those patterns and reverberations were in turn affected by the 'matrix set up by the axis for prayer, or qibla, in one direction and the curvature of the river (Rhine) in the other'. At the apex of the complex is the mosque itself. The architect also describes the building as a 'fractal space', generated by Islamic geometry, the symbolic and physical properties of water, the metaphor of calligraphy and the methodology of patterns. All of which gives a highly complex explanation behind a poetic, flowing form.

Zaha Hadid is known for conjuring buildings that, even if they do not get built, are beautiful renderings which themselves have the appeal of exquisitely drawn calligraphy. Here, in a scheme that comprises secular and religious functions, she has taken hold of symbol, metaphor and thematic concepts and laid them like ribbons across a practical plan. For the form does indeed resemble ribbon-like strips draped over a series of volumes – the undulations visibly responding to the waterside setting, like waves lapping at the bank. Among the peaks and valleys the shapes of modified arches are discernible, as are the swirls and flourishes of Islamic script. Elements that are often used in two-dimensional or relief patterns, have been brought by Hadid to three-dimensional life.

The scheme is not all flourishes; there is a very concrete logic to the arrangement of buildings that makes the poetic a realistic proposition in the urban context. To begin with, the mosque is elevated to the second level, along with an enclosed entrance courtyard. So the entrances to the secular facilities are all easily accessed at ground level, while the entrance to the mosque brings visitors to more enhanced aesthetic aspects of the scheme. Nonetheless, the ground floor will benefit from the structure

2 The model shows the 'mosaic or fragmented skin' which would be achieved using concrete panelling interspersed with glass and ceramics.

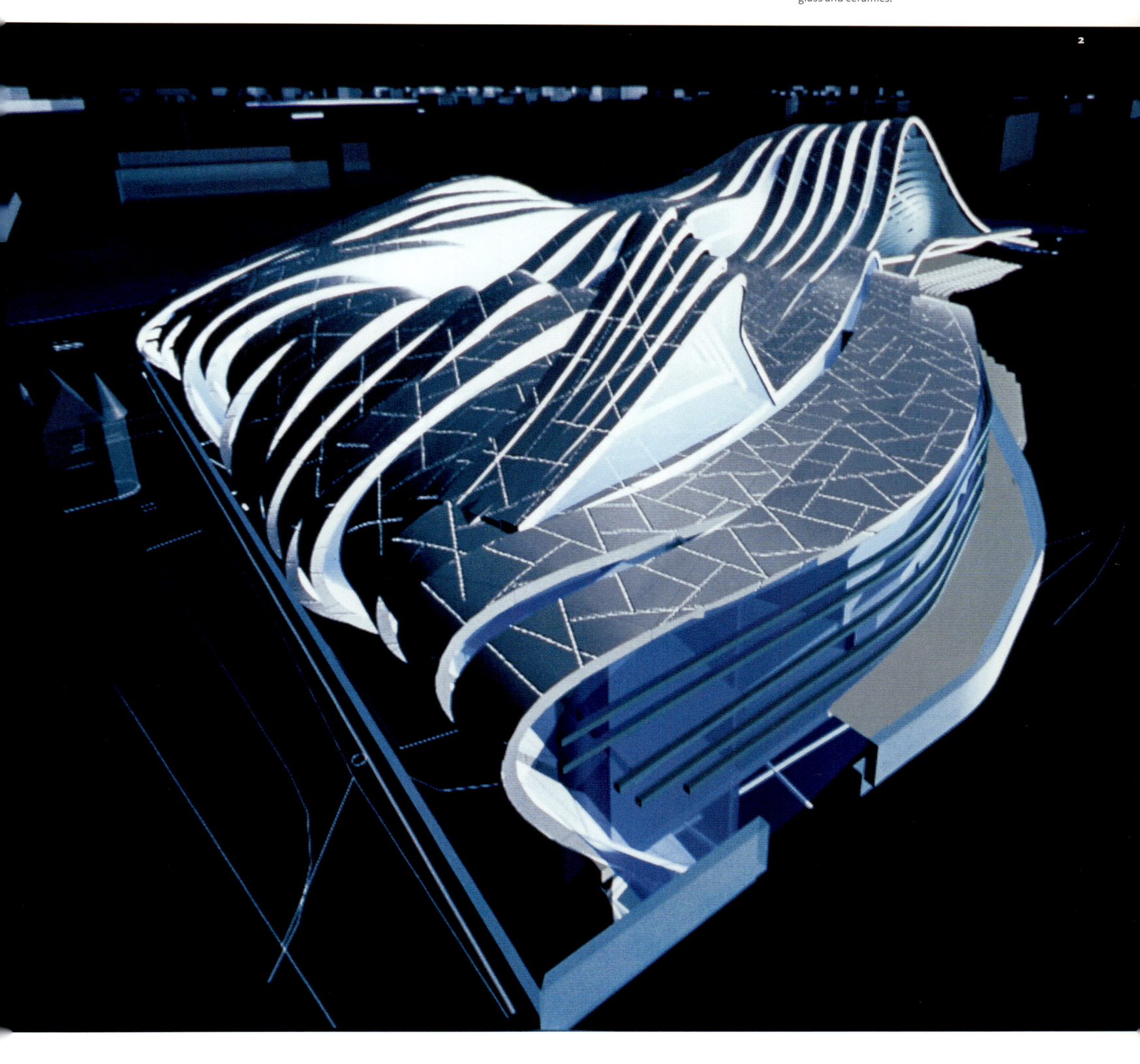

3 Here the model demonstrates how the undulating shape would sit within the built environment and how its flowing form responds to the curving river.

4 The design of the complex consists of public spaces on the ground floor while the prayer spaces are housed on the second floor, beneath the dramatic apex of the structure.

above, since slits at the mosque level will allow the light that permeates the roof and courtyard to fill the area below. The secular rooms, while important, are viewed as 'semi-autonomous pieces', acting as 'a collection of fragments ... similar to the pavilion arrangements of a citadel'.

Upstairs, the raised courtyard is insulated from outside noise and distraction by the adjoining buildings – the auditorium, library and kindergarten. Designed as an area of contemplation and transition, the courtyard also provides additional prayer space on holy days. This arrangement, though imbued with particular drama by Hadid's treatment, follows the Islamic tradition of using passages and transitional spaces so that the prayer space is removed, as 'an embracing and serene enclosure'.

The use of water, an element of great importance in the Koran, is also a traditional aspect of Islamic architecture that Hadid has gracefully inserted. 'Channels drift across the plan,' the architect explains, 'on the ground floor level and in the courtyard, forming parallel lines to the qibla.' In this way, the traditional rows of worshippers facing the qibla are re-created beyond the walls of the prayer space, and the 'gentle distraction' of flowing water serenades visitors to all parts of the complex.

Structurally, the form is based on the arch – but an arch that has been softened and stylized with reference to the flowing forms of calligraphy and the desire to slope toward the river. Reinforced concrete forms the primary structure, while a secondary layer of concrete panelling interspersed with glass and ceramics will, again, take traditionally decorative elements and make them perform much larger duties.

The interior of the prayer space will also benefit from the stylized calligraphic patterning that Hadid has brought to form. Eschewing a traditional screened gallery space for women that is set off from the main prayer space, Hadid proposes a separate hall. 'This enriches the innovative perception of the scheme,' she says, 'while acknowledging the contribution of women's spiritual and material culture in Islamic society, a role they have maintained since early Islam.'

Though it is as yet unbuilt, this is a scheme we can look forward to seeing in some adaptation or further development. The ideas it proposes are radical within the traditional or, better yet, bring the traditional elements (such as calligraphy) to radical new proportions and form – a form that deserves to be seen and admired.

2 INTERVENTIONS FITTING INTO THE BUILT LANDSCAPE

Christ Church, Donau City

A cathedral was once the centrepiece of the western European town or city; the church, the focal point of the village. Mosques, though usually located at the periphery, were often the largest buildings in a city.[1] In a modern, industrialized city populated by skyscrapers or overtaken by urban sprawl the task facing the architect of the religious building has less to do with creating a new centre or landmark and is more about responding to context. This is complicated by the fact that the need for harmony must be reconciled with the desire for a building to resonate with particular purpose, and enclose a sense of physical and spiritual retreat from the urban fray. Context can be a strongly mitigating factor, and it is the deft work of designers and their patrons that allows the growth of meaningful architecture within the framework of tolerance, faith and diversity.

The built landscape is sometimes flagrantly dictatorial, as in the case of the design for a jamat khana, or Ismaili prayer facility at the University of Natal in South Africa. The constraints in this case demanded an exterior that matched the materials of an existing building, but Yusuf Patel and his team from Architects' Collaborative managed to achieve much more than a seamless integration. So, too, did the architects of Office d'A, whose task was to create a prayer facility within an existing building and whose entrance leads from nothing more distinguished than a public corridor.

It is often almost impossible for architects to derive a harmonious link with the physical environment due to the inherent disharmony of the cityscape. Architecture Studio's giant cube, seemingly suspended within a three-dimensional metal grid, has no obvious associations with the 1970s high-rises and other modern buildings surrounding it. The imposing skeletal metal frame is meant to 'create transition between the secular world and the sanctuary' and only relates in pattern to the metal-and-glass gridded structures nearby. Similarly, Alfred Jacoby's Kassell synagogue and Lamott Architects' church in Völklingen emerge from their nondescript surroundings with affirmative force, not just as religious buildings but as potent reminders of aesthetic possibilities, drawing on subtle associations with materials and shape to connect with the built environment.

A different pressure is brought to bear on any building emerging from the ashes of destruction, such as the Kassell or Dresden synagogues (chapter 4). In many cases architects decide the best response is to leave a blank in the landscape in order to acknowledge the previous structure rather than try to emulate it in some way. The Chapel of Reconciliation in Berlin lies on the site of a church that was first trapped by the barriers of the Berlin Wall and then later destroyed. Reitermann and Sassenroth's new building is a small but powerful note of reconciliation that takes up a fraction of the old site, leaving space for memory and revelation.

Calm is the feeling inspired by Raj Rewal's Ismaili Centre in Lisbon, the first such facility for the Ismaili community in continental Europe. Its enlarged geometric patterning recalls both traditional Islamic and historic Portuguese architecture while offering a garden-centred bastion in the heart of the unspectacular urban fabric. Two continents away, Josh Schweitzer's synagogue in Hollywood brokers a similarly unprepossessing site and was further constrained by the need for ample parking in a city totally reliant on motor transportation. As a reaction to an even more densely packed location in a commercial district of Vienna, Heinz Tesar created a small, dark box of a church that looks inward, away from busy thoroughfares and looming skyscrapers, and explodes with warmth on the inside. The small, block form is in marked contrast to the towering skyline, a suggestion that in today's increasingly dense urban context the best response often lies in a quiet, graceful opposition.

1 The perfect cube sits in its tridimensional grid which acts as a buffer between the cityscape and the sacred space.

2 The cube structure is located at one end of a rectangular site, with an open plaza at the other end, all within a tightly packed urban area.

3 The exterior is clad in recycled paper hardened in resin and coated with a transparent protective anti-UV layer on to which words of prayer have been inscribed.

2.01

OUR LADY OF THE ARK OF THE COVENANT CHURCH

PARIS, FRANCE

ARCHITECTURE STUDIO

1998

Striving for perfection, spiritual or otherwise can be a noble aim. For the design of the new church in Paris's 15th arrondissement the Architecture Studio team chose a 'perfect volume ... that of a cube, because of its simplicity' and because 'the equal sides of the cube reflect the presence of the one and only'. Here is a grand statement of spiritual objectives, but a statement that must be rendered through architecture. The team at Architecture Studio have not merely set a perfect cube floating as some ultimate minimalist symbol; they have adulterated that perfect volume, like any grand church, with iconography and elements that invite interpretation.

Before visitors enter the cube, indeed probably before they perceive its form, they are confronted with the three-dimensional stainless-steel grid that holds it in seeming suspension. However, the grid is not structural; it is intended, the architects say, to 'create a transition between the secular world and the sanctuary'. It is as if the perfect cube is being protected from the outside world while at the same time remaining highly visible in its pristine form. The metal structure also helps to mediate the urban environment, since the architects had a limited amount of groundspace they could use to create any sort of barrier or entrance buffer. Stainless-steel members in similar proportion to the main grid are also used in a circular vertical form for a bell tower and, attached to the main building by a bridge of galvanized steel, for a symbolic and somewhat deconstructivist wedge-shaped structure that represents the traditional façade, leaving a space between it and the nave for the narthex. The stainless-steel framework

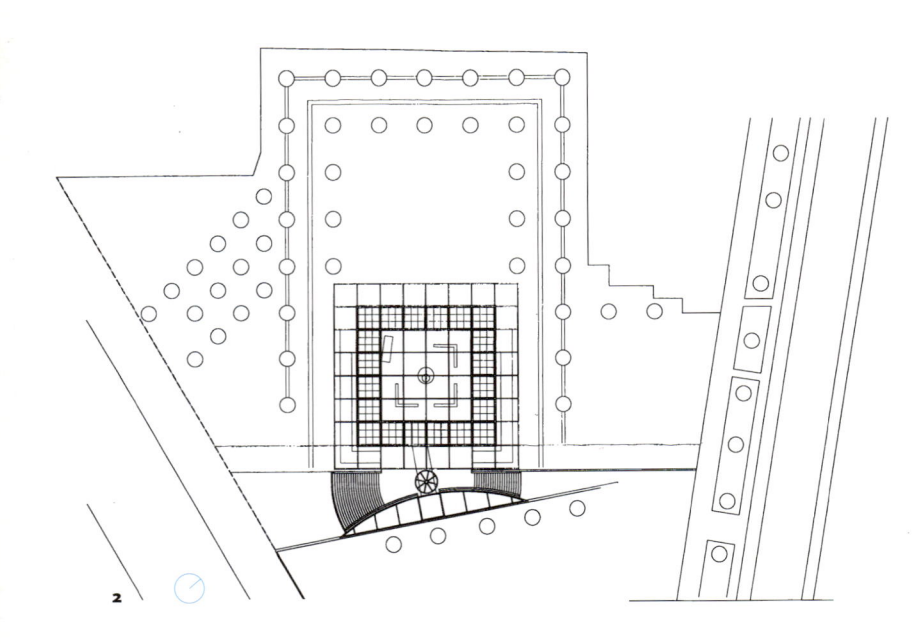

3

4 The grid is extended and used to form traditional elements like the bell tower.

5–6 The plan at the bottom shows the outline of the interior within the cube, while the plan immediately below shows how the arrangement within the simple square creates an apse and transepts.

7 The cube sits on 12 piles which raise it above ground level. The grid form at right is meant to suggest the presence of a grand façade, which is normally associated with more traditional church buildings.

creates delicate approximations of traditional elements while leaving almost total transparency around the sacred volume.

The interior maintains this theme of orthogonal purity marked by symbolic intrusions. The steel grid pierces the cube at the transepts, functioning again to outline the traditional structure of the church while leaving the cube intact. The main worship space is a smaller square within the floor area; however, the transepts are actually created by extending the floor plan beyond the sides of the square to form a cross shape. Extra seating is tucked into the extensions of the transept at ground level and in galleries on the first and second floors. Two six by six metre (20 by 20 foot) stained-glass windows placed at either end of the transept light the worship space. Smaller windows light the passageways between the galleries that form the cloisters, which are lined with louvred wood sections that separate them from the main worship space but allow light to filter in both directions. The exception to the square, the curved apse, is still contained within the cube but features a parabolic-shaped glass that shields a lighted symbol of the Cross and extends upwards toward infinity.

The pure form is also a model for the architects' predilection for unexpected materials. The flooring is black riven schist. The walls are made from recycled paper hardened with resin. The same material is used on the exterior but has an added transparent anti-UV coating which has been serigraphed with the words to the prayer of 'Hail Mary'.

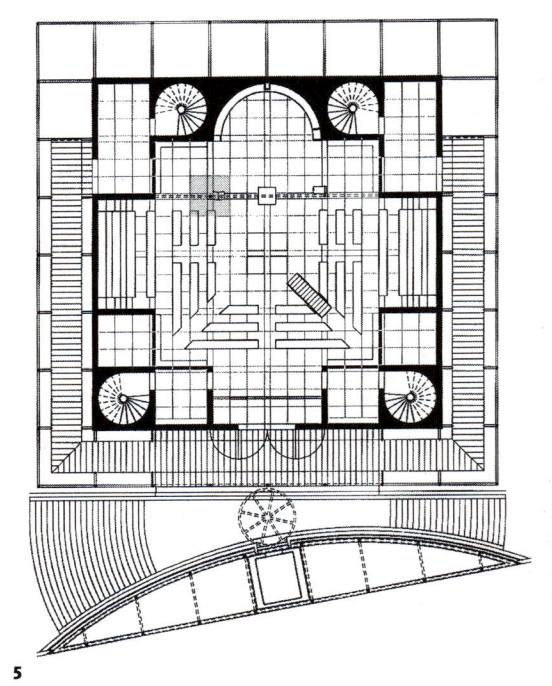

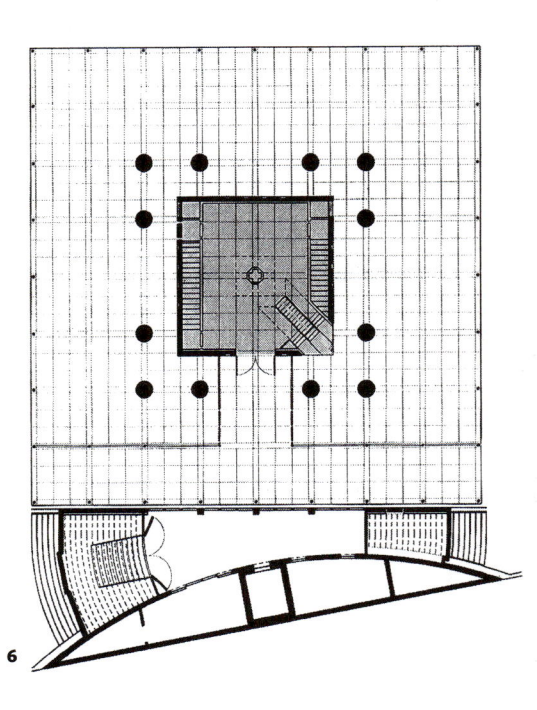

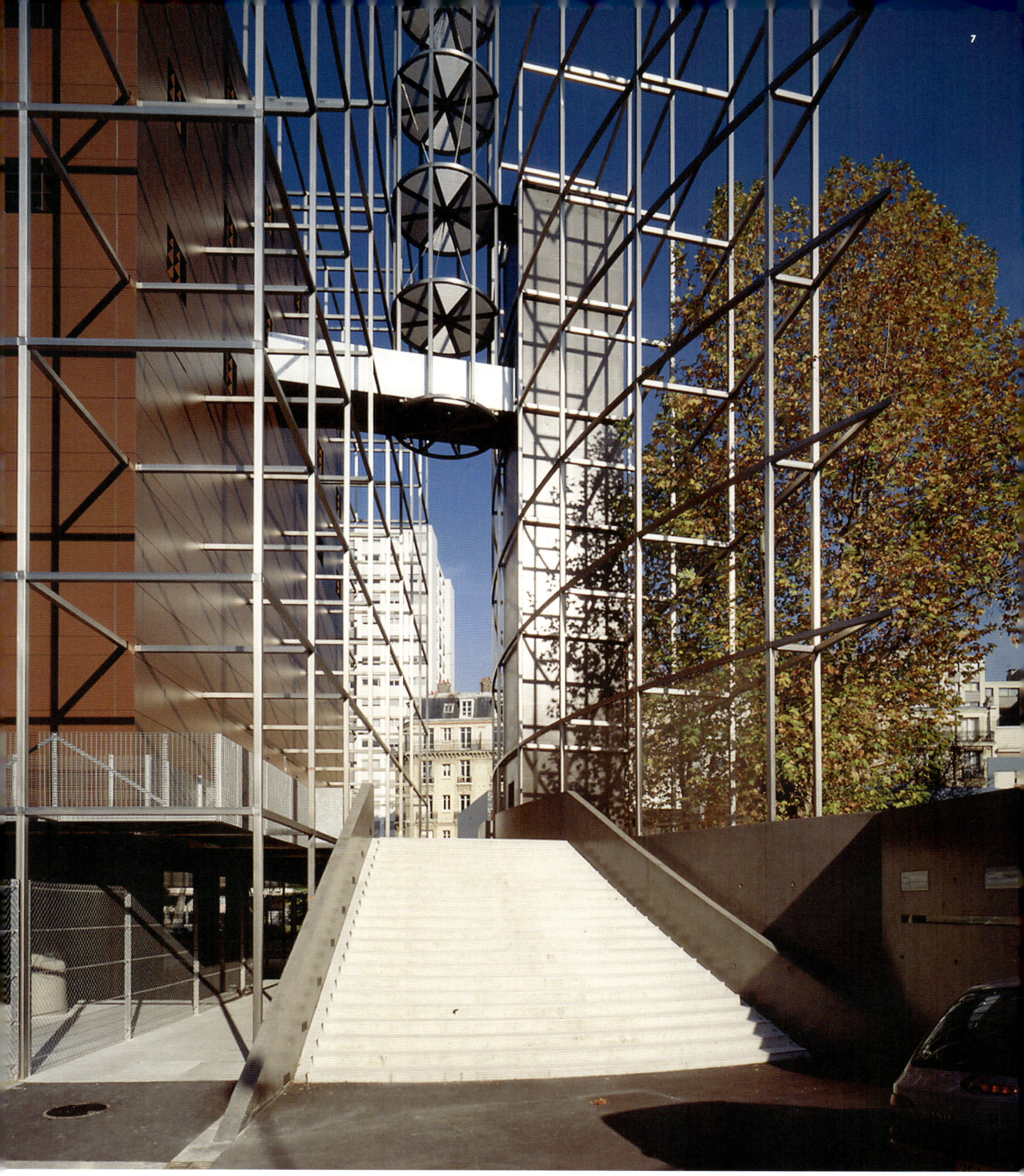

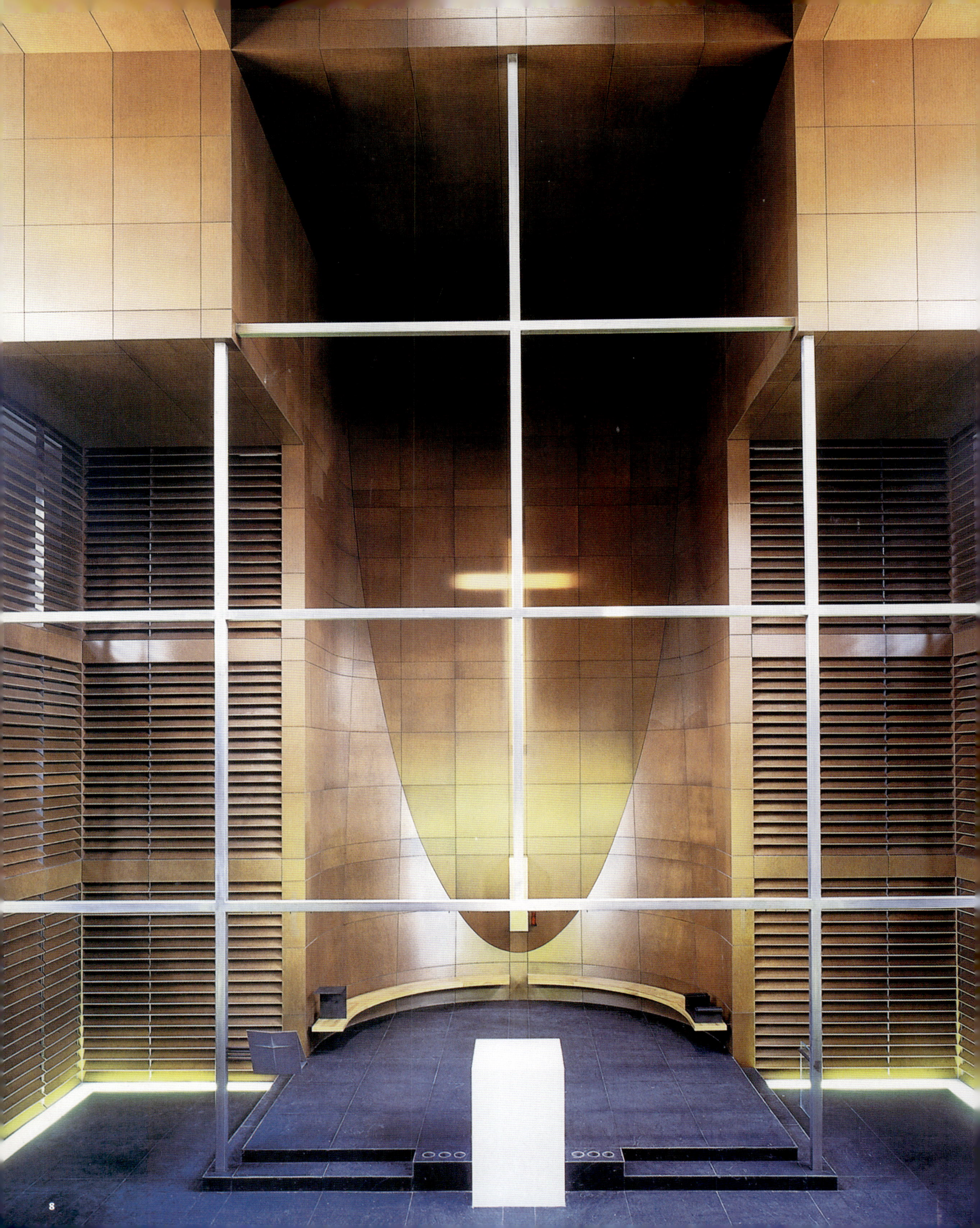

8 The grid pierces the interior space. The apse is formed by interior woodwork, while the glass panels in the floor allow light into the basement baptistery.

9 The section shows the different levels created inside, with stairways and access located along the periphery of the square.

10 The square plan is broken at both sides to create the transepts. Stairwells are hidden behind the louvred panels.

11 The elevation shows the relationship between the cube, the surrounding grid, the bell tower and the 'outlined' façade.

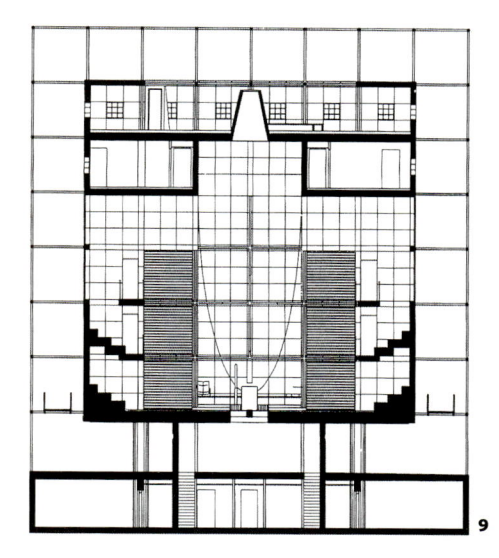

Symbolism is used from the ground up, with 12 piles, for the 12 Apostles, supporting the cube and surrounding the crypt and baptistery which are contained in a smaller box that drops below the floor of the cube to ground level. Trees and shrubs mask this space beneath the elevated volume, giving credence to the idea that the stainless-steel grid is actually supporting the mass of the structure. A real sense of procession is created with the wide entrance stair that begins at one end of the wedge-shaped metal 'façade' and leads up to the narthex/porch beneath the bell tower and then to the weighty main doors. Progressing from the street into the defined space of the grid, up to the main level provides a preparation not totally unlike the colonnaded entrances of the old basilicas. Such strong links with past traditions usually come at the price of innovation; here, however, the elements are easily readable without being dominant. Great symbolic importance lies behind the design, but its manifestation is unique, provocative and puts the viewer in mind of what it is like to strive for an ideal.

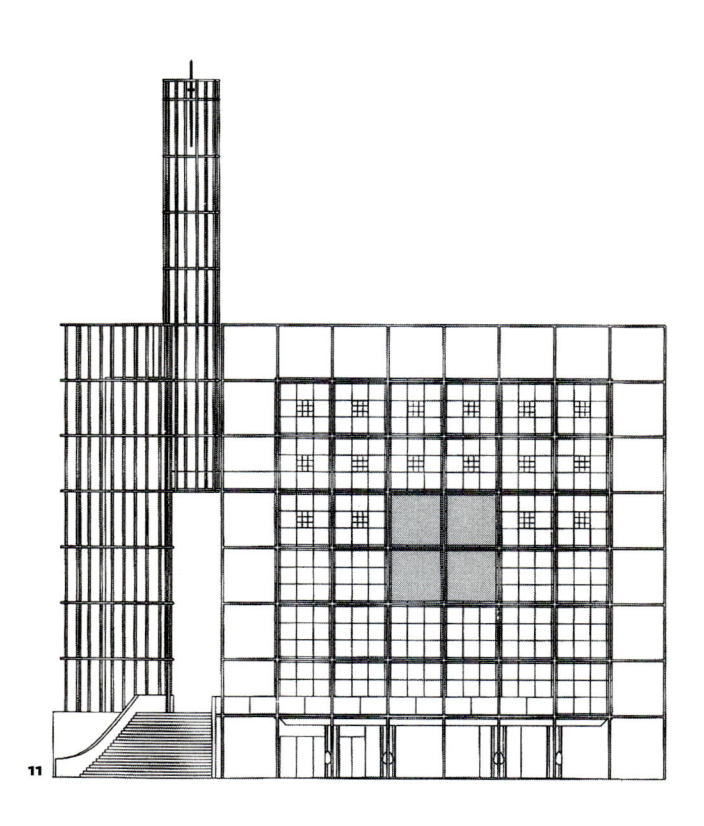

2.02

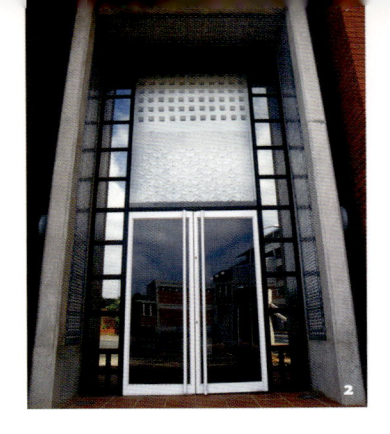

JAMAT KHANA

UNIVERSITY OF NATAL

DURBAN-NATAL, SOUTH AFRICA

ARCHITECTS' COLLABORATIVE

1995

This is a project in which the religious aspect was viewed by the architects not only as less than a constraint, but as something they would have happily recognized had they been allowed. However, the brief for this prayer facility on the campus of the University of Natal precluded the design of a traditional religious structure. After allowing the university's 1,000 or so Muslim students and faculty to make use of a temporary facility for Friday prayers, the university decided to take back that facility but bowed to demands for a new space. A 19 x 19 metre (60 x 60 foot) plot of open car park area was allocated for the project with the specific requirement that the building be not only free from religious references on the exterior, but that it match the neighbouring Shepstone Building – which houses the university's School of Architecture – in the use of red brickwork and off-shutter concrete. Yusuf Patel of Architects' Collaborative found the conditions challenging, but he concludes they also 'allowed us a flexibility we would necessarily not have enjoyed' had they been asked to design a traditional Islamic prayer space.

'Islamic architecture, particularly in respect of mosque design hasn't progressed very far in the nineteenth and twentieth centuries', Patel argues. 'We have a great legacy but whilst there has been the adoption of new materials and structure, very little development has taken place. Most of what is going around is a replica of traditional forms, arrangements, etc. I think we were able to synthesize the elements of the mosque and present them in a contemporary way.' The architect explains that a jamat khana, as opposed to a mosque, is a 'congregation house' and can be on leased land, while a mosque cannot, and its use can change over time. The resulting structure is a thoroughly contemporary-looking design and is a thoughtful, sculptural building. It has the added accomplishment of successfully jumping through religious and secular hoops – that is, it does not appear religious but it fulfils the requirements of a centuries-old religion for which tradition is paramount. Nothing on the exterior indicates that this is an Islamic structure, except perhaps the tiny pattern on a narrow fin-like panel projecting from the leaning qibla wall which is covered in a delicate interlocking geometric patterned zalij (Moroccan-style mosaic) and denotes the placement of the mihrab inside. For those unaware of the building's purpose it is simply a small but beautiful detail on an otherwise blank but nicely articulated façade.

The arrangement of wedge shapes, cubes and triangles that make up the visible structure account for the very modern appearance, but can also be taken as the continuation of the Islamic tradition of using geometric and abstract motifs – only here they are structural rather than decorative. The concrete and red brick were dictated by the neighbouring building but other details were not. The canting of the 'wing' walls at 15 degrees, for example, and the thousands of tiny holes that, somewhat like a mushrabiyah (traditional carved screen), allow light and air to pass through the concrete without loss of privacy are evidence of the architects' aim to 'create a building that would have all the elements of mosque design, but

1 The red brick and concrete were meant to match a nearby existing building, but the angular form and arrangement of the materials make the building highly distinctive.

2 The main entrance is inlaid with zalij and, along with the mihrab, it contains the only external decoration.

3 The leaning concrete 'wing walls' define the prayer space portion of the building.

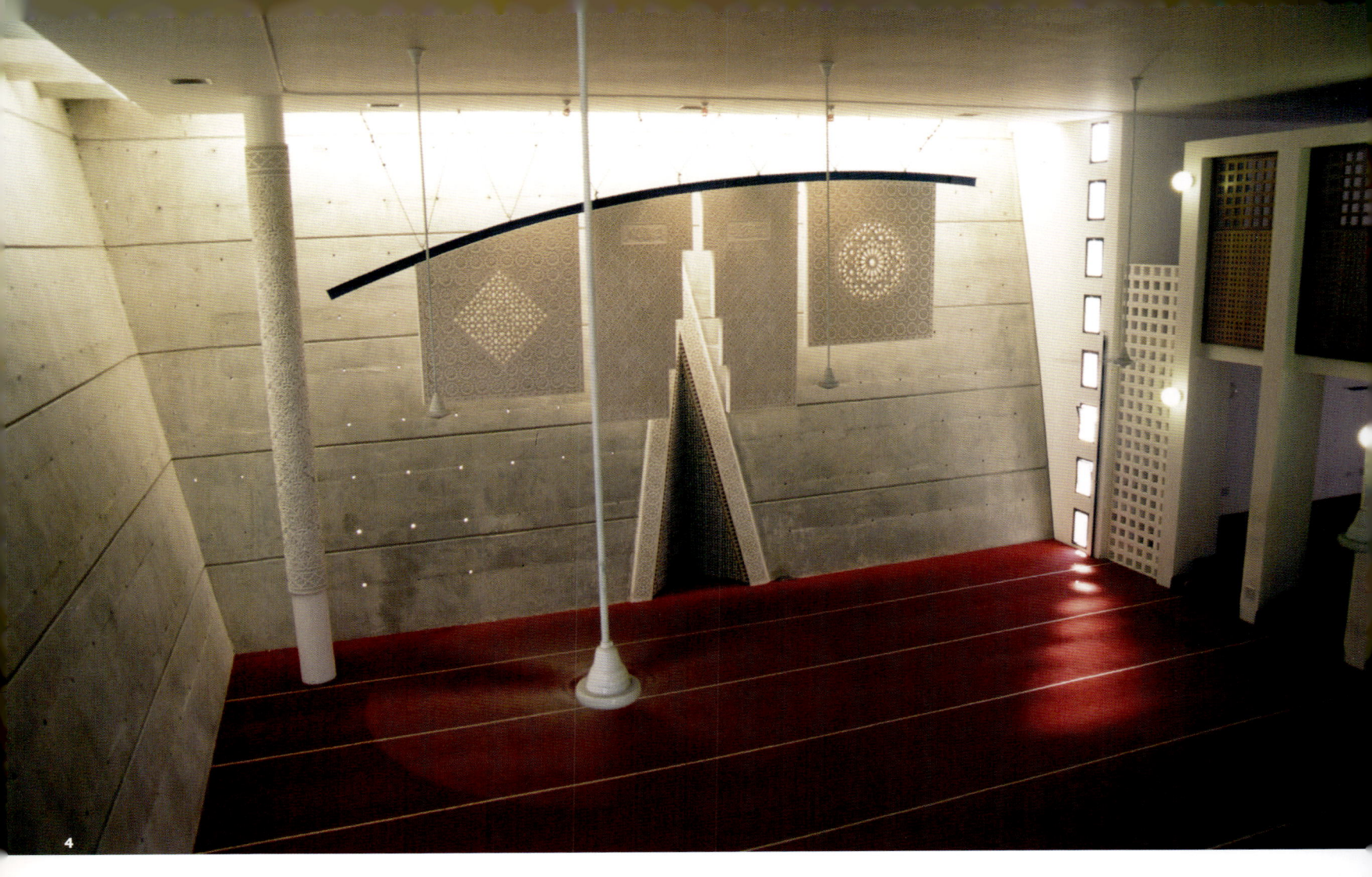

4 The main prayer space is lit by a combination of toplighting, rows of small, rectangular openings and tiny piercings within the wing walls, all set within the wing walls.

5 The mihrab is expressed as 'an elongated prism' accentuated with delicate carving and zalij.

would not look like any other mosque'. This philosophy extended to the interior decoration. The main prayer space is left open, with skylights and some artificial light enhancing the small area. Fretwork wooden screens separate the women's prayer space as per tradition but there are also innovations. The lines etched in the exterior concrete echo the pattern of the carpet in the main (male) prayer space. The carvings carried out by experienced Moroccan craftsmen are given greater attention due to the spare backdrop. The architects gave them further significance by asking the craftsmen to construct separate panels, rather than carvings to set onto walls or other surfaces, so that they are backlit by peripherally placed skylights. These add to the gravity-defying feeling that Patel says he wanted to impart. This, in the face of the heavy burdens imposed by both tradition and conformity, is the stuff of thoughtful innovation.

6 Ground-floor plan
1. male prayer hall, 2. committee room, 3. male shoe lobby, 4. male ablutions, 5. sahn (entry courtyard), 6. male toilets, 7. kitchen

7 Upper-floor plan
1. main hall, 2. library, 3. female toilets, 4. female shoe lobby, 5. female ablutions, 6. female prayer area

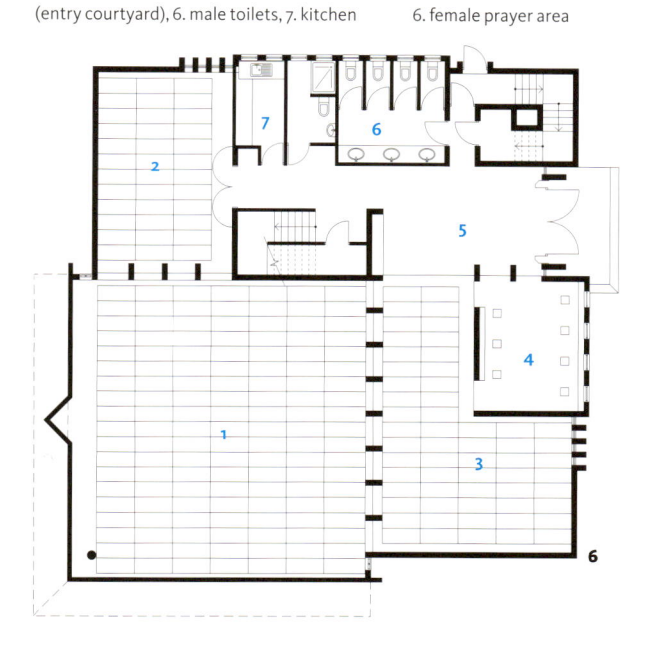

8 The main prayer space with the female prayer area located on the upper floor behind the wooden screens.

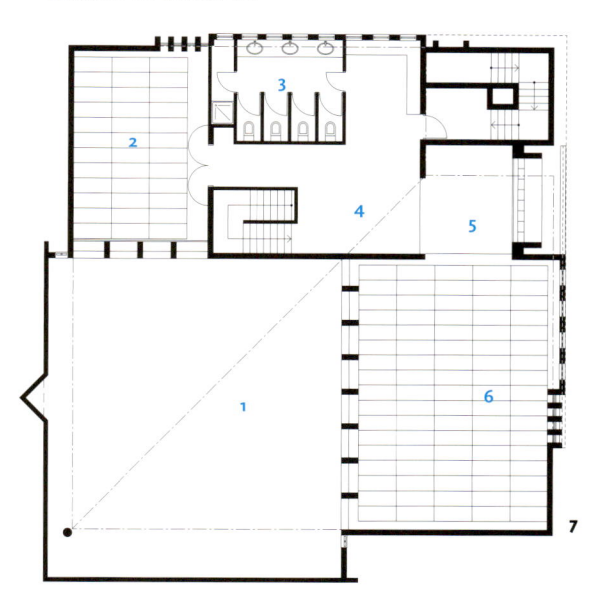

1 Backlit transparent wall panels provide ambient lighting in a windowless room.

2 The exploded axonometric shows how all the three interior surfaces were treated as building parts so that the design is a complete structure within the existing space.

2.03

INTERFAITH SPIRITUAL CENTER

NORTHEASTERN UNIVERSITY

BOSTON, MASSACHUSETTS, USA

OFFICE D'A

1999

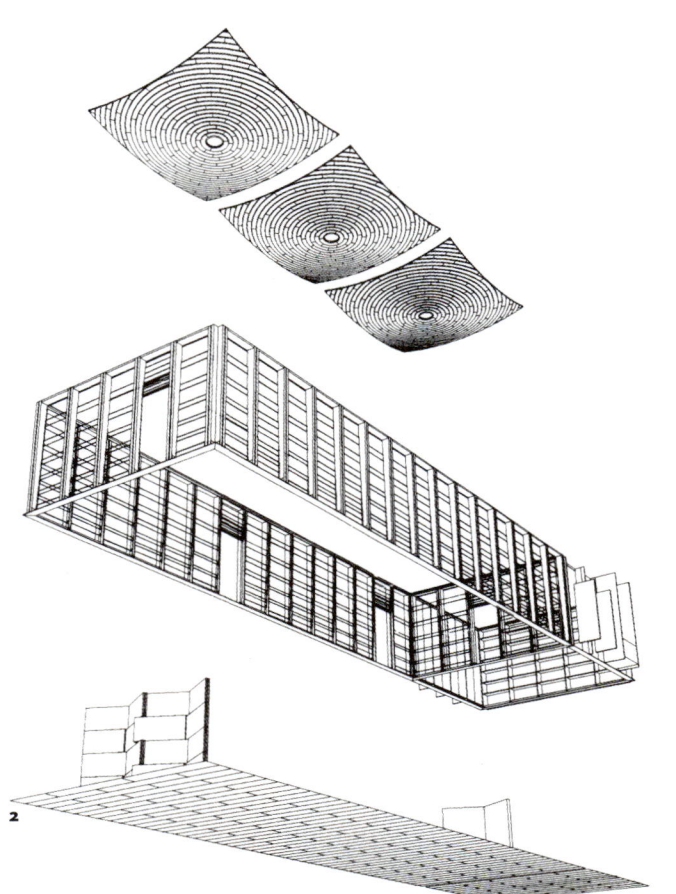

Office d'A are a young, innovative practice based in Boston, Massachusetts. Their brief for a multi-faith worship/communion facility at Northeastern University was to create a space 'where people of different spiritual, religious and cultural orientations may come together under one roof for prayer and reflection as well as constructive dialogue'. The architects point out how this aim differs from that for 'conventional university halls of prayer' which, they say, 'are conceived as non-denominational chapels – sacred spaces for no specific religion'. The idea here was something that could be adapted to suit different religions specifically. So, rather than a nondescript space, it was to be a changeable venue that accommodated distinct types of ceremonies and gatherings.

To achieve this the architects produced something like the typical large, unadorned interior that one would expect, but they gave that interior a beauty of surface and atmosphere that is remarkable and transcends religious boundaries rather than ignoring them. Two ante-rooms 'function as mediators and collector spaces for the various user groups', that is, they provide a meeting room and small library with storage units for the 'reli-

3 Surface finishes and textures are intrinsic to the design, in the ablutions room as much as in the main space.

4 Movable furnishings, along with the three ceiling shutters, can be used to orient the space for specific ceremonies.

5 Highly polished wood provides a reflective surface to respond to the varied lighting devices and gives a real sense of warmth.

6 A prayer rug is laid out for a Muslim service.

7 The plan shows the three ceiling domes with their rotating shutters, the entrance off the main corridor and the rooms for storage and ablutions.
1. entrance, 2. ablutions, 3. main space, 4. storage

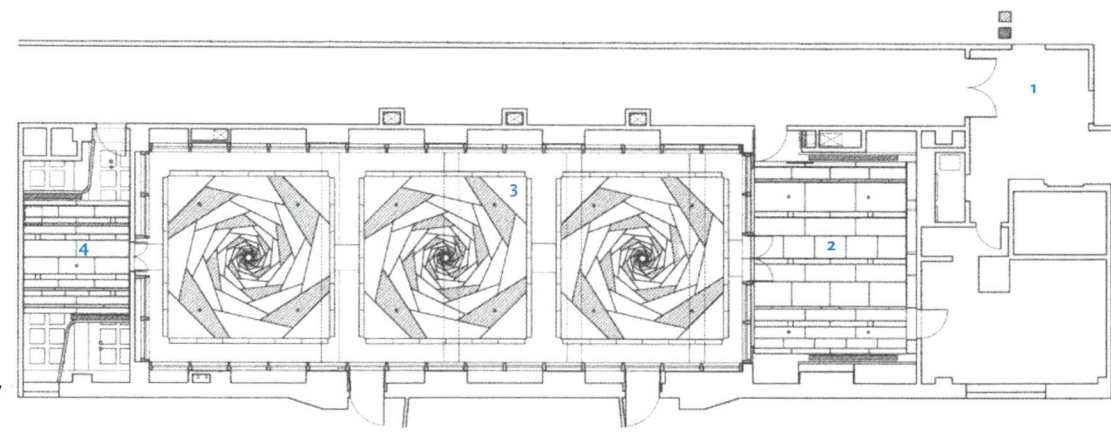

gious and ceremonial artefacts' and a room for ablutions as required for mosque and synagogue attendees. Neither of these rooms is given any sacred association and both are meant to be primarily utilitarian so that the focus of the religious intent is on the main space. This is a room shimmering in polished wood and gleaming surfaces with subtle reminders of the morphing shapes and innovative materials that architects Monica Ponce de Leon and Nader Tehrani have become known for. Since this is a space in an existing building, the light comes from frosted-glass wall panels that have been backlit to emit a soft, inviting glow. The light can be modulated for different purposes. The floor is covered in Brazilian cherrywood, which is also used for other elements around the room. It is of a hue and shine that speaks of a certain aesthetic awareness and intensity. This is not a hollow hall; it is an absorbing, womb-like space.

As many religious buildings are concerned with the focus and filtering of light, so too is this multi-faith room. The design also had to contend with the lack of natural light, something it does quite successfully, managing to create an ambience that seems more purposefully attenuated than artificial. Perhaps the most intriguing element is the series of domes suspended above metallic, rotating shutters that can modulate light but also shift the focus of the room according to need: toward the east, west or centrally. Light also appears around the periphery, as is common in mosques and churches. The reflective quality of the highly polished wood and of the metal shutters enhances the quality of light, so that the fact that this is a space within a busy campus building is lost to those who gather here.

It may be a small project but it is one that excels beyond spatial limits in its attention to finely crafted details, from the panes of glass set between wood panels to the mechanics of the domes, to the sculpture of the furnishings and even the light wood, deep blue curtains and articulated stainless-steel footwash bowls in the ablutions room. Whether chairs are set out for Christian or Jewish services or a prayer rug laid out for Muslim worship, the space bespeaks a beauty and solemnity of craft. This is all the more remarkable as the Interfaith Center is entered 'circumstantially from a corridor, like any other classroom in the building' say Ponce de Leon and Tehrani 'without the characteristic sequence of spaces that anticipates places of prayer or spirituality'. But what it lacks in processional space it more than makes up for in a distinctive atmosphere that makes crossing the threshold an act of transcendence.

1 The sketch shows how the new church sits in the corner of the old building's footprint with the outer shell aligned on the axis of the old church and the inner shell turned toward the east.

2 When lit from within the transparency of the louvred outer wall makes the building act as a lantern.

3 The site plan shows the small presence of the church in the 'death strip' of the Berlin Wall.

2.04

CHAPEL OF RECONCILIATION

BERLIN, GERMANY

REITERMANN/SASSENROTH ARCHITEKTEN

2000

The site presented to architects Rudolf Reitermann and Peter Sassenroth was a palimpsest of the terror and division that had come before. Once the location of the Neo-Gothic Reconciliation Church built in 1884, this area became divided by the erection of the Berlin Wall in 1961. Sitting in the no-man's-land between sections of the wall, the church was seen as an unnecessary obstacle and was taken down in 1985 in order 'to increase security'. In 1996, architects, investors and artists were invited to present ideas for a competition to erect a new building. Reitermann and Sassenroth's winning entry confronts the tensioned themes of old and new, built and unbuilt, memory and progress with unusual lightness and grace in a setting that is heavy with history.

The louvred structure appears slight and insubstantial, as if it makes no claims to its own longevity in an area so resonant with political-military flux. It is also small: nine metres (30 feet) high and 18 metres (60 feet) wide at its furthest point. An oval shape encloses another, smaller oval centred on the same point but turned within. This point was determined by the

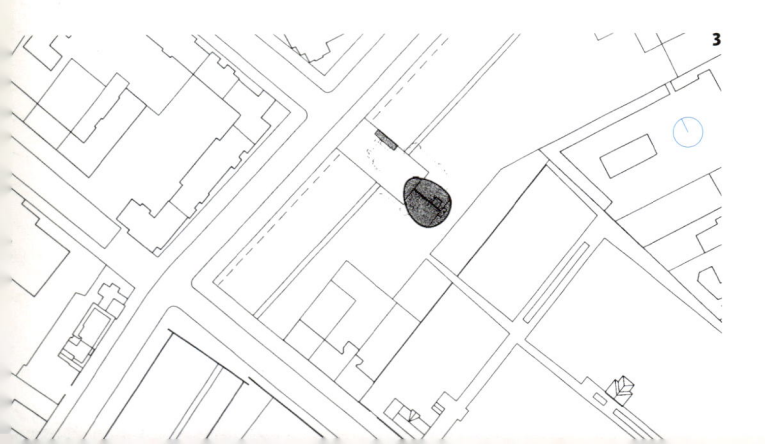

4 The church is separated from the built-up surroundings by land that has been left open.

5 During the day, the slatted wall presents an unadorned surface that is appealingly textured.

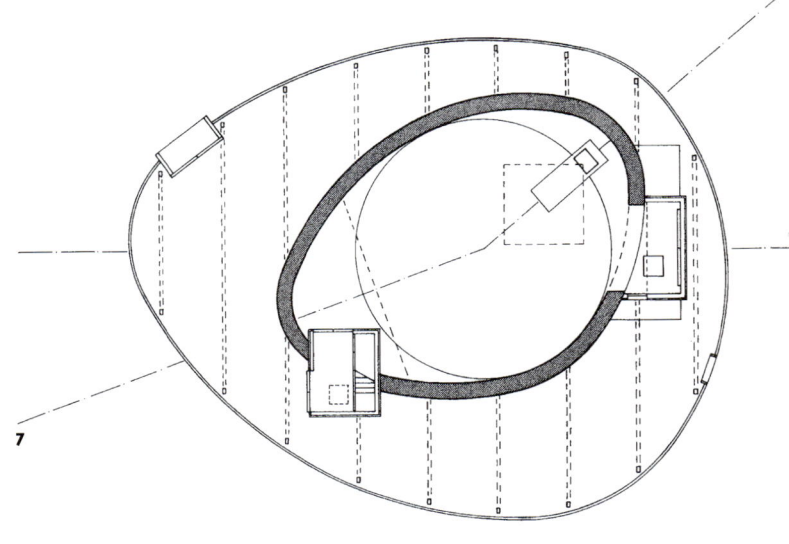

intersection of an east–west axis and one that runs from north-west to south-east and is drawn parallel to the central axis of the old church. The interior structure is like a more solid centre but with some interesting properties. The curved wall, overseen by specialist Martin Rauch, is made of compressed loam (also called rammed earth) with brick fragments, taken from the old church, and flax fibres. The solid form of the altar was also made from loam to Rauch's design.

The compressed loam is solid enough to help carry the roof load and its solidity has great symbolic value for the architects as well. Within the open framework of the slatted outer wall, made from Canadian Douglas fir, they say 'the loam is visible and is the core or heart of the building. The precise position of the inner space refers to the altar and choir of the former church.' It also conveys a real sense of centred gravitas that imbues the structure with genuine meaning against the open framework of the outer shell. As the wooden skin contrasts with the inner structure in form and in position, it also creates an oscillating open-air corridor around the main worship space that emphasizes the break in strict geometry. As the more regular form of the outer wall corresponds to, and sets the building in alignment with, the outline of the former church inside, the shape is bent to acknowledge another, less physical orientation, as well as a certain dis-connected-ness from the outside world.

The church is now surrounded by ample green space, and the choice of creating such a negligible mark on the land was deliberate. By placing the building in a small portion of the site of the old church, whose physical foundations are still visible in parts, the architects say, 'the body of the building does not become the focal point of the plot but leaves as much free room as possible to indicate the volume of the former church'. They also wanted to maintain the open area in order to make 'a poetic space within the built environment around it', and leave an appreciable degree of separation. 'It is not a multi-purpose room,' they point out, 'but rather a very special sacred place in the middle of the former "death strip" of the Berlin Wall.' With so much history and emotion weighing on it, this is a project that remarkably defies heaviness of reference or iconography. Instead, light and transparency are prized, along with inner strength.

6 Within the oval of the outer wall is the loam, or rammed-earth, wall that forms the sanctuary and contains earth and fragments of the former church.

7 The inner shape is deliberately off-axis with the outer wall. The inner wall is breached by the entrance box (on the left) and by the niche for the reredos at the east point (on the right).

8 The sketch of the inner, loam wall shows the point of intersection between the east–west and the north-west–south-east axes.

9 The layers of compacted earth and fragments are visible in the loam wall. The reredos, a nineteenth-century carving of the Last Supper, came from the former church and had been vandalized. Below it, the basement of the old church can be viewed through the window in the floor.

1 The entrance façade. The metal cut-outs on the window spell *tzedek*, the Hebrew word for 'justice'. The main panel features symbols for light and is surrounded by quotations from the Book of Psalms.

2 The building blends in with the profile of the built-up area while possessing distinguishing qualities of texture and detailing.

3 The letters here spell *shalom* ('peace'). The architect has used different tones and textures in the stucco rendering to distinguish elements of the building.

2.05

KOL AMI SYNAGOGUE

HOLLYWOOD, CALIFORNIA, USA

SCHWEITZER BIM

2002

The commission came about over a tennis game, says Josh Schweitzer, the architect of a new synagogue in Hollywood. Schweitzer has become a famous son, responsible for a string of high-design restaurants built during the 1990s when Los Angeles's craze for fusion was matched only by the hunger for holistically designed eateries in which everything from the wall panels, to the matchbooks to the cutlery bore the trademark of the architect/designer. But Schweitzer emerged with solid credentials and ambitions, as he related to his tennis partner. 'I said that my dream project would be a religious building. She said that she was part of a small congregation that was looking to house themselves in their own space, having used a Christian church for many years.'

It is a far cry from achingly trendy restaurant work, but the Kol Ami Synagogue bears witness to an author who knows how to fit in with the local environment while at the same time making well-wrought, detailed design. The building rises from its small, lacklustre site on the corner of a busy traffic intersection, looking distinctly Californian with its adobe-esque surface and softly rendered Mission-style box shape. The exterior's brushed green-brown look is achieved with 'brown coat stucco' which the architect explains 'is the second step in a normal three-part application. I prefer it in this stage because it has an incredible texture; very rough and

3

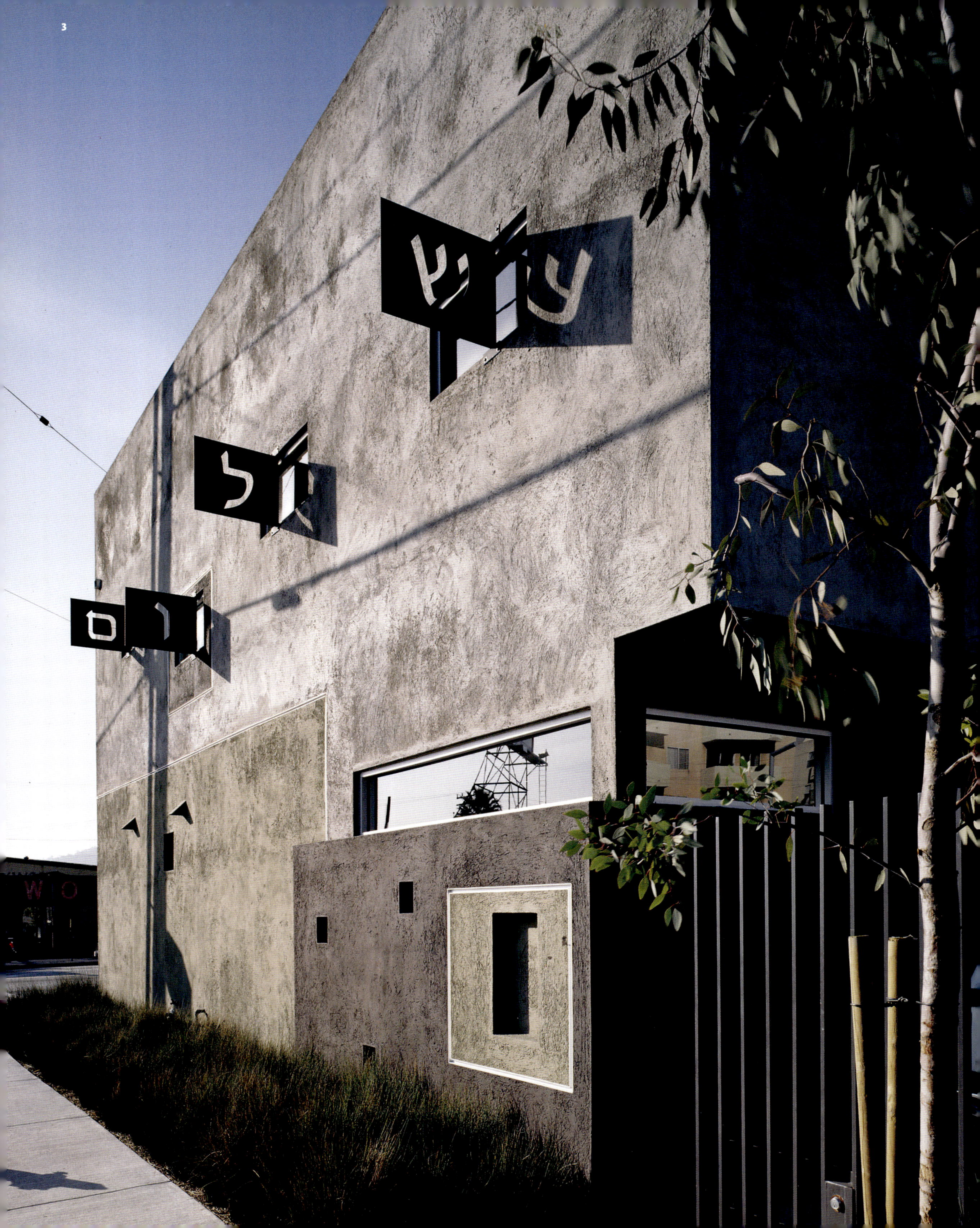

4 The ark, with its ten etched-glass panels, was designed by artist Laurie Gross.

imperfect.' This imperfect texture, together with the planted palm trees, may make for a very typical Southwestern picture, but it is an atypical synagogue building. Schweitzer's penchant for powder-coated aluminium elements has been expressed here with protruding window screens that are cut out with the name of the synagogue in Hebrew lettering. Another cut-out metal panel greets visitors at the main entrance and features the symbols for light, and text from the Book of Psalms. Although Schweitzer has used similar elements elsewhere, these finely honed, enigmatic details reminiscent of the California Craftsman Style work well as potent symbolic gestures that distinguish the building without overwhelming it.

Kol Ami is a Reformed synagogue with a large gay and lesbian membership and so is perhaps less fettered by tradition than more Orthodox communities. However, work still required consensus between architect and committee – 16 members of the congregation, including the rabbi, cantor and several board members. In addition, this being Los Angeles and a Reformed synagogue to which people will drive their cars, one of the greatest constraints the architect had to confront was car culture. 'Parking requirements drive the size of the sanctuary,' he explains, 'so there was considerable time spent on maximizing the space, given the number of cars we could fit into the parking area.' All of which makes the building even more of a triumph.

Though Schweitzer is not Jewish and so had to leave the Hebrew lettering and religious symbolism to others, he did spend 'many hours of study in order to understand the symbolic elements within Judaism and to understand the differences within the different sects of the religion'. The fruits of his research are most evident in the emblematic interior space. 'The suspended ceiling is an inverted symbolic gesture referring to the parting of the Red Sea that focuses on the Star of David as the guiding light,' he says. 'The coloured glass windows on the west are keyed to the days of creation, etc.' The main worship space is subdued while the 'parted' ceiling allows light down a central corridor of skylights. A painted frieze is made up of inspirational concept-words chosen by the architect and the rabbi and written in both English and Hebrew. Despite such attention to symbol and detail, it is the green-brown exterior with its traffic-blown palms that is most remarkable, with its nod to the natural and historic context that sets the non-traditional house of worship firmly in its modern-day community.

5 The interior continues the theme of simplicity, with cut-out panels in the walls and pendant lamps the only ornament.

2 The site plan shows the relationship of the three courtyards which are the basis for the scheme.
1. entrance, 2. main courtyard, 3. exhibition hall, 4. prayer hall, 5. prayer hall court, 6. social hall, 7. community courtyard, 8. multi-purpose hall

1 The Ismaili Centre complex is located in an area of urban sprawl.

2.06

ISMAILI CENTRE

LISBON, PORTUGAL

RAJ REWAL ASSOCIATES

2002

The Ismailis are a sect of the Shiah Muslim community for whom the Aga Khan is the spiritual leader. Though they trace their tradition back to the eighth century, the Ismaili community makes up a small minority of Muslims and has never had a major place for worship and communal events within Europe. The Ismaili Centre in Lisbon is the first such establishment on the continent and also serves as a base for the activities of the Aga Khan Foundation, a non-profit philanthropic organization which has been involved with promoting development primarily in Asia and East Africa since 1967. This project was the result of an invited competition held by the Aga Khan Foundation, which chose New Delhi architect Raj Rewal's plan of machine-worked geometry.

Looking to the historic specimens of the Alhambra and the Great Mosque of Fatehpur Sikri in India, Rewal produced a scheme that, he says, 'is based on three interconnected enclosed gardens fulfilling distinct functions'.

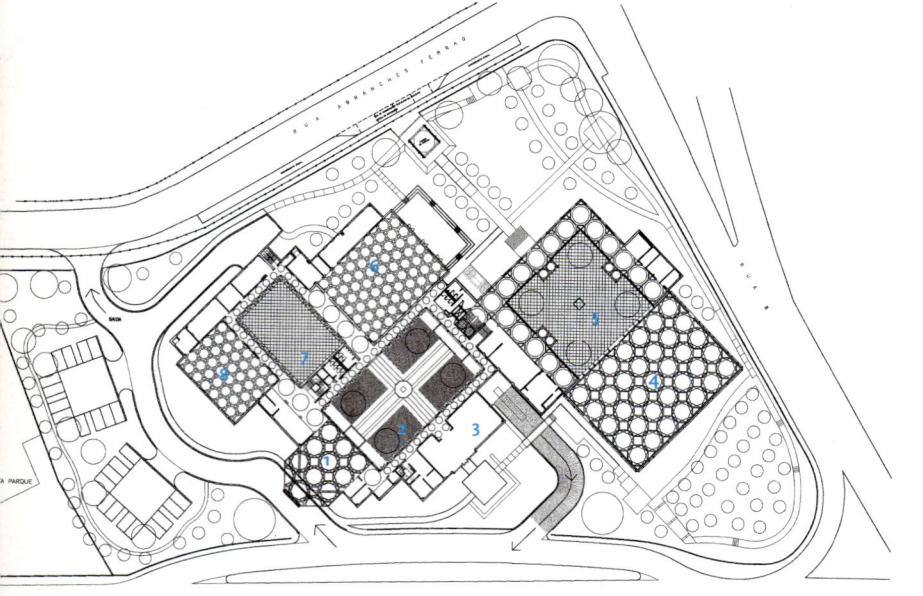

3 The entrance sets the theme of expanded geometric elements.

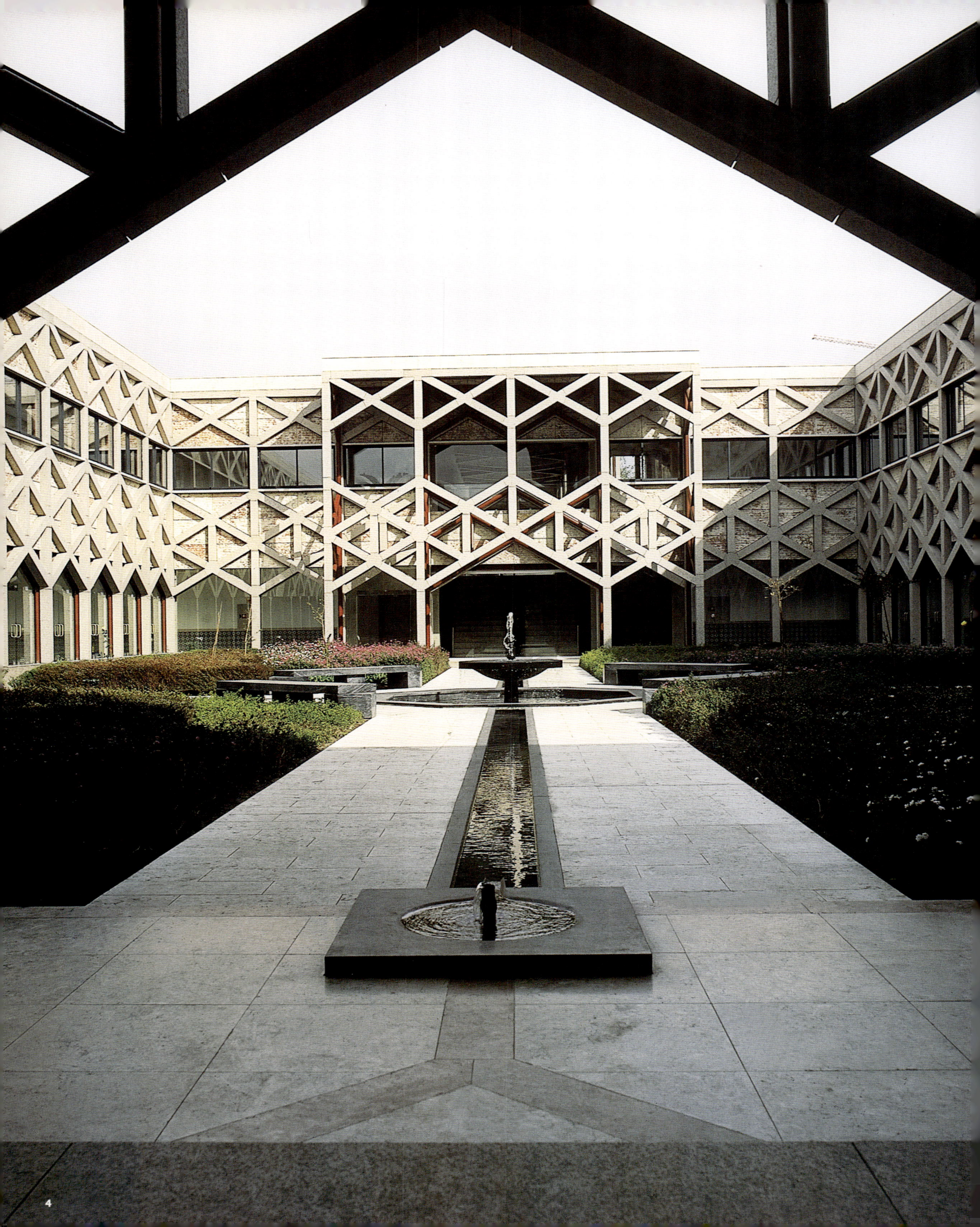

4 The main courtyard is flanked by public and exhibition spaces, and makes a peaceful transition from an urban to a sacred environment.

5 Using CNC (computer numerical control) technology, the architect had local pink granite cut to shape the giant geometric fretwork.

6 The drawing shows one of the geometric patterns repeated in the design of the jamat khana.

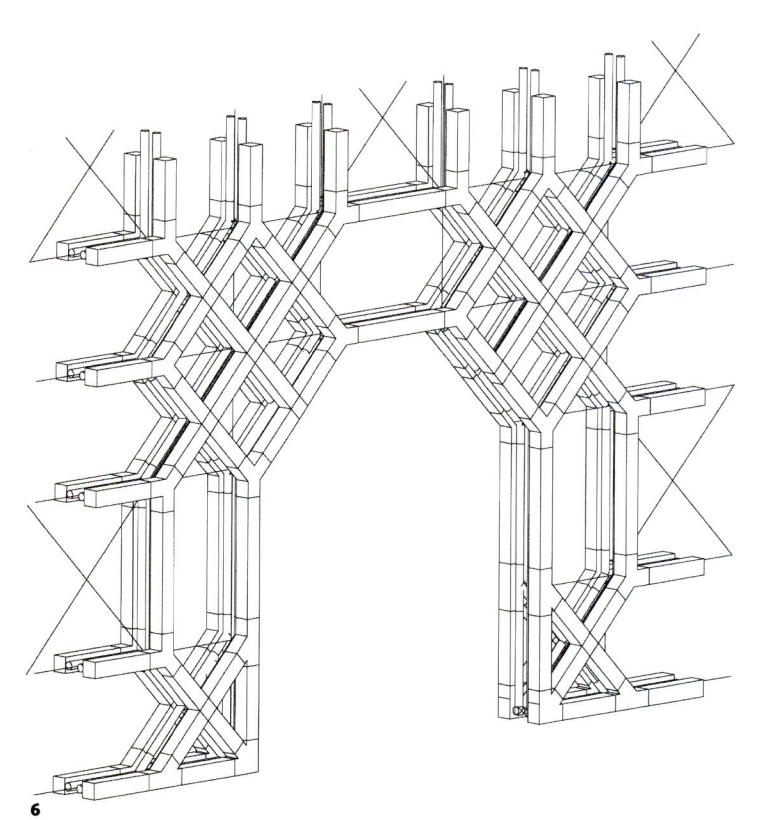

The lush plantings of the Alhambra have not been reproduced here; neither have the elaborate carved stone screens and fanciful elements of Fatehpur Sikri. However, the flowing succession of rooms and courtyards enhanced by ponds, fountains and reflecting streams that determine the design of the Lisbon centre are traceable to these architectural marvels, as is the play of geometric patterns. The scale, too, not obvious from photographs, is decidedly grand, signalling a centre of cultural, religious and communal importance, which was one of the reasons for the project in the first place, providing a solid, meaningful base for the Ismaili community.

Like its historic progenitors, the Lisbon centre devises a captivating, peaceful retreat from urban tumult. A semi-enclosed porch forms the entrance through which visitors reach the central courtyard. With its linear pool leading the eye to the fountain of the courtyard, where white marble paving contrasts with low-growing plants and shrubs and the patterned walls create a latticework backdrop, this is the most picturesque aspect of

7 The main prayer space (jamat khana) is approached by a separate courtyard.

the scheme. Intended to welcome the visitor, the courtyard space was designed on the principle of char bagh (the quadrite garden). According to the architect, 'the aim is to transform the mood of the visitor from the external stress to internal calm'. The courtyard is flanked by an exhibition space on one side and rooms for public and communal use on the other. Straight ahead is the prayer hall court and next to it the prayer hall itself.

The prayer space is not held in the central womb of the building as is generally the case with mosques contained within larger complexes. However, the prayer hall (jamat khana) and court are separated from the central courtyard and public spaces by a narrow corridor with a gateway and change of level that mark a further separation from the world outside, while the other buildings and octagonal cloisters run along the perimeter. Once through the gateway, visitors encounter more open spaces characterized by the transparency of the architect's specially conceived cut-stone square, diamond and octagon pattern. Inspired as they were by historic Islamic buildings, Raj Rewal and his team embraced the potential of new technology. The geometric shapes were cut by computerized machines in local pink granite, and are strengthened by tensioned steel elements and the compressive strength of the stone.

Rather than using a single dome or arrangement of prominent domes, the architect chose to punctuate the ceiling and roof with a proliferation of domes, with the greatest concentration occurring over the prayer hall where domes alternate with three-dimensional diamond shapes formed by the steel members. Filled out in stone, these would indeed begin to resemble some of the elaborate relief work of Fatehpur Sikri. As they are, however, they are part of a vast room, almost completely open to the courtyard, with only the wall and ceiling patterns for ornament. Whereas traditionally the geometric latticework would be employed as mushrabiyah screens, here, being of such a great size, the shapes reveal more than they hide, so the room's scale becomes even more awesome.

There is historic precedent here, but Raj Rewal's aim was 'to capture the essence without mimicry of past historical styles'. In this he has succeeded, adding subtlety and modern elegance to a haven of peace.

8 The prayer hall (left), with social hall and multi-purpose hall (far right).

9 The elevation shows the change in pattern from the main courtyard to the prayer hall court (left), as well as the higher elevation of the prayer hall court.

10 The interior of the jamat khana is alive with geometric patterning on the walls, floor and ceiling.

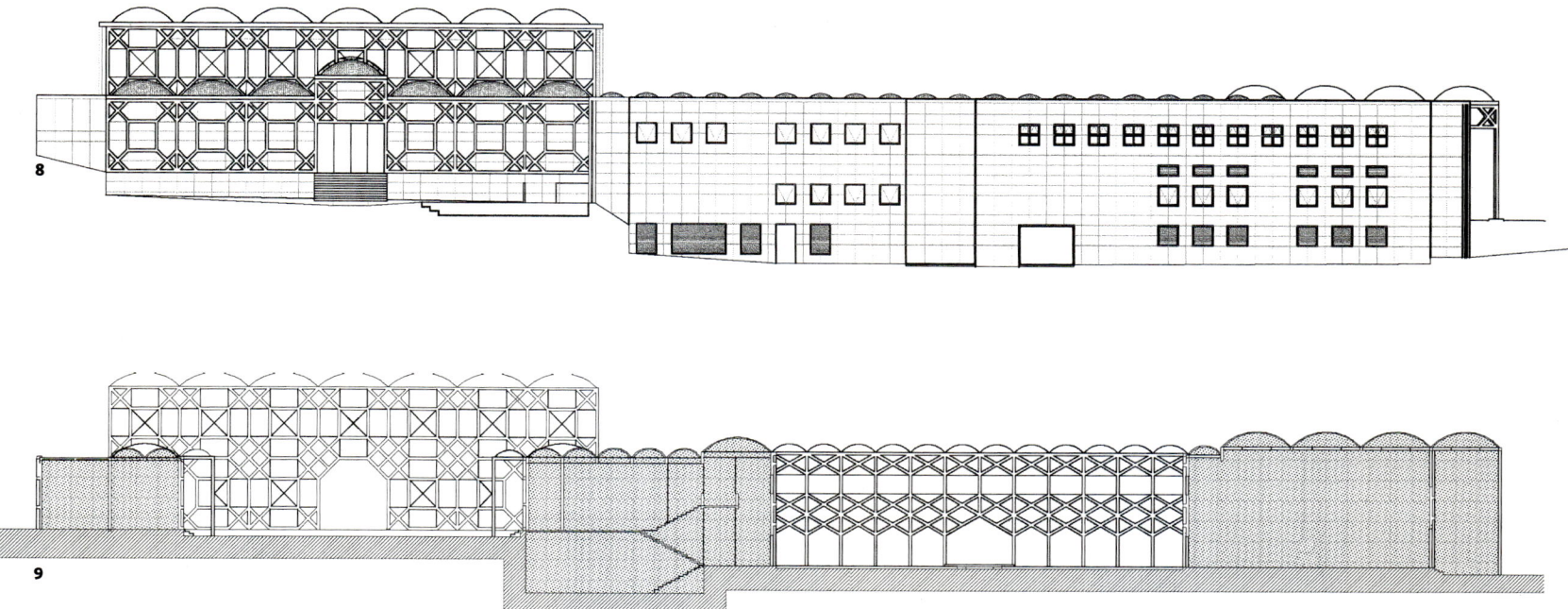

1 A series of detached planes creates space for reflection and illumination.

2 The intersection of water, wood, concrete and metal brings the church together with the courtyard and public area.

2.07

SACRED HEART CATHOLIC CHURCH AND PARISH CENTRE

VÖLKLINGEN, GERMANY

LAMOTT ARCHITEKTEN

2001

Superannuated industrial communities face particular obstacles to renewal. A former steel town, Völklingen is located within a mining area just outside of Saarbrücken. Its disused steel mill is now a landmark of historic preservation, and its old community centre was torn down because of subsidence. Yet the town continues to thrive as a community, sufficiently so to require a new community centre with provision for public rooms, kindergarten and a new church. The setting for the project is in a quiet neighbourhood of single-family housing and retirement homes so, the architects maintain, 'a lack of architectural definition and a diversity of building styles challenged us to seek contrast rather than context'.

The contrast is expressed in a low-lying arrangement of buildings that plays with solidity and transparency, strength and light. Long, concrete orthogonal planes are topped by extruded flat roofs. Free-standing concrete walls define and protect glass-enclosed spaces. The International Style and hints of Mies' Barcelona Pavilion come to mind at first glance, but the scheme produced by Stuttgart-based Lamott Architekten imbues the iconic planes of minimalism with specific themes and references. The L-shaped form is made up of public facilities along a north–south axis with the church set perpendicular to them and separated by a semi-enclosed courtyard. Steel used for trusses, purlins and columns recalls the town's industrial heritage, while the white concrete also carries industrial connotations.

Extending the historical manufacturing theme, the architects surrounded the church in specially prerusted Cor-ten steel sheets whose burnished colour is in tune with the larch used on the courtyard façade of the church and parish buildings. The wood siding is horizontally grooved, a pattern which maintains the pure lines of the building but softens the appearance. Four long, white concrete slabs punctured with narrow horizontal openings also maintain the low profile of the scheme and define the separate

2

3

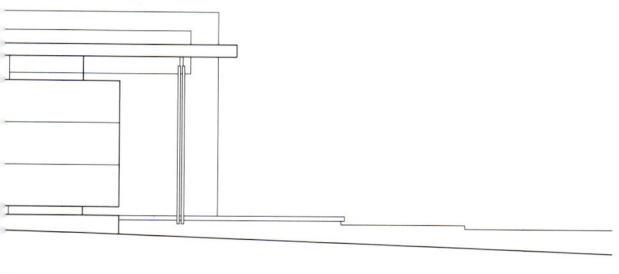

3 The elevation shows the linear harmony between the church at right and the community centre building at left.

4 The church building demonstrates the beauty of planar forms and contrasting materials.

5 The plan of the church shows the protective concrete wall on the north-east side, which is set in a linear pool and breached by the entrance bridge. The Cor-ten steel walls enclose the building at bottom and right, while a wood façade faces the courtyard at left.

6 The plan of the complex shows the profusion of straight lines and right angles. The chapel is located in the south-east corner with the parish centre on the western side of the site.

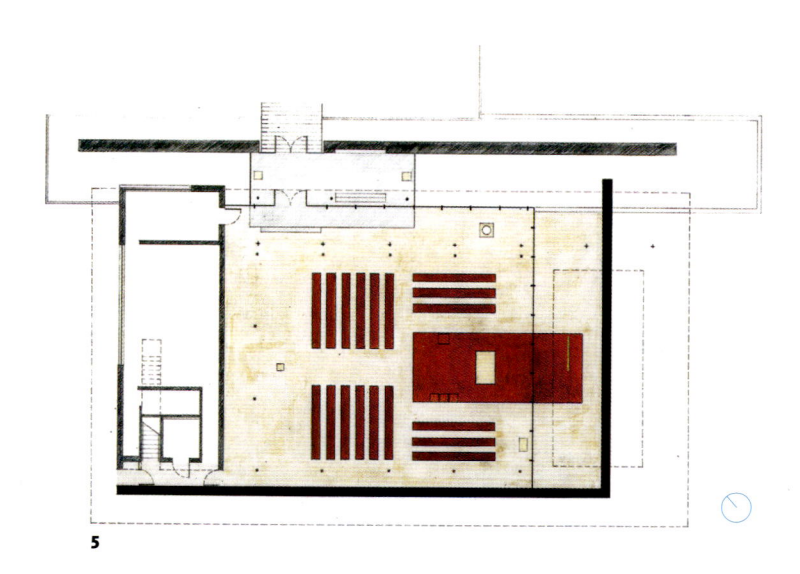

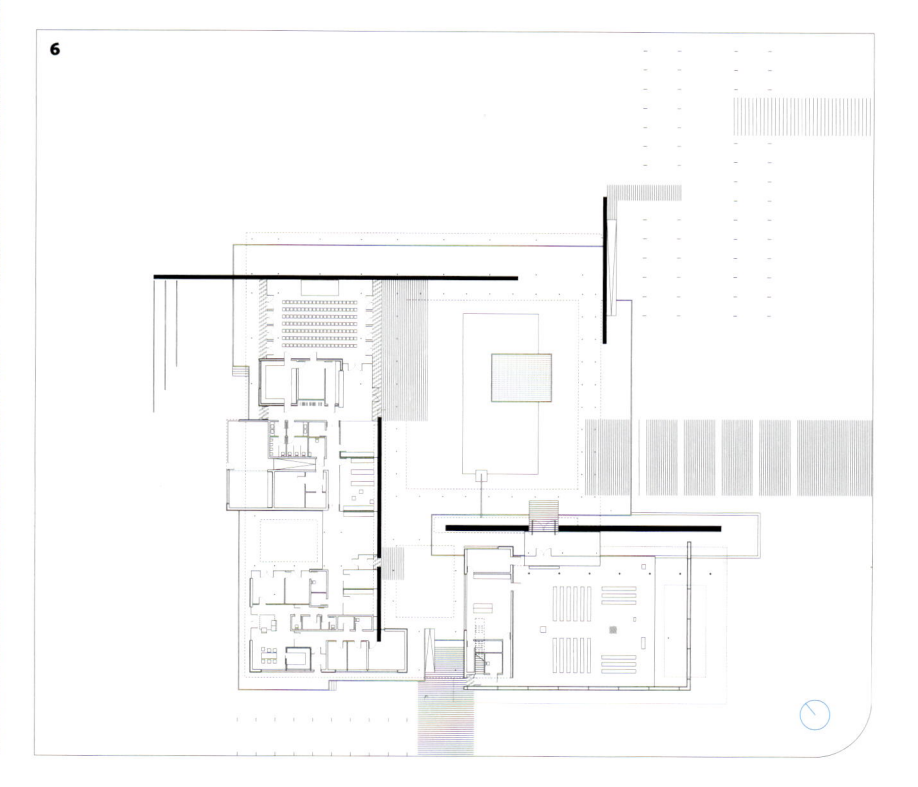

buildings around the courtyard. The concrete panel alongside the church stands in a shallow pool of water and is used by the architects to 'symbolize the threshold into the sacred interior of the church'. That threshold seems almost impregnable, with the squat rusted-steel church doors sitting in the thickness of the wall and reached via a wooden bridge. It is the use of materials rather than an enfilade of spaces that lends the great sense of sobriety and ceremony.

Inside, the more vulnerable aspect of the building appears in the two glass walls that are shielded by the concrete and wood façades. The other two, steel-clad, walls contrast in their solid density, but are hung, leaving space above and below for light to penetrate and to imbue bulk with weightlessness. So much light and transparency countered by the separate solid barriers of the stand-alone walls gives the interior a sense of freedom and openness that is perhaps greater than it would be in an all-glass structure where the degree of exposure is a limiting aspect. Here in the spare interior, the protective embrace of the outer walls and the transparent lucidity of the glass inspires a state of special grace and suspension between opposing physical attributes. Particularly in the evening when the dusky natural light is enhanced by the rows of single ceiling-pendant lamps, the interior hovers between light and shadow.

Ornamental details are minimal, in keeping with the form of the building, and make a spare worship space. A poured concrete pulpit, altar and baptismal font, and contrasting dark wood benches go along with the architects' stated aim: 'To relay a sense of formal simplicity and minimalism through shape and selection of materials.' The glass door-panels etched with excerpts from the Book of Revelations are one concession to iconography, but otherwise the sense of emptiness is deliberate, intended to enable worshippers to 'find the mysterious presence therein'.

7 The entrance consists of a set of Cor-ten steel doors and an inner set of glass doors.

8 The interior is surrounded by an inner glass skin that rises up to meet the roof, producing a clerestory along the perimeter and separating the interior from the hard barriers of concrete and steel walls.

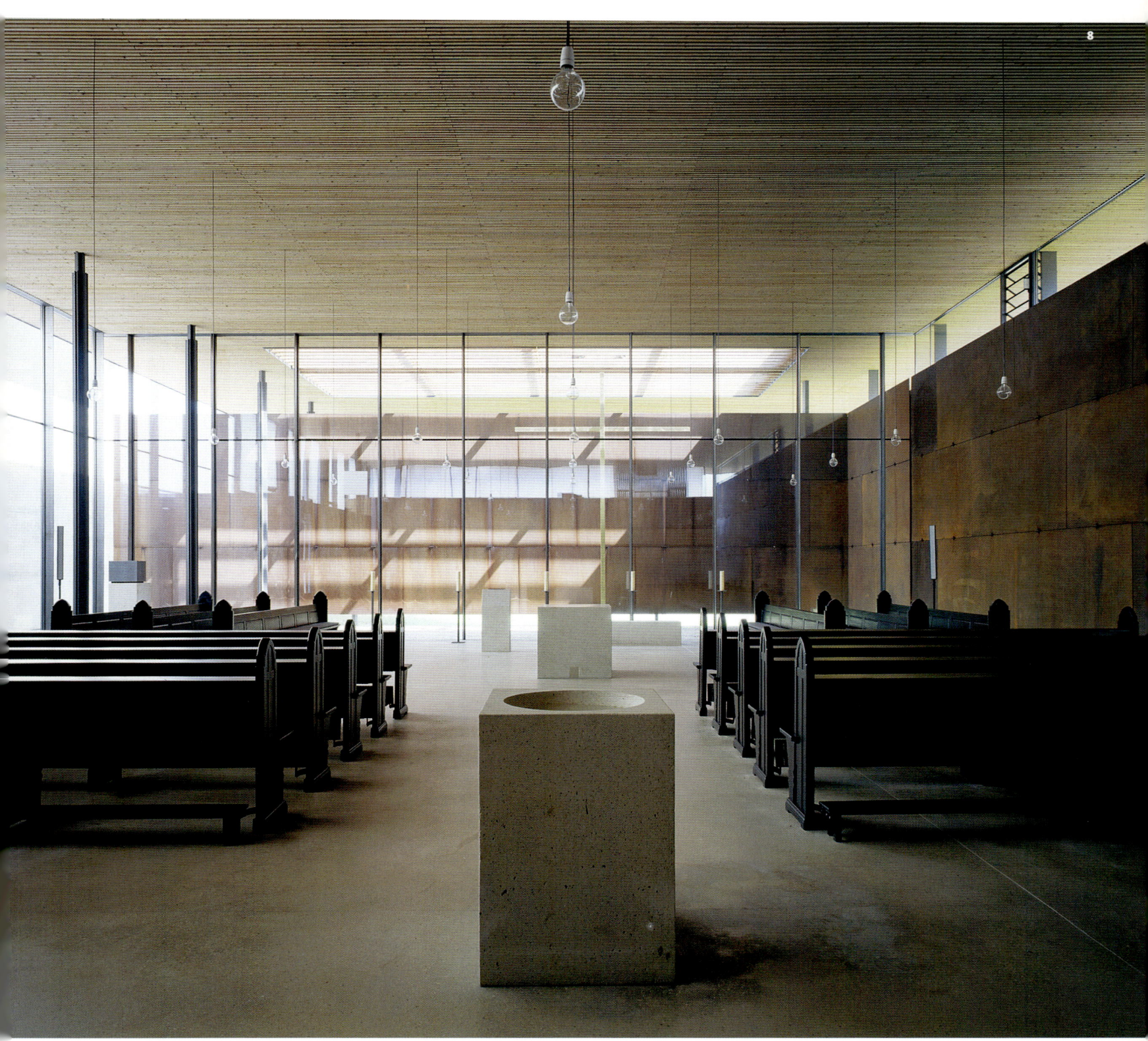

1 The church is clad in panels of chromium-steel Inox plates that have been washed in an acid bath. Each panel is one-eighth of the length of the façade.

2 The elevation shows how the building extends below ground level.

3 In a landscape dominated by skyscrapers and transportation routes, the architect says the church 'had to be the most pure geometry possible'.

4 The west façade features the largest window opening. At left, the pergola bell tower sits on elevated ground.

2.08

CHRIST CHURCH

DONAU CITY, VIENNA, AUSTRIA

HEINZ TESAR

2000

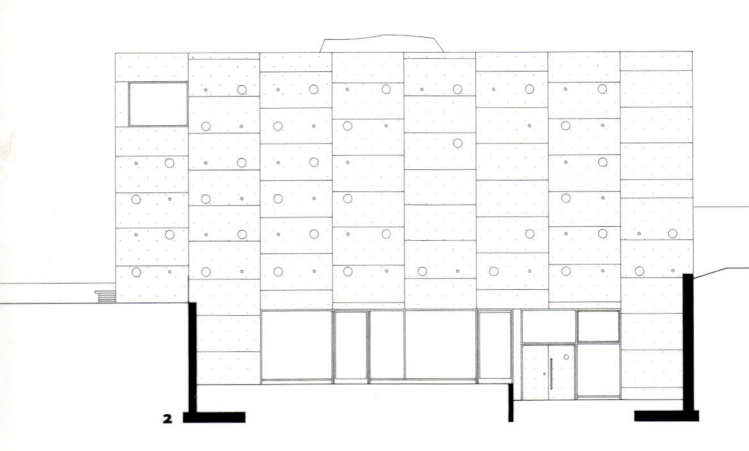

Donau City is a modern, master-planned area of Vienna which, architect Heinz Tesar explains, 'was intended as a complementary city-centre to the historic nucleus of Vienna, capable of representing the twenty-first century'. Not surprisingly, it has become home to a few architectural expressions, if not experiments, by well-known adherents of the high-tech, sweeping vertical and near-Brutalist style. It is a city coursed by wide, heavily trafficked streets, subway lines and an elevated rail line. When the archdiocese of Vienna set up a restricted competition for the building of a new church in this context, they must surely have hoped that something would make its mark in this setting, though it is doubtful they could have foreseen just how it would do so.

The urban church at the turn of the twentieth century is a special interest of Heinz Tesar, who has designed 11 sacred buildings during his 30-year career and is working on a project for 'seven chapels' in Herzogenburg. For the Roman Catholic church of Donau City, Tesar explains, 'my inspiration came from the fact that the site is located in direct visual connection with the UNO-City building', which was designed by Johann Staber. 'We wanted to build a church for the twenty-first century. Thus to offer a space of meditation and contemplation for many people in a multi-cultural context.'

However, if Tesar viewed the Y-shaped, concrete-and-glass United Nations building as a starting point, he also viewed it as a point of departure. The hard, solid exterior of the church seems more forbidding than some of the monumental towers, but it hides a light, airy and altogether uplifting interior; being highly conscious of the harsh cityscape outside, peaceful and glowing inside. A 'crossed cube', the building appears as a block of darkened steel made up of panels perforated with small and large circular openings. The low, weighted bulk is in distinctive opposition to the multi-storey surrounding structures. A terrace of lawns steps toward one of the nearby buildings; however, the church sits on a flat site, in a largely tarmac void, emphasizing its nearness to the ground. Its refusal to compete with vertical gestures is palpable, as is its concern with texture. Set at an angle to buildings on either side, it possesses a tactile quality that comes from the tone and sheen of the oscillating chromium-steel surface and from all those Swiss-cheese holes as well as thousands of tiny pinpricks in the metal, all so

5 The north section showing the upper ground level at right and lower level entrance, left.

6 The baptismal font in the north-east corner of the church.

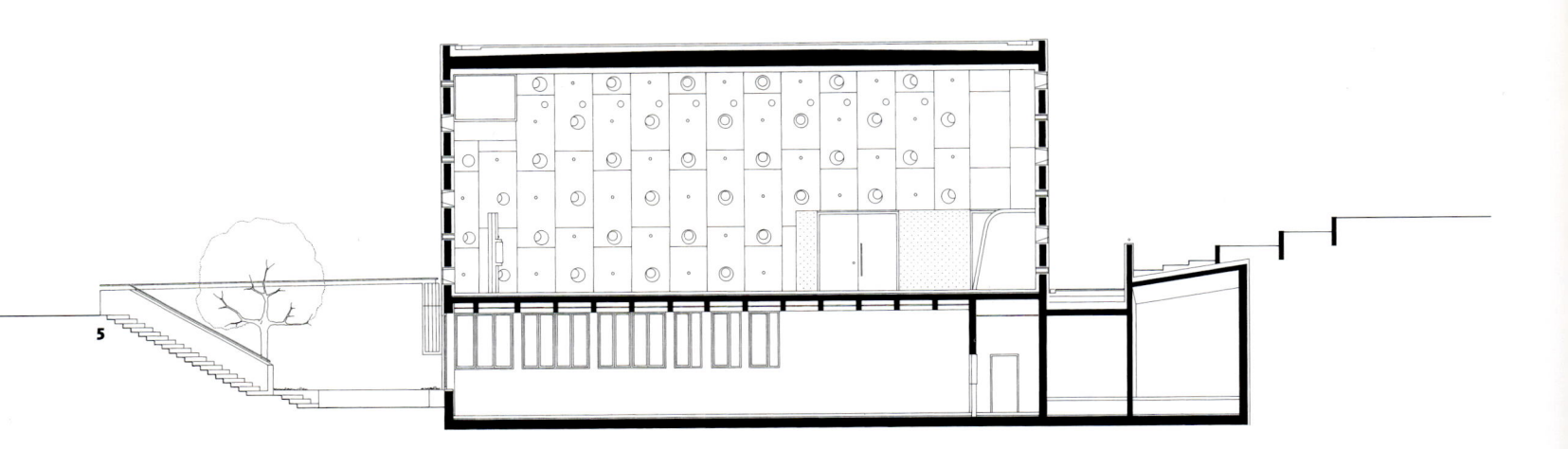

close to ground level and so touchable. Tesar even shrunk the traditional bell tower, opting for a pergola-style structure that holds three bells in a steel frame. Located on the west side of the building where the ground is elevated, the bells attain height without the need for a rising tower.

Inside, where the obvious contrasting gesture would be a stark white box, the architect chose instead to clad the walls, ceiling and floor entirely in birch and Canadian maple, creating a warm embrace. The four corners of the building have been inverted and glazed in different sizes – the smallest being one-eighth the length of the side, the largest four-eighths (eight referring to the 'newest day', according to Tesar). These corner windows, together with the exterior holes, which are tunnelled through the thickness of the wall, allow a spectacle of natural light to play through a golden interior. A skylight and an asymmetrical cross finely inscribed in the apse area marry the natural light with iconic imagery. The curved benches that encircle rather than face the altar pull the energy toward the centre, an interior world very much apart from what lies outside in terms not only of materials but of focus, illumination and exuberance.

Remarkably, this gesture against a competing gesture, this acknowledgement that the centre has already been claimed, manages to centre itself like a pillar of solidity and, in many ways, of faith.

7 The benches are aligned on concentric circles. The sculptural skylight, dozens of light circles and inverted glazed boxes at the corners make an interior of striking illumination.

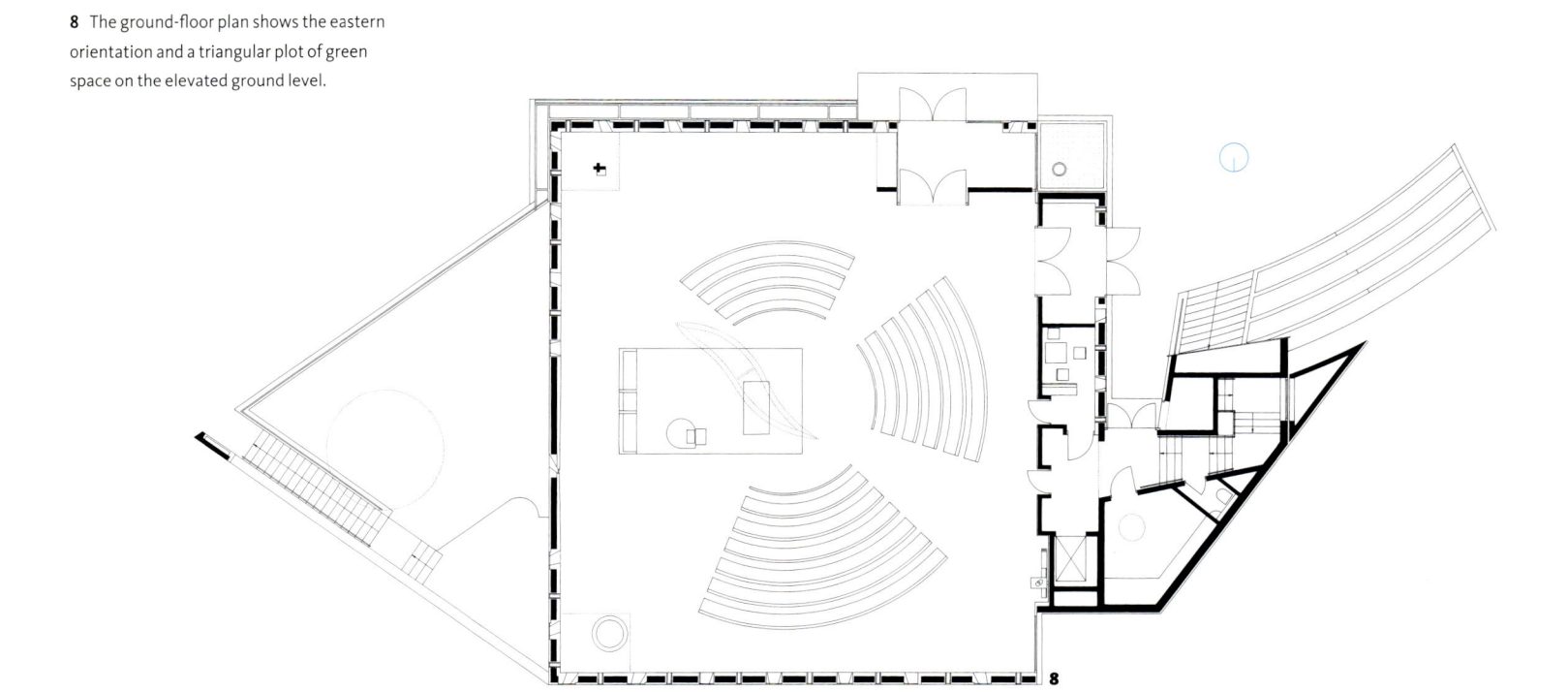

8 The ground-floor plan shows the eastern orientation and a triangular plot of green space on the elevated ground level.

2.09

KASSEL SYNAGOGUE

KASSEL, GERMANY

ALFRED JACOBY

2000

As prolific as he is, it is a wonder how Alfred Jacoby manages to turn out buildings with such singular appeal. In this, the architect's sixth synagogue project, he shows his predilection for wood, for playing with rectilinearity, for worship spaces that transcend the boundaries between physical and ethereal beauty. Though he has said that he does not seek to emulate the elaborate synagogues of the past that represented an elite society of wealthy Jewish patrons, Jacoby manages to infuse his humbler versions with a sense of grandeur nonetheless.

The Kassel synagogue project was a commission that came from a desire to replace what the architect describes as 'an unspectacular ... structure of 1961, which had become too small and needed replacement due to the immense growth of the community over the past ten years'. This has been the case in many German cities, where Jewish communities decimated by the Second World War and post-war flight have begun to re-establish themselves. Here the architect's approach was dictated somewhat by the need to stay within the area of the old site while creating substantially more space and, at least in its finished form if not in the planning, a more celebratory building.

As with the Chemnitz synagogue (see p. 52), completed two years later, Jacoby created a sacred space that rises out of a plainer volume, making a spectacular contrast between the more prosaic rectilinear building and the synagogue's distinctive form. It is a contrast of both shape and materials, where the squared-off white concrete of the surrounding structure serves as a frame for a natural wood-clad central volume that arcs from a point almost level with the lower building to project the synagogue up and outward. In this way, the architect explains, 'the curved central space of the sanctuary as well as the eastern (misrach) wall step out of the cubic volume'. The projected eastern wall is further distinguished by a slatted panel within the wood cladding that allows light to enter through a near floor-to-ceiling window. Together with a glazed strip along the roof, the window brings light into the prayer hall, light that is diffused through a notably Jacobian grid of blue-tinted panels.

On the inside, the window becomes an incandescent source, radiating blue light into the space, clad with swathes of cedar wood along the walls, and the coffered ceiling which rises to nine metres (30 feet) in height. The great span of wood and diffuse blue light create an intensity that one does

1 The shape amplifies the misrach wall, revealing the internal focal point of the synagogue from the exterior.

2 The synagogue sits squarely on a street corner without the benefit of shielding elements.

3 The prayer space volume rises out of the block form with contrasting cedar shingle cladding.

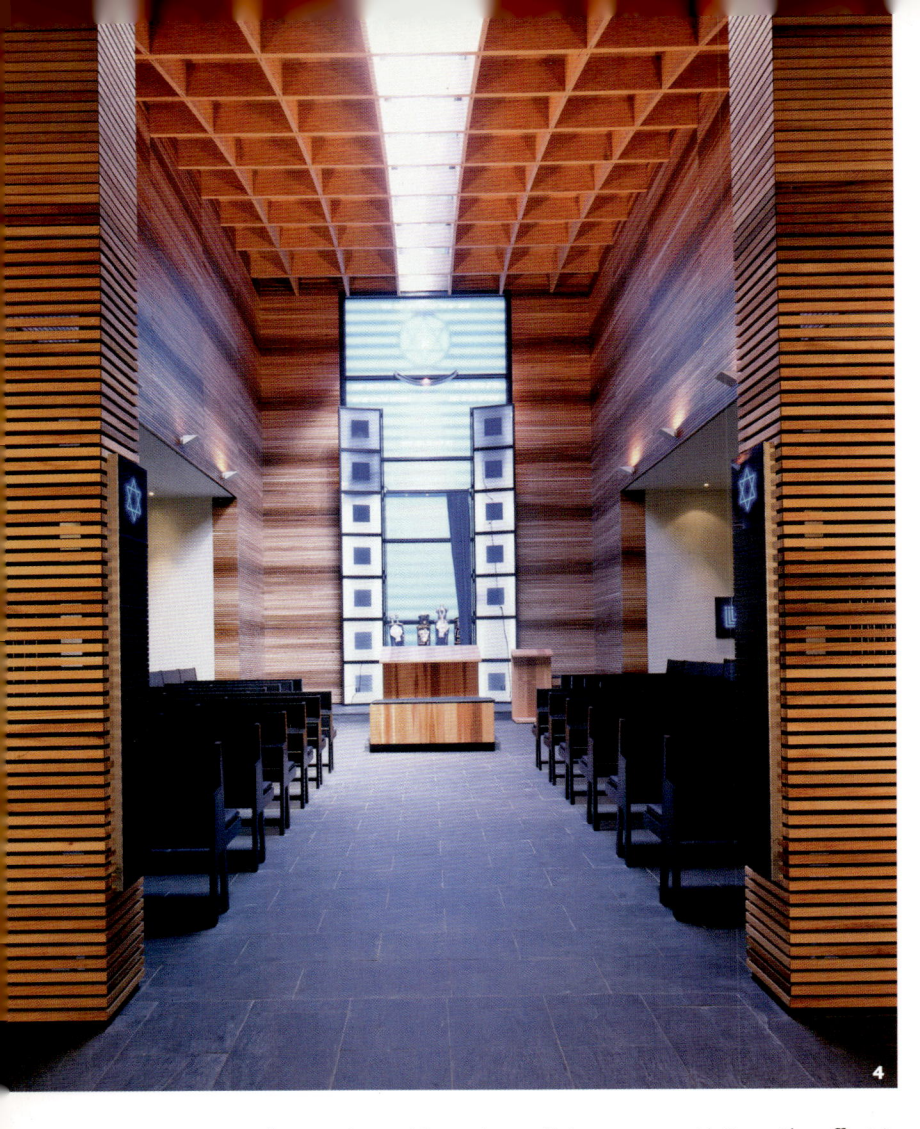

4 The coffered ceiling rises to a height of nine metres (30 feet) at the stained-glass window. A skylit strip illuminates the space from above.

5 The ground-floor plan.
1. synagogue, 2. conference room, 3. offices, 4. foyer, 5. library, 6. cloakroom, 7. apartment

not usually associate with modern religious spaces. At times the effect is akin to that produced by the rich pigments of Byzantine church interiors. Though Jacoby has consciously forgone the use of gold, there is richness still in the colours and textures he has chosen. The cedar is a response, Jacoby says, 'to a request in the Torah to build the temple with the cedar of Lebanon', though the degree of exuberance and warmth achieved with the material is to the architect's own credit.

Other materials, like the black-tinted oak of the benches and the black slate on the floor, show Jacoby's determination to add tactile experience to the sensory engagement of the space. As if to signal this point, he created at the entrance the concrete-and-cedar bench that draws visitors immediately to appreciate the combination of materials, and makes them aware of a building with a deliberate physical touch that urges the spiritual. As Jacoby notes, none of the physical is perfect so among the beautiful glass panels of the Torah shrine, one is cracked; and in the carved continuous piece of cedar wood that forms the bimah, the irregular graining is clearly visible.

These are small and subtle imperfections in a space that has an overall quality of fine finish and detail. If it is Alfred Jacoby's intention to raise the sacred space from the mundane built environment, he has succeeded in that aim. With the clear focus and restrained grandeur used here, he might also succeed in raising the spirit and the mind.

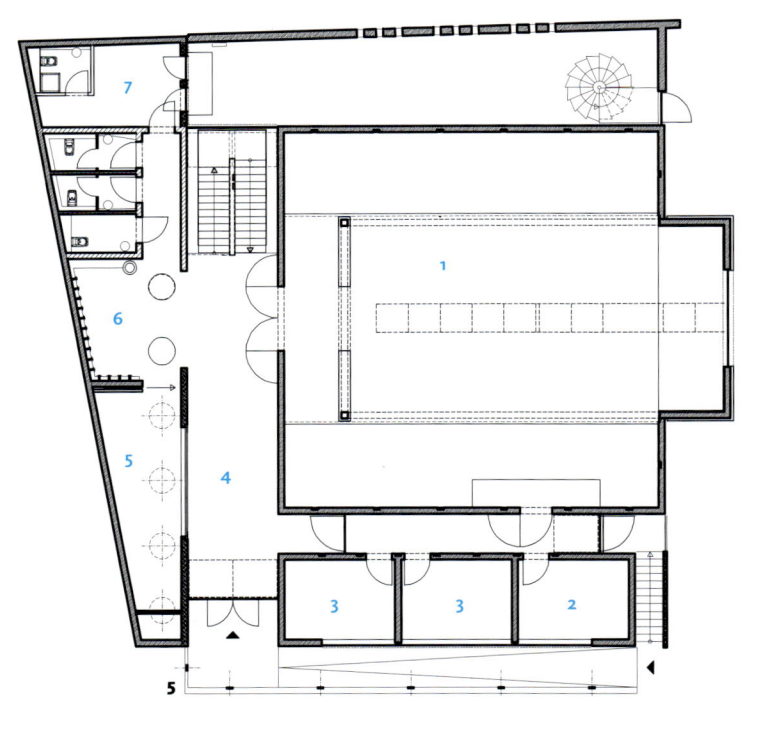

6 The front elevation shows a highly ordered rectilinear arrangement of spaces. The entrance is at left, with a common room and plant room below the synagogue.

7 The use of cedar shingle continues inside the space. The floor is black slate and seats are black-tinted oak.

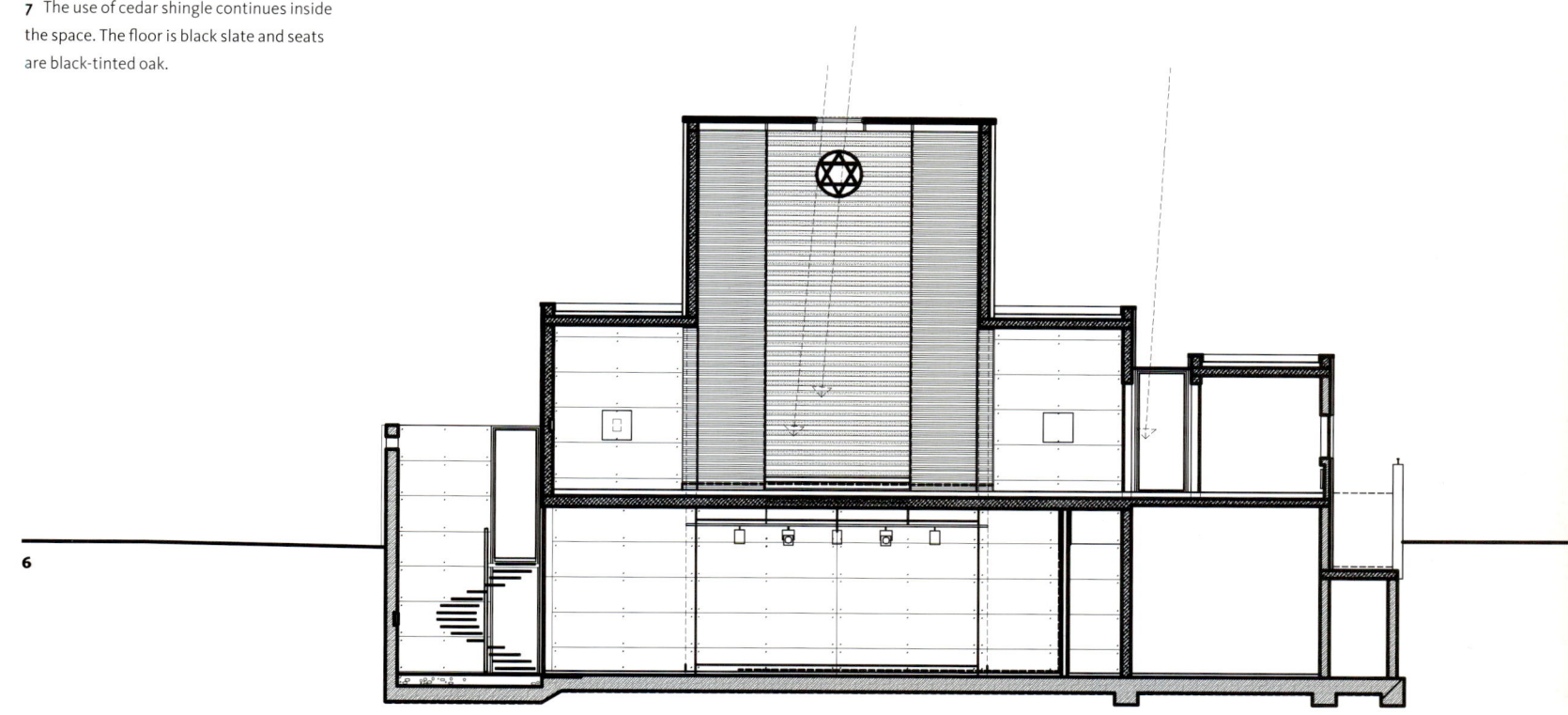

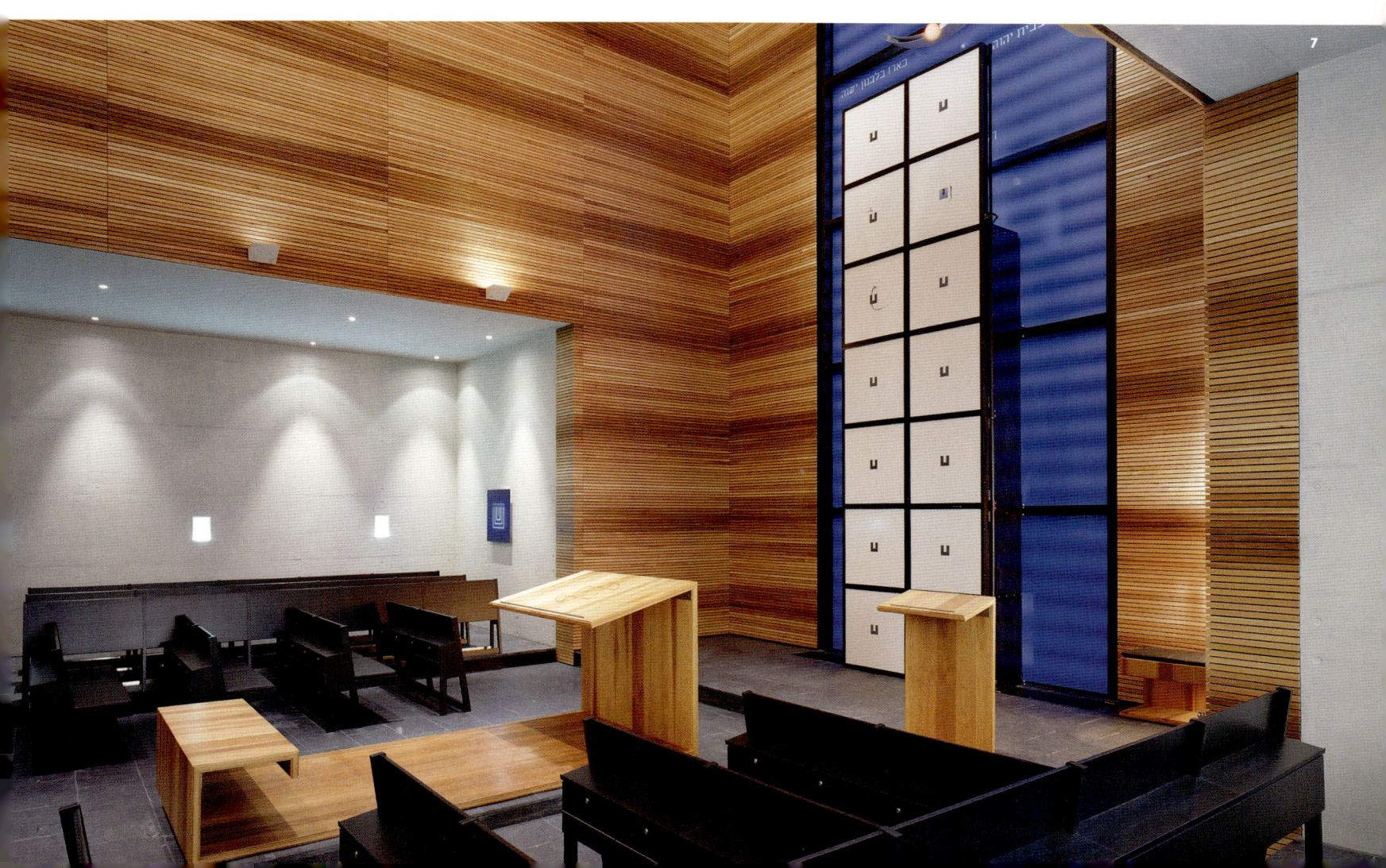

1
The ornament of an existing building on the sacred site (foreground) contrasts with the simplicity of the new temple.

2 The architect's rendering attests to the symmetry of the design.

2.10

KOMYO-JI TEMPLE

SAIJO, JAPAN

TADAO ANDO ARCHITECT & ASSOCIATES

2000

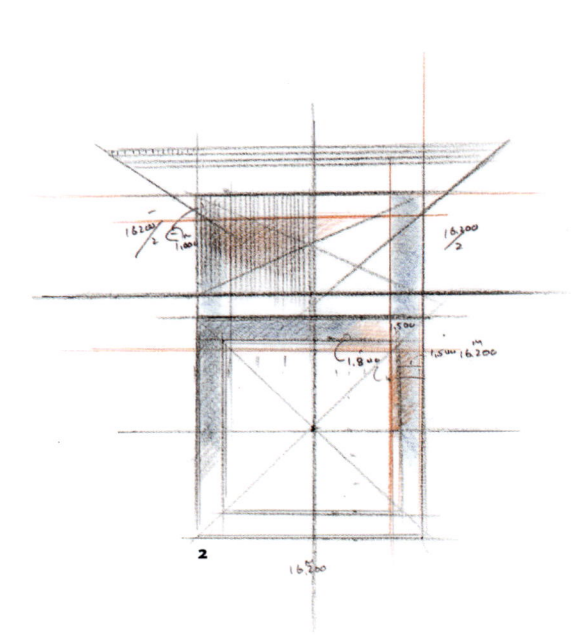

Tadao Ando has created some of the late twentieth century's most evocative buildings, but a series of spiritual spaces has put him at the forefront of new religious architecture. His Peace Chamber designed for UNESCO in Paris (1995) and his Church of the Light in Ibaraki Japan are structures possessing a serene beauty that few would believe possible to achieve in hard concrete. In his latest spiritual commission the architect turned to traditional Japanese wood construction to replace an Edo-period temple for the Pure Land sect, but here again he has located a remarkable presence in a common material.

The association of Buddhist temples with minimalism is largely a modern construct. While the asceticism of the monks might accord with the ideal of pared down simplicity, Buddhist temples have in the past presented highly elaborate designs – perhaps most perceptible in their involved roof constructions. Tadao Ando looked to some of the most compelling examples – the Great South Gate of the Todai-ji temple and the Amida Hall of the Jodo-ji temple (both twelfth century) – for inspiration, but not in any restrictive sense. Both buildings are masterworks of 'assembly' – as Ando describes it, 'the essence of Japanese architecture'. The traditional construction of the tall, pitched roofs with scrolling eaves involves a system of massive timbers, purlins and rafters, with pillars supporting stacked brack-

3 The surrounding pool refers to the city's many waterways and also helps to set the building apart. An existing Edo-period building is at right.

OVERLEAF
4–5 The section (4) shows the urn hall and priests' quarters which the architect also designed. The south elevation (5) shows the ornamental gateway to the car park (on the right) and the new office and guest hall building.

OVERLEAF
6 The vertical slats continue into the eaves and, seemingly, into the water.

4

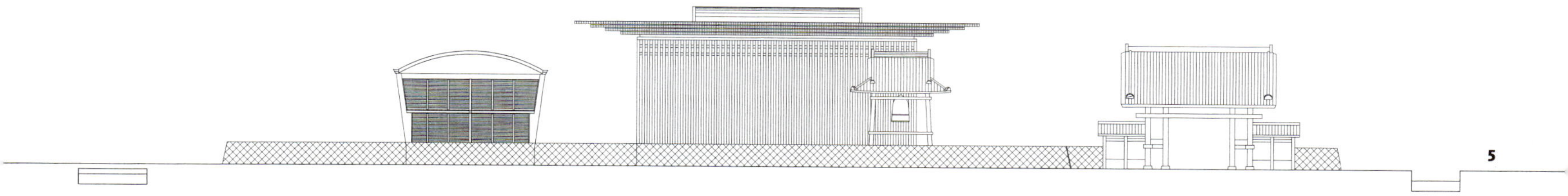

5

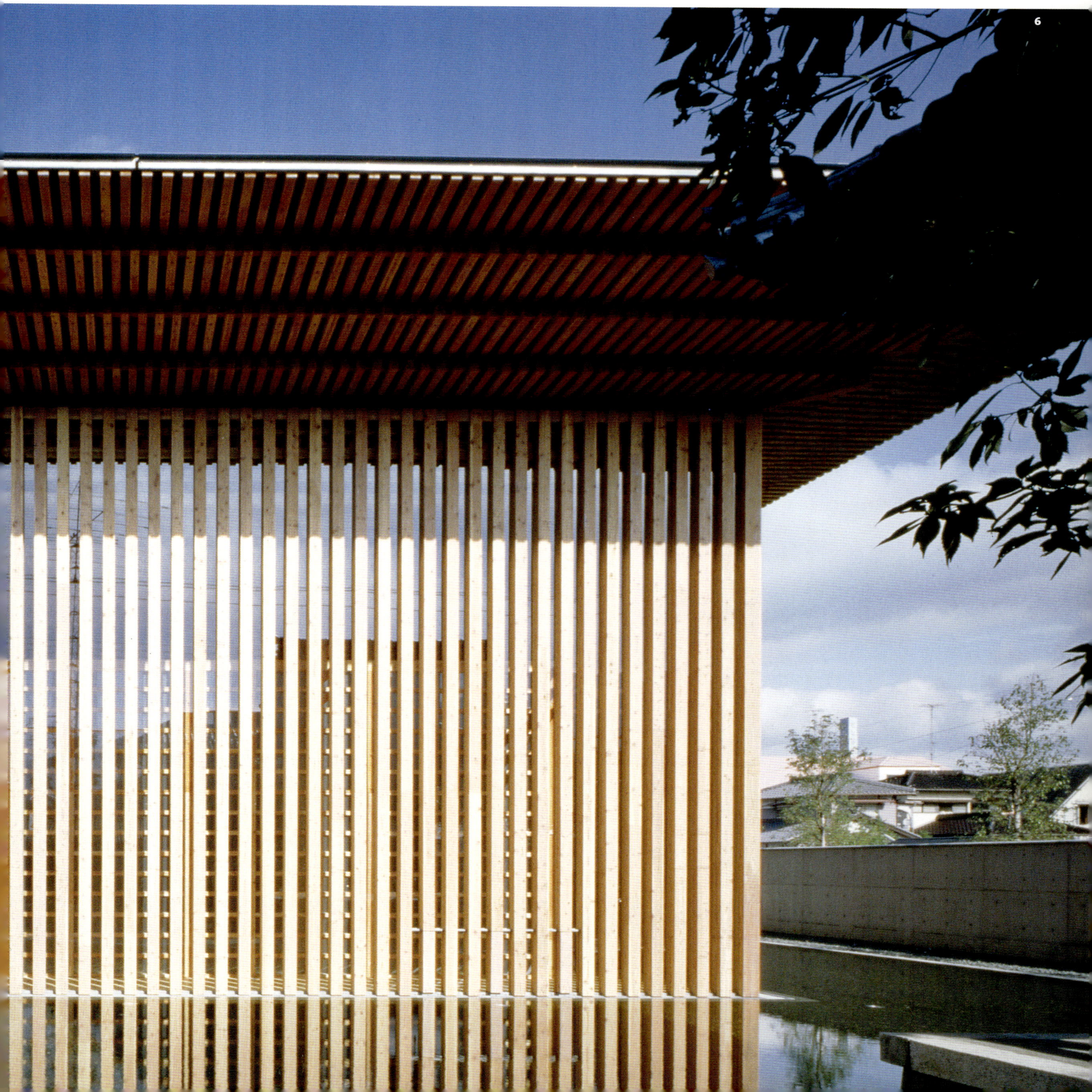

6

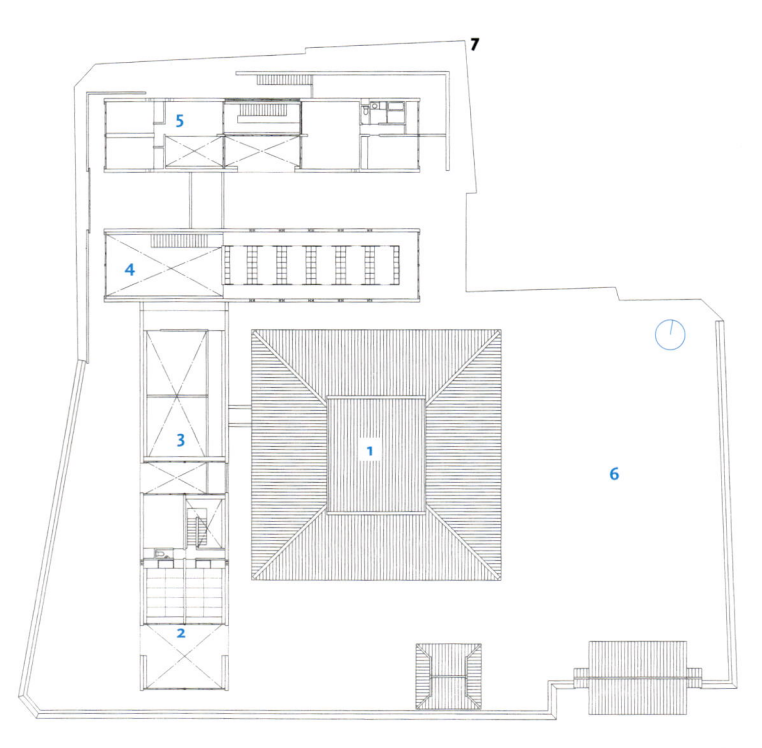

7 The site plan
1. temple, 2. offices, 3. guest hall, 4. urn hall, 5. priests' quarters, 6. car park

ets that raise and amplify the roof space well beyond the tops of the walls. Finished examples have the appearance of complex, interlocking wood puzzles – and this method of fitting elements together is what the architect focused on, rather than any predetermined historical design. 'I wanted to create a space that would return to the origins of wooden architecture,' he explains. 'It would be a simple structure made up of multiple parts, each full of tension.' He also wanted the framework 'to express the image of people gathering and joining hands, supporting each other in a single community'.

The team conceived a building 'in wood, shrouded in gentle light and floating over water'. As the city of Saijo is on the Inland Sea and is a gateway to Mt Ishizuchi, western Japan's highest mountain, it is criss-crossed with waterways running off from mountain streams. The idea of setting the building on water emphasized the dramatic physical environment while creating a sense of peaceful isolation. The light-shrouded effect was achieved using three layers for the enclosing walls that allow light to flow into and out of the building: interlocking beams frame the inner 'screen' of frosted glass, which is surrounded by a corridor that is then protected by the exterior lattice wall of closely spaced square-cut wood posts interspersed with glazed strips. The pattern of the exterior posts continues through to the exposed eaves, so that the structure appears from a distance almost solid. It gains transparency as you approach, the building's solidity dissolving between the reflected shapes and the sky that becomes visible as you see through the interior to the other side.

Inside the room is bathed in diffuse light, and Ando's own version of 'assembly' can be appreciated in the layered beams and rafters of the ceiling. These acknowledge the traditional stacked, interlocking method but have been simplified and improved with the use of laminated timber, which offers strength and uniformity without the wastage of cutting solid wood members. 'Since the material itself is made up by layering smaller parts, it seemed especially appropriate to the intent of this design,' Ando explains. At night the internal glow radiates outward and, together with the water-borne reflection, makes for a 'mystical appearance'.

Apart from the fact that 'it is a wooden structure, and the roof has gently sloping eaves, this building has almost nothing in common with traditional Japanese wooden architecture,' the architect freely admits. But the structure would not have been possible without that precedent, of which Ando is keenly aware. The project gave him 'a chance to rediscover and become conscious of the origins of my own architectural methods', he says. 'Water, wood, history and landscape.' His hope is that these elements will 'come together and speak to the visitor'. They do speak and, in the manner of Ando's best work, the building suggests the beauty of light, form and material with a gentle urging toward something beyond the physical presence.

8 The ceiling of the main hall reveals the complex assemblage of wood elements that is intrinsic to traditional temple architecture.

3 RETREATS RURAL SANCTUARIES

White Temple, Kyoto

Perhaps one of the most universally appealing aspects of a religious building is the space it offers for peaceful contemplation, an activity that is enhanced when the structure is removed from the built environment. Leaving the urban context and getting closer to nature is often a spiritual act in itself, and even some non-religious buildings assume an otherworldly air when set in a larger context of natural beauty. People have long linked spirituality with the natural world, and there is an age-old tradition of meditative structures set in nature.

We admire architecture that attempts to harmonize with the environment rather than dominate it, but this does not always produce admirable buildings. The religious spaces shown here exist in varying natural contexts, and respond to them with refreshing ingenuity by using recent developments in building methods and materials or simply new ways of looking at building in the landscape.

Computer-controlled milling techniques do not sound like a means to an environmentally sympathetic building, but London designer Thomas Heatherwick will be applying the technology to create a form that is very much in tune with the dramatic site of his new building. Presented with a site located on a steep hillside and across a lush valley from an active volcano, Heatherwick responded with an undulating form that the architect says was inspired by the folds in the fabric of monks' robes, but which creates a gentle imitation of the ascending hillside and heightens the awareness of both the man-made and the natural topography.

A world away, another highly innovative Buddhist temple, designed by John Frane and Hadrian Predock, sits like a serene winged creature in the flat desert landscape of scrub and red earth, surrounded by jutting sandstone cliffs, of the New Mexico desert. The form stands out in its sculptural simplicity but also utilizes ecologically friendly materials that make it responsive and responsible to the natural environment.

In somewhat milder climates architects have embraced the opportunity to create structures that are open to nature. Bernard Desmoulin's meditation centre for a veterans' cemetery in Fréjus, France, exemplifies this freedom. Offering symbolic rather than physical shelter, it provides an anchor in the landscape, but not a retreat from it. As with Gerold Wiederin's 'chapel' for nocturnal pilgrims in Austria, the larger setting easily overwhelms the structure, which appears like a sculptural folly on the horizon.

Takashi Yamaguchi's White Temple also has the air of a folly, its pure, simple form limiting its impact on the surroundings and helping to call attention to the natural context through its modest size and contrasting bright form. It also stands in contrast to a building like Tony Fretton's Faith House on the west coast of England, which is consciously linked with the surrounding forest, meadow and sea.

Such links are sometimes more historical than physical. John Pawson's Cistercian monastery in the Czech Republic and Álvaro Siza's small chapel in Portugal are part of established rural communities. They take their cue from past structures and are connected with the environment through local materials and tradition. Though both do so with very modern, minimal styling. Nature is not so much the focus in these buildings, but all of the projects in this chapter signal a particular kind of harmony that is possible when natural beauty is the starting point for inspiration.

1 The slatted open-air shelter sits low in the landscape, blending in with its colour and texture.

2 Plan: the two facing rectangular structures each contain two meditation areas. The dark blocks represent the location of the steel wall containing the scripture for each faith.

3 The panels at left slide from side to side to vary the enclosed area.

3.01

MEDITATION CENTRE AND CEMETERY

FRÉJUS, FRANCE

BERNARD DESMOULIN

1997

While non-denominational facilities have been in the public landscape for some time, it is a different act to produce multi-denominational spaces; that is, to recognize specific religions and give prominence or space to their iconography, tradition and sacred texts all in one designated site. The brief for a meditation centre for a French war cemetery in Fréjus, southeast France, was to accommodate the needs of families and friends of Muslim, Christian, Buddhist and Jewish soldiers buried there. The solution, presented by architect Bernard Desmoulin, was to construct four shelters that provided defined space for contemplation but were open to the semi-wild landscape.

Two elaborate pergola structures, both made of steel supports with slatted roofs and sides, sit square with one another, making a transparent form against a natural backdrop. Panels of cedar slats define four separate 'rooms', each of which contains a small free-standing wall made of rusted steel. Where in the mosque, prominence is given to a mihrab or in a synagogue to the ark, here Desmoulin has inset each of the walls with a stone slab that has been engraved with text sacred to the relevant religion. This also provides a point of focus, as does the altar or presbytery in Christian

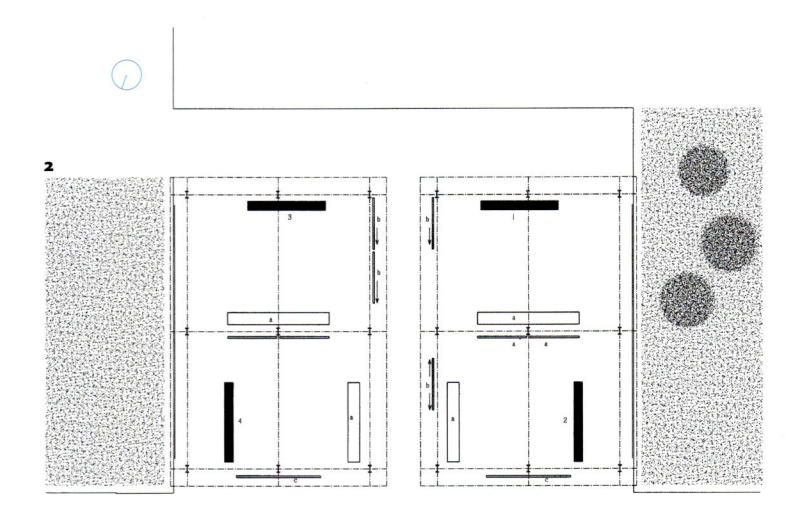

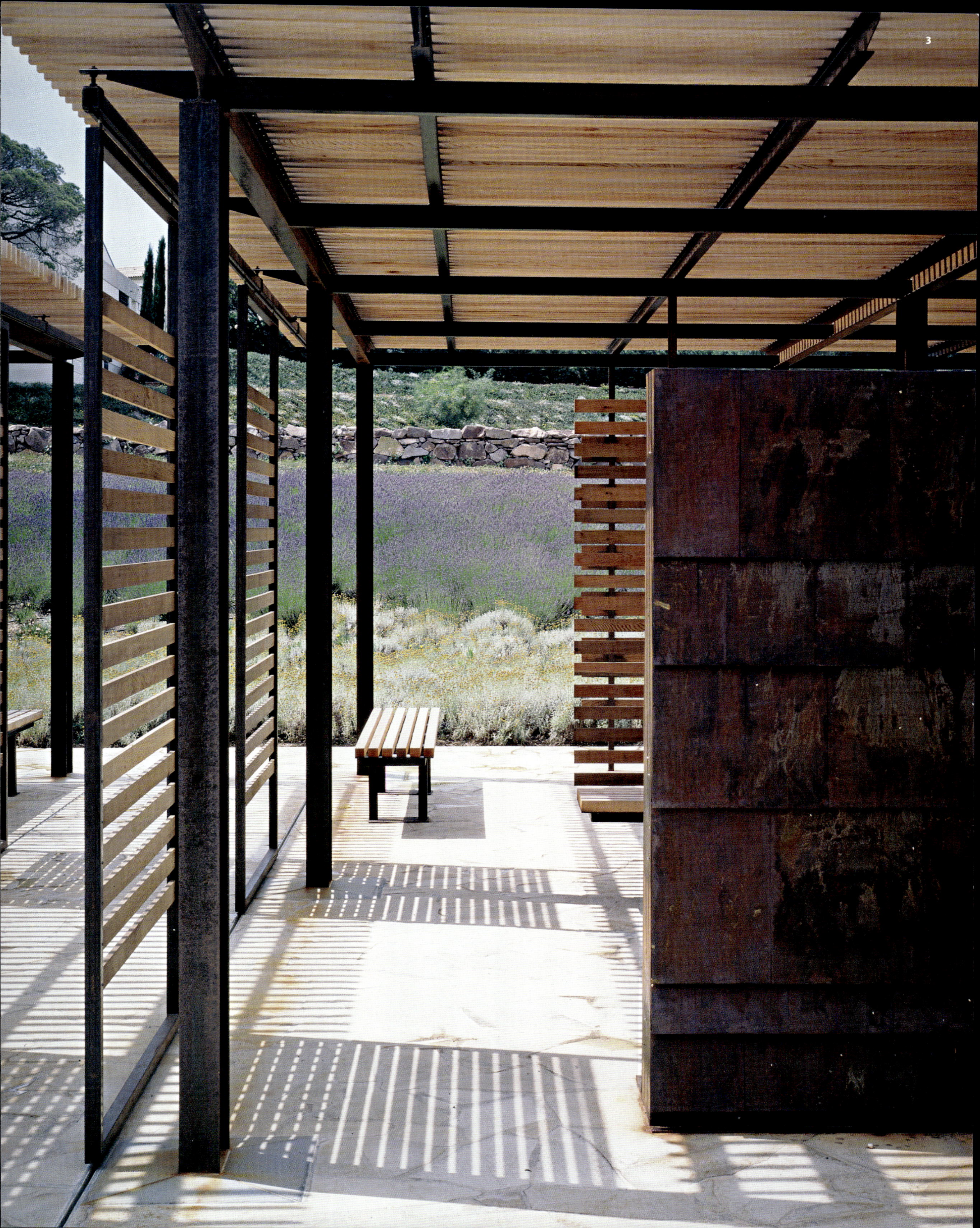
3

4 Pierre d'Hauteville stone flooring, red cedar slats and weathered steel make a hardy but inviting structure.

5 The rendering shows the ivy growing up the vertical wires on the east and west sides, as the architect intended. Desmoulin also designed the surrounding necropolis with 'wild' landscaping.

6 One of the steel panels with the niche that will hold the engraved stone slab.

structures or the shrine of a temple. The roof is steel-framed, with red cedar slats that allow sunlight and shadows to mix freely across spaces, emphasizing union rather than the division of the four areas. The slatted, pergola-style roof is reminiscent of the vine-covered structures of this region and allows rain through. 'I thought that when one is praying or meditating, rain can be a way of being closer to God,' says the architect. Providing separate areas for people of each faith while at the same time making them share an overall openness and a general character of design was, the architect says, his attempt to 'unite them in the same place and to respect each'.

'Before this,' Desmoulin explains, 'I had never worked on religious projects.' He had, however, worked on a small structure before, which he found 'a particularly interesting scale for focusing reflection, which is essential in architecture'. He was also struck by the idea that 'because of its metaphysical value, religious architecture frees itself from a strict adherence to utility to achieve a mystical and poetic dimension. In this regard it corresponds generally to a real demand of architecture.' As interpreted by Desmoulin, the awareness of the mystical dimension becomes manifest in a lack of encumbrance. These pergola-like structures, set formally on a generous stone base, present themselves as objects in the landscape through which the landscape can still be seen and felt. Desmoulin designed the necropolis and laid out the wild planting, which is at its best when the lavender and other meadow plants are visible through the slatted walls and add colour to the gold and brown of the open interior. As part of the landscape, the steel, stone and cedar weather with age and the elements, and the roof is becoming covered in ivy.

Tensioned wires strung vertically between the roof and the stone floor indicate the east and west sides of the buildings, so that worshippers who need to orient themselves can do so easily though there is no dominant icon indicating direction. While the idea is not to favour any characteristic building style, there is an element of the open Japanese temple in the design and a similar sense of calm in both the use of materials and the gentle intrusion of the shelter in the landscape. While it is meant to speak to four religions separately, this bare essence of structure is also meant to facilitate quiet contemplation, remembrance and peace; and what it mostly speaks of is the ethereal beauty of silence.

1 Faith House, designed by British architect Tony Fretton, was voted the best English building of 2002 by the *Guardian* newspaper.

3.02

FAITH HOUSE

HOLTON LEE, DORSET, UK

TONY FRETTON ARCHITECTS

2002

A charitable trust dedicated to the aid and spiritual growth of disabled people, Holton Lee maintain a rural complex of accommodation and activity facilities on 140 hectares (350 acres) of farmland overlooking Poole Harbour on England's south coast. Their stated mission is 'empowering and resourcing people, particularly carers and disabled people through creativity, environmental awareness, personal growth and spirituality'. The complex includes a holiday residence called 'the Barn', a crafts pavilion and the new Faith House completed in 2002, all surrounded by natural habitat, with accessibility the watchword for everything from the structures to the nature trails. With a remit to create a masterplan for the existing buildings and new structures to fulfil the trust's plans for expansion, British architect Tony Fretton, along with partner Jim McKinney, created a calm and calming pavilion. The structure speaks to the natural setting with its unobtrusive low profile and warm wood cladding of Western red cedar that will change with age to darker brown and perhaps to a mellow silver. Surrounded by mature trees and overlooking a wild meadow that spreads out to the sea below, the building functions as refuge from inclement weather, meeting house and place for solitary meditation. Fretton invited nature indoors with a glazed seaward façade across the meeting room and meditation space, and unmilled tree poles lining the walls of the meditation area – which is painted a reflective silver that seems to radiate inward while also echoing outward to the natural environment.

The simple rectilinear structure features a sheltering porch that is slightly incongruous alongside the Modernist tendencies of the squared form, but entirely in keeping with the theme of accessibility that is paramount at Holton Lee. Another touch that makes this more than just a simple, elegant Modernist box structure is the green roof planted with grass that will continue to grow, die and green again with the seasons. Seen against the backdrop of great mature trees, the wisps of grass coming off the building and the ageing cedar make the building genuinely blend with the scenery, as it responds visibly to weather and light.

Fretton was recommended by a neighbouring arts board to help Holton Lee expand their scheme, which was originally much larger but was reduced due to funding restrictions. Though this is his first commission for a spiritual building the architect says that in the past 'people have said that they feel a certain peace and contentment in buildings we've done, an ambience'. Fretton himself does not follow any particular religion, and, he says, 'I couldn't make a building that is religious, because I'm not religious.

2 The architect's sketches show the Modernist lines of the building.

3 Glazed doors and panels on the seaward side of the building make for inspiring views.

4–5 The elevations demonstrate the elegant simplicity of the design with its timber framing, flat green roof and glazed façade.

6 The plan shows the wheelchair-friendly path leading directly to the meditation area of the building. 1. quiet room, 2. quiet garden, 3. meeting rooms, 4. sun porch

7 The meditation area at left, meeting rooms at centre and open porch at right are all easily accessible.

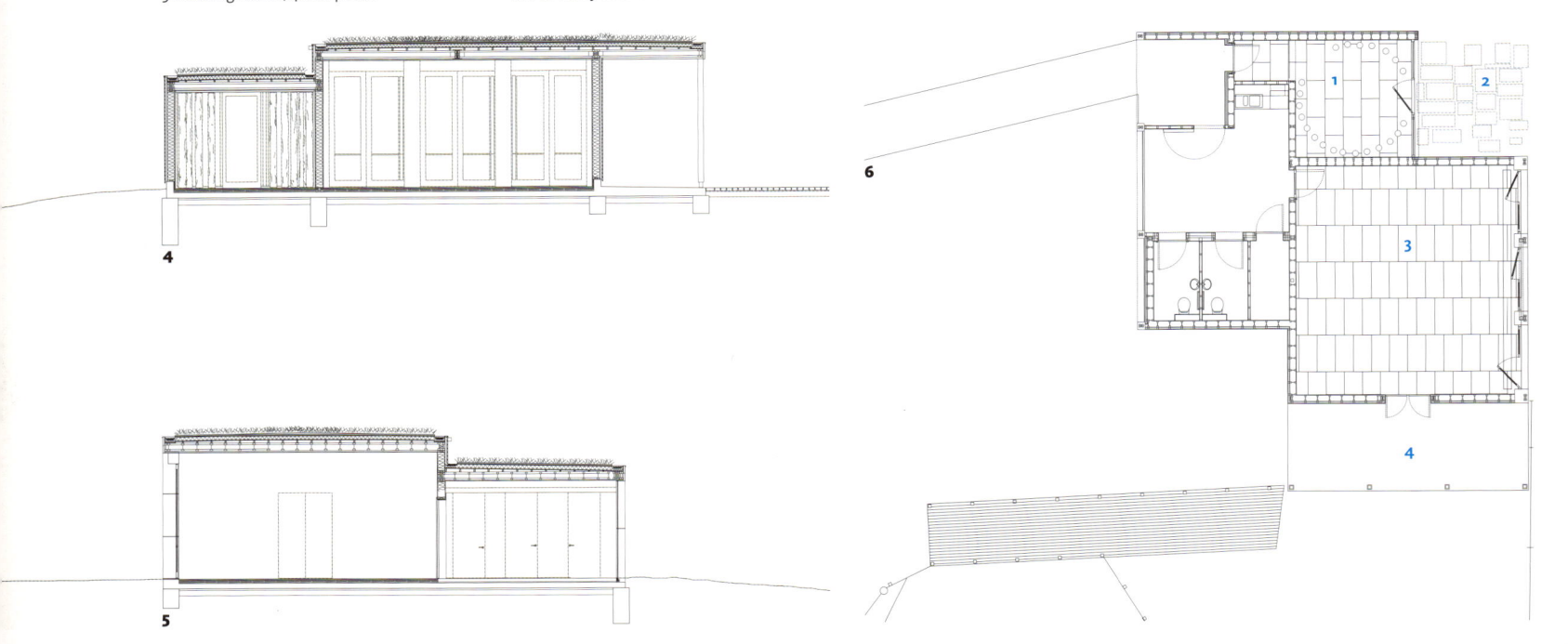

8 The building is covered in strips of Western red cedar which can be used without preservative or paint.

9 The meditation area is painted a silvery hue and lined with timber poles culled from the surrounding forest.

10 The sketch shows how the new building has been integrated with the existing structure and the natural setting.

But I can make a building that allows people to practise religion in it.' This he feels is due in part to 'an ambiguous quality' with which such a building is imbued. But it is an ambiguity of distinct purpose, not of the building's own aesthetic integrity; that is clear enough.

Holton Lee started as a communal Christian organization but now supports people of all faiths, and this building was intended to be totally non-denominational, without any religious symbolism, so that, as Fretton explains, 'anybody could feel at home here'. As Holton Lee evolved from a religious organization and acquired land courtesy of Sir Thomas Lee and his wife, Faith, it took on a nature-conservancy role, becoming active in the protection of the local plant and wildlife. Culling trees is part of its ongoing activities and some were reclaimed for the meditation room of Faith House. The building is environmentally friendly with low 'embodied energy', that is, the energy required to produce the materials is low, since it is mostly wood with only one piece of steel and the framing was prefabricated so that transport energy was also minimized. It became a memorial for Faith Lee, who died before the building was completed and after whom it is named. It is also a tribute to the beauty and spiritual connections inspired by nature, eloquently translated into form.

3.03

SHINGON-SHU BUDDHIST TEMPLE AND OSSUARY

KAGOSHIMA, JAPAN

THOMAS HEATHERWICK STUDIO

IN PROGRESS

When British designer Thomas Heatherwick was approached by members of the Shingon-Shu Buddhist order to build a new temple and ossuary in Japan he was, he said, 'elated', but also felt a very keen sense of responsibility. 'We're not Japanese, or Buddhist and we had never built a temple, but they said they wanted someone who would be objective. We felt very trusted.'

It was a sense of trust that permeated the project. 'We asked them to give us four months to leave us to our process, to not contact us. No client has ever allowed that before but they said OK. Perhaps it's the Buddhist sensibility but they are happy to take time over things.' The time proved useful in a number of ways. The team needed six months just to work out how all of the spaces required in the brief would be organized before they even considered what the building itself would look like. Part of that aesthetic was culturally informed if not prescribed: the clients brought Heatherwick to Kyoto to look at a range of traditional temples. 'They told me, "We want you to understand these but not to copy them".'

Though unhampered by a diktat, Heatherwick found the project was affected to some degree by the site, a revered historic battleground on a hillside outside Kagoshima. It is not far removed from the city but on a dramatically steep slope and facing a volcano across the valley. 'It is a sacred site,' Heatherwick explains, 'where the last Japanese samurai hero committed hara-kiri.' He did so after a battle in which 20,000 troops were killed, so although the area is important to the local population they also feel somewhat haunted by the massive bloodshed. 'They're happy that there is a priest here now to purify the site.'

Heatherwick's design for the temple is an organic form that displays his tendencies for flowing, sculptural shapes produced through intricate workmanship. Though he favours a single material or as few as possible, that material is often used in a highly organized and painstaking fashion. Here he achieved a design that was, he says, 'inspired by experiments manipulating fabric. I looked at the fabric of the robes that the priest wears and the Buddha and found these amazing undulations.' A beautifully rolling plywood structure, the building will be made of a series of layers, 'each the height of an average step, so that those can be pulled out of the walls wherever necessary'. The purity of form is achieved through computer technology, which will determine and cut each piece of each layer. It is a technology now widely used, but only recently on such a scale as this. The layers cannot be made in a single piece but they can be made to look as if they are.

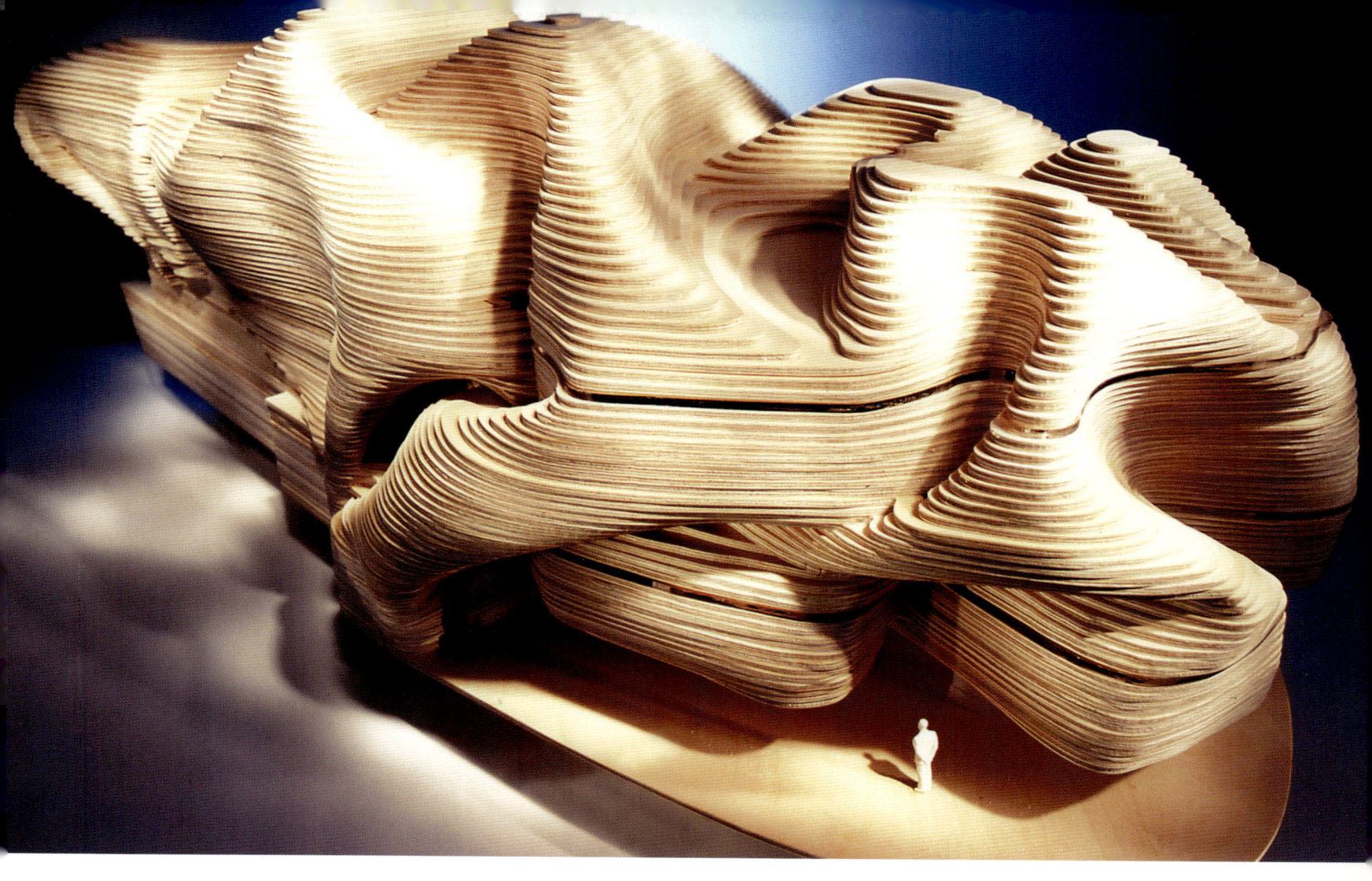

Interspersed between the plywood will be blocks of coloured glass, which will take up entire layers. Because they will be in numerous small segments instead of custom-made giant curves the cost is minimal. Concrete floors also keep the overall budget in check. Because of the threat of earthquakes, the entire structure is bolted to a steel typhoon frame.

Though it is not yet built, the temple is exciting to see in model form as different levels are removed to show how the interior spaces are set within the cloud-shaped structure. Though the affinity with fabric is discernible, there is also a topographical influence that Heatherwick says was unconscious, but which is definitely there. Every room has a different shape, which is affected by the undulating walls, and the temple is much like a series of caves but with an infusion of natural light. Stairs between levels, being formed as they are by the existing layers of plywood, are like natural steps emerging from the bedrock.

Since statues of the Buddha must face south or east and the architect was eager to have a relationship with the nearby volcano, due east of the building, the temple Buddha will solemnly confront the great natural wonder across the valley. Worshippers will have their back to the volcano, but will surely be aware of its presence. The building will have a distinct presence of its own, one that responds to the powers of nature and history.

The new building combines a temple and ossuary in one integrated plan, a traditional practice that has been lost in recent decades.

1 Polycarbonate side panels allow the building to glow in the nighttime desert landscape.

3.04

CENTER OF GRAVITY HALL

NEW MEXICO, USA

PREDOCK_FRANE ARCHITECTS

2003

Surrounded by sloping desert hillsides, near red volcanic cliffs, the Bodhi Mandala Zen Center brings together students and Buddhist monks for teaching and meditation within the dramatic natural setting of a river valley high in the mountains of northern New Mexico. The Center of Gravity Hall is an addition to the existing complex, parts of which are remnants of an old Boy Scout camp, and will function as 'the symbolic heart for teachings, meditation and ceremonies'.

California-based architects Hadrian Predock and John Frane were asked to create a scheme for various new facilities, of which the Center of Gravity Hall is the first to be completed. The idea of a Buddhist retreat in the middle of the American desert would seem to excite more dissonance than harmony, but the rural setting – with its sparse vegetation and rugged terrain – has proved an apposite context for the architects' blend of Zen, native Southwest and modern method and practice. 'While being programmed for a traditional Zen Buddhist practice,' the architects note, 'the building itself has been highly responsive and sensitive to its unique position.' Combining characteristics of the free-flowing interior–exterior space of traditional Buddhist temples with a determined environmentally sympathetic structure, they have produced a building that sits calmly and gracefully in the landscape.

The structure is basically a large room that has been given strength of character through the chosen materials and adaptive approach. While the folded, triangular metal roof certainly departs from traditional building types of the American Southwest, its low profile and hardy qualities make it ideal protection from desert thunderstorms. Cantilevered well beyond the building frame, the roof also provides a sheltered space for walking meditation. The rammed-earth walls are a more modern and efficient take on the adobe construction indigenous to the region and practised by native Americans for centuries. Using a mixture of 'highly compacted local earth and cement', which, says Predock, 'has been finely tuned to relate to local sandstone cliffs', the architects created the massive 460 to 660 mm (18 to 26 inch) thick walls that ground the building and make it thermally efficient: the walls keep the heat out during the day and, at night, radiate what heat they do absorb. The mass of the earth walls is efficiently countered by the use of translucent polycarbonate panels that echo the light-filtering qualities of rice-paper screens. The polycarbonate is set within

2 The rammed-earth wall at left is thermally efficient and ecologically friendly.

3 The section shows the minimal intrusions that the building makes on the site with its gently sloping roof and efficient pinpoint foundation work.

4 Humble materials were used to create dramatic sweeps of line and texture.

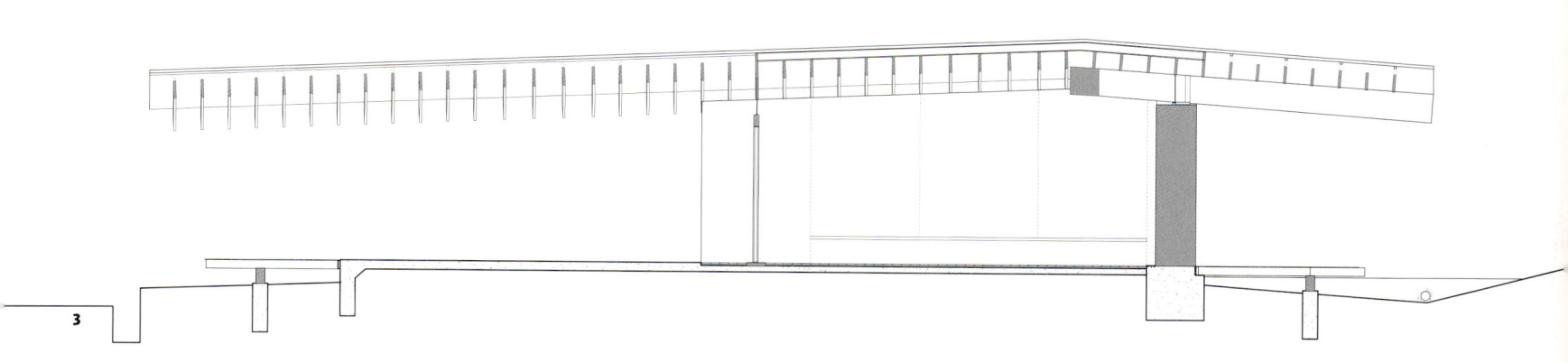

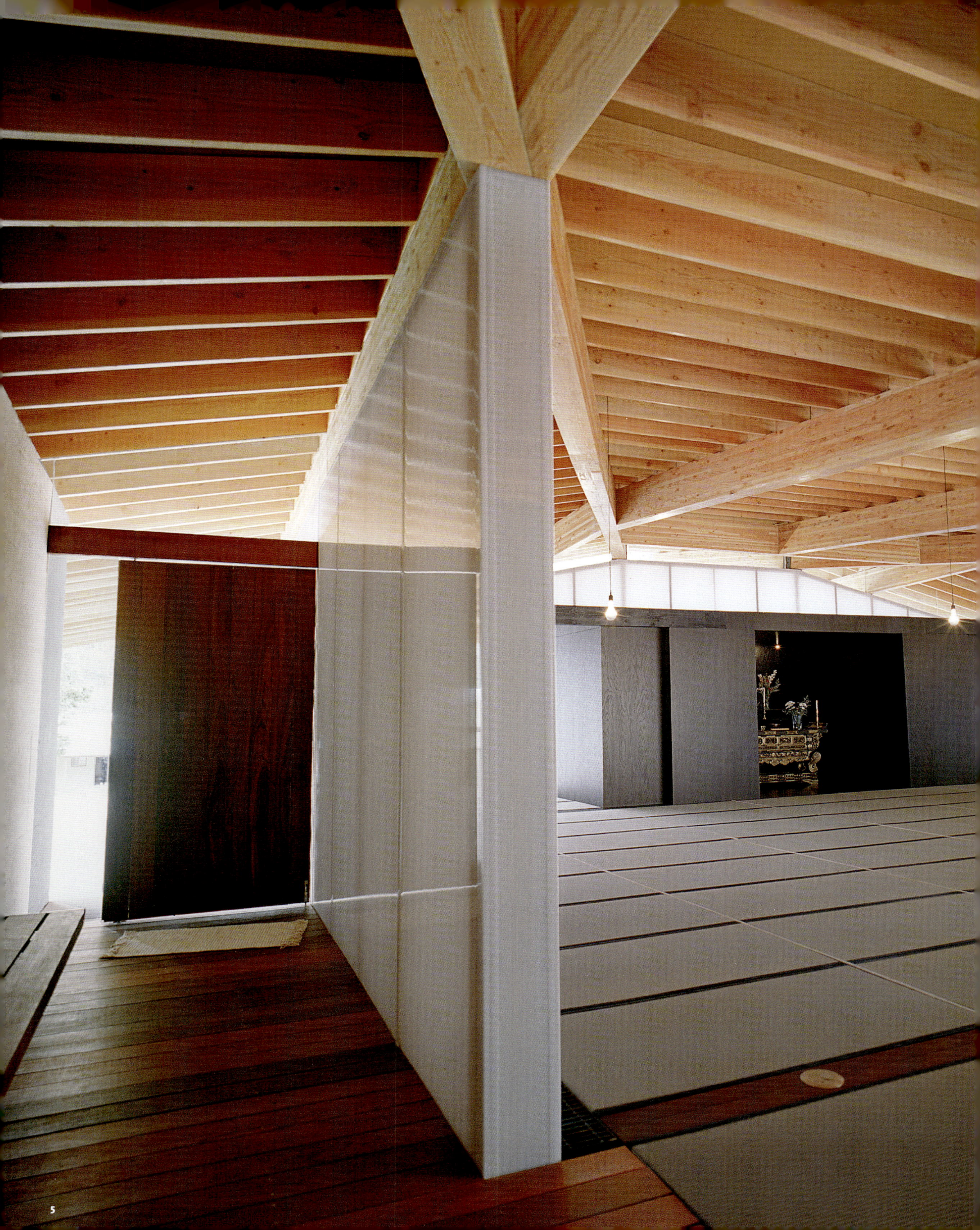

5 Polycarbonate sheeting is used to create an entrance enclosure that maintains the free flow of light.

6 The ceiling construction, using highly strengthened glu-laminated beams, resembles the open beam-and-rafter sequences of traditional temples.

7 Sliding wood panels lead to a small Zen-style garden and allow the room to be opened to the outdoors.

8 The exploded axonometric shows a tightly controlled range of elements and angles, all developed around the presence of the shrine, students and monks.

9 The plan shows the shrine located on the west side with the sliding panels opposite. The rammed-earth walls envelop the eastern corners.

10 Tatami mats create a seating grid in lines echoing the wall planes and ceiling structure.

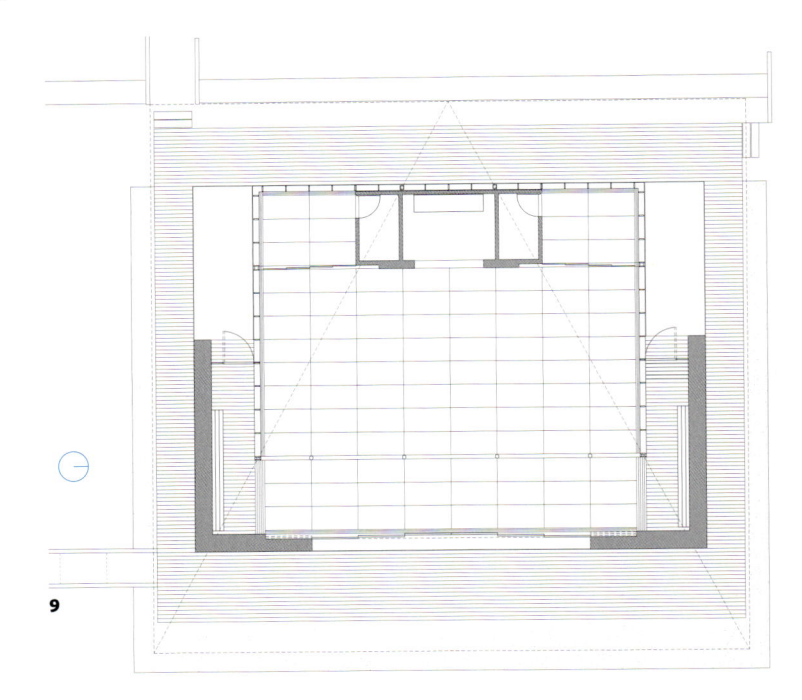

the boundary of the earthen walls, which overlap to create a dramatic entrance hall that is both protected and light.

Like many traditional temples, the Gravity Hall benefits from the ample use of wood. The metal roof sits on chunky fir purlins and glu-laminated wood beams that give the overall effect inside of a traditional beamed and latticed ceiling structure with the warm coloration that comes from natural wood. The floor and exterior decking are all made of pau lope, a sustainably harvested Brazilian hardwood that has the rich tone of cherrywood. To emphasize the relationship between interior and exterior, the architects have made a long wall out of slatted wood verticals through which natural light streams at angles and creates changing patterns of light and shadow across the room. By using one 11 metre (36 foot) long structural beam at this end, the architects have made it possible to completely open the slatted panels that make up this wall, so that the interior will be open to a 'reinterpreted' Zen garden.

While Predock and Frane have made sure the building sits well in its context they have also set it apart slightly. Surrounded by wood decking beneath the eaves of the overhanging roof, it is further separated by a swathe of white pebbles around the perimeter, suggesting the act of crossing from one world into another, or at least moving between two environments. Because of an approach that is both thoughtful and innovative, the movement from the natural into the man-made feels both easy and inspired.

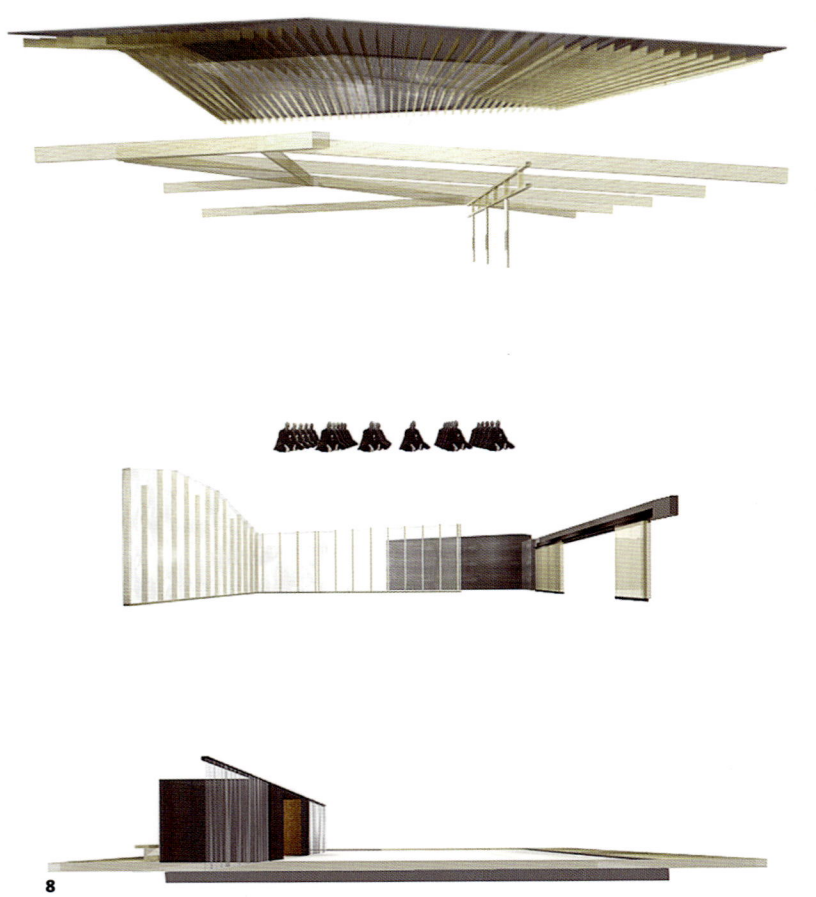

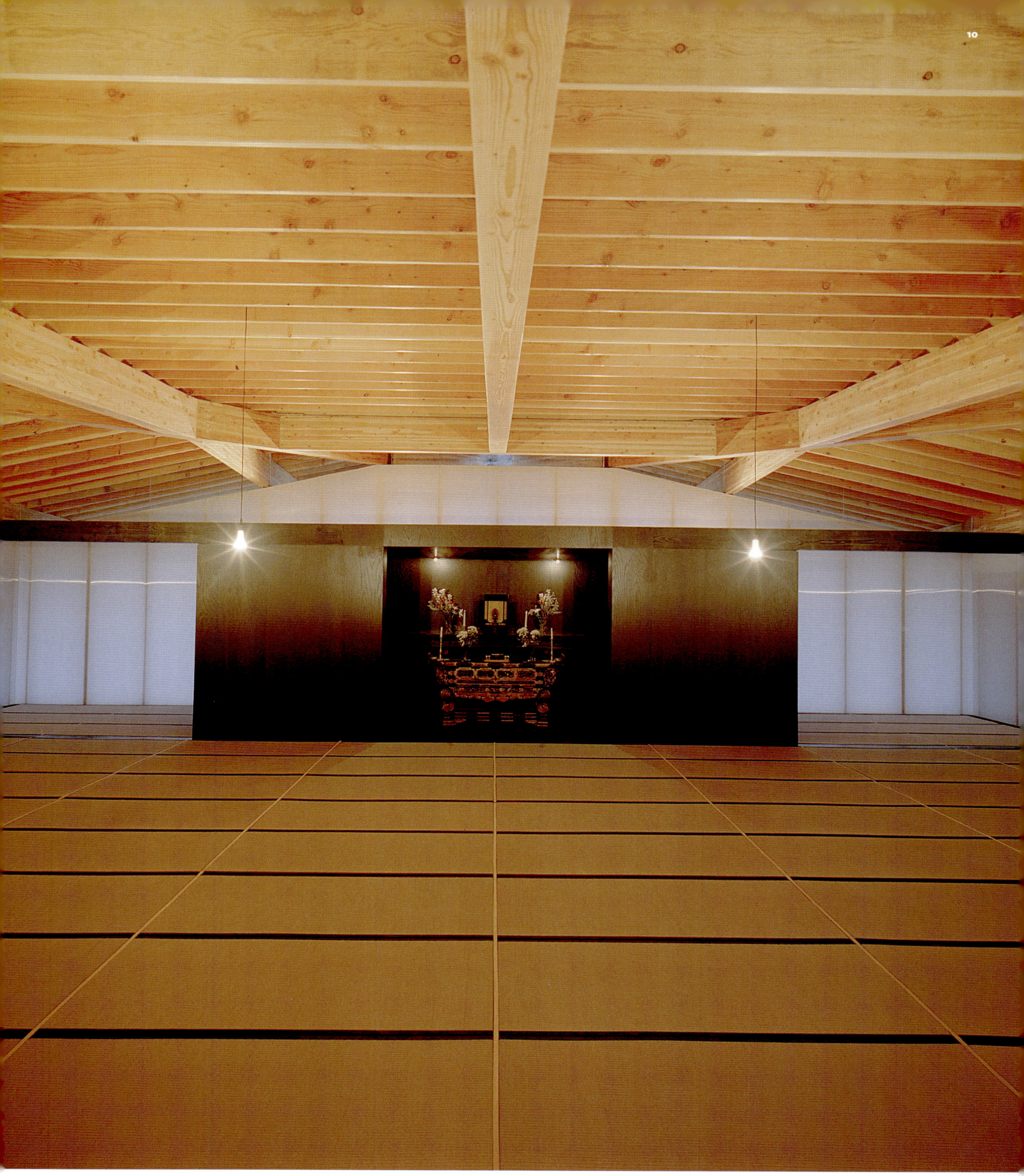

1 The white interior has a flowing, sculptural quality.

2 The refectory room demonstrates the simple beauty of the interiors.

3 The south elevation exterior showing the manor house, left, and new wing with refectory, right.

4 East elevation from the courtyard, with the church at left.

5 A corridor lining the central courtyard combines the purity of the white interior with that of the uninterrupted glazed surface.

3.05

MONASTERY OF NOVÝ DVUR

PLZEN, CZECH REPUBLIC

JOHN PAWSON

2004

The Gothic style was born under the Cistercians when, in the twelfth century, Abbot Suger transformed the abbey church of St Denis into the grandly austere prototype. He was happily congratulated by the ascetic St Bernard, known as the second founder of the Cistercians,[1] who went on to preach that monks should renounce 'all precious and beautiful things for Christ's sake'.[2] Here he seems to have been slightly at odds with his Gothic collaborator, Suger, who believed that God was made manifest through material beauty. In defence of his use of fine objects and materials in the church of St Denis, he wrote of his 'delight in the beauty of the house of God – the loveliness of the many-coloured gems [that] called me away from external cares.'[3] However, the two approaches dovetailed with an architectural–historical Big Bang in the mutual embrace of the Gothic. The eschewing of ornament for ornament's sake and the love of the graceful, gravity-defying vaults and pointed arches that raised the Gothic from the great massed volumes of the Romanesque satisfied both Suger's desire for inspiring beauty and Bernard's Cistercian commitment to purity and simplicity. These latter qualities were now celebrated, perhaps incongruously, to exhilarating effect.

In a somewhat similar fashion, John Pawson has brought an exhilarating simplicity to the Cistercian monastery of Nový Dvur in a remote part of Bohemia. His team refer to this collaboration as 'one of the more unlikely consequences of the fall of communism in former Czechoslovakia'.[4] While

3

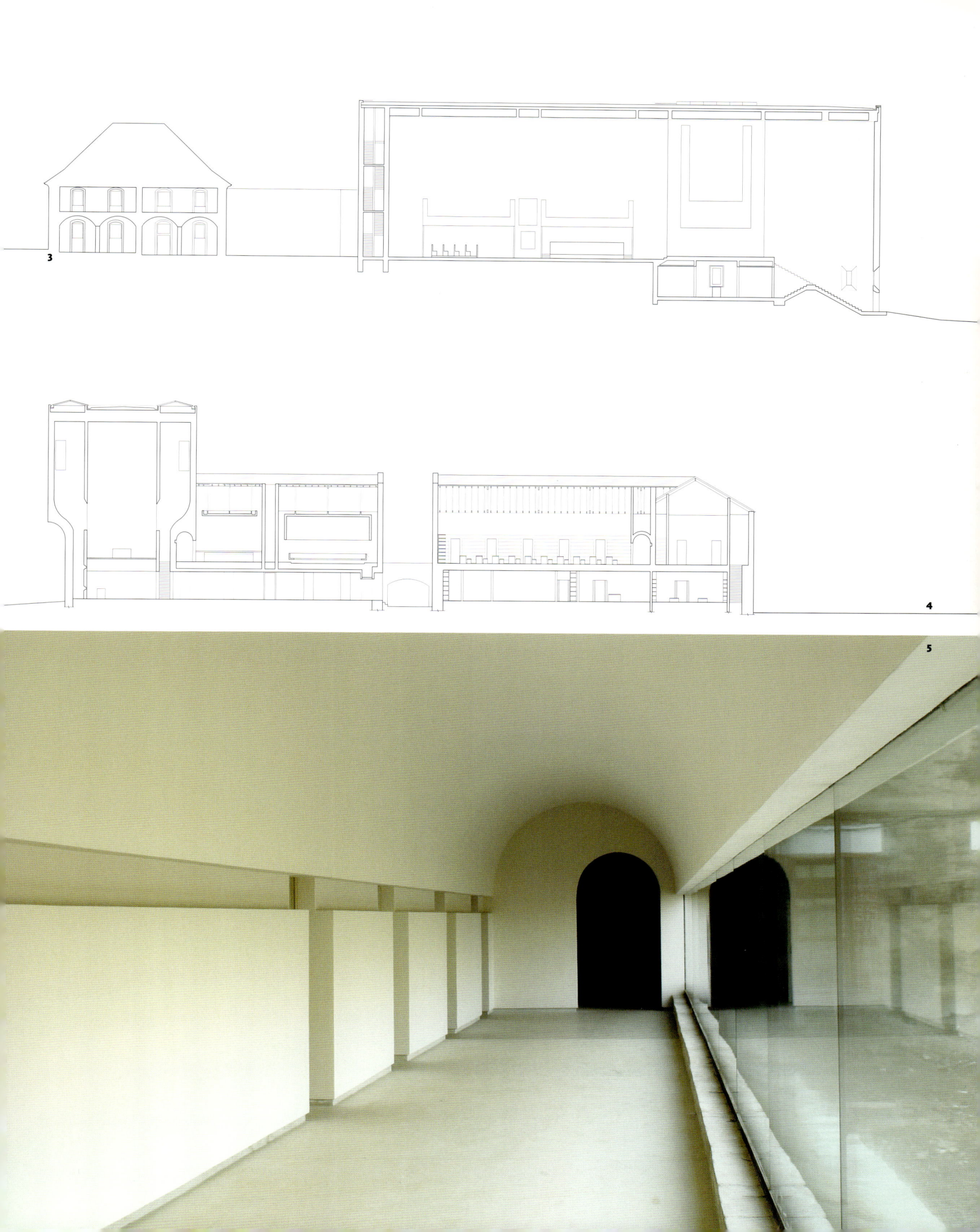

4

5

6 The model shows how light is filtered through sculptural openings rather than stained glass.

the monks of Nov Dvur have not set out to redefine the parameters of a monk's existence, as Bernard before them had, they have returned, after venturing abroad to Burgundy following the Velvet Revolution of 1989, to establish a new monastery for the Cistercian Order. The site they chose contained 'a Baroque manor house with runs of agricultural buildings framing a courtyard', which had been uninhabited for decades. Pawson's brief included creation of a church, cloister, chapel, kitchen, refectory, cells and classrooms.

The decision was made to restore the manor house but to replace the agricultural buildings with new structures. The general plan, however, of buildings set around a square courtyard, was maintained and Pawson's new church inserted into the north-east corner of the square with deft adherence to linearity. Suitably for Cistercian asceticism, the church makes its most obvious appearance with the apse located on the opposite side from the manor house (now used as offices and classrooms). Here, the curved frontage rises up and the projecting lightboxes that define the transepts become visible. From inside, one appreciates only the light admitted through the window openings without being aware of the lightbox structures hovering at either side of the choir.

In another way it seems that Pawson has taken the airborne quality of Gothic a step further, making the cloisters, too, sit above ground level – though here it has been done to negotiate a steep gradient. The cloister is at ground level next to the manor house, where the site is highest, but is entered at the first-floor level on the east side where the land slopes, so that a single level is achieved even as the ground drops away. The cantilevered cloister is without precedent, being wholly unsupported by columns. Instead of the monks pacing the grounds of the garden they circle it from above, overlooking it, their sight – should they lift their gaze – drawn by the windows at each corner that break out of the curved white ceiling tunnel with a view of open countryside and sky. The cloister ceilings, like the church and monastery interiors, are Pawson white, meaning they are painted white but have a sculptural essence. And the white is contrasted with glass walls and wood floors, and serves as a backdrop to highlight even the simplified objects of the Cistercian lifestyle. Though he has made his name with private houses for wealthy clients, high-end shop design and a certain luxurious minimalism, Pawson seems particularly well suited to the task of creating monastic beauty. Making forms that reveal their essence gently, over time and changes of light is something with which he seems entirely at peace.

7 The plan shows the arrangement of buildings around a central courtyard with the church at the north-east corner.
1. presbytery, 2. monks' choir, 3. nave, 4. courtyard, 5. chapel, 6. conference room, 7. administration/former manor house, 8. refectory, 9. scriptorium, 10. sacristy, 11. cloister

8 An early construction image shows the pure cylindrical shape of the apse.

9 Easter Mass was celebrated in the unfinished church.

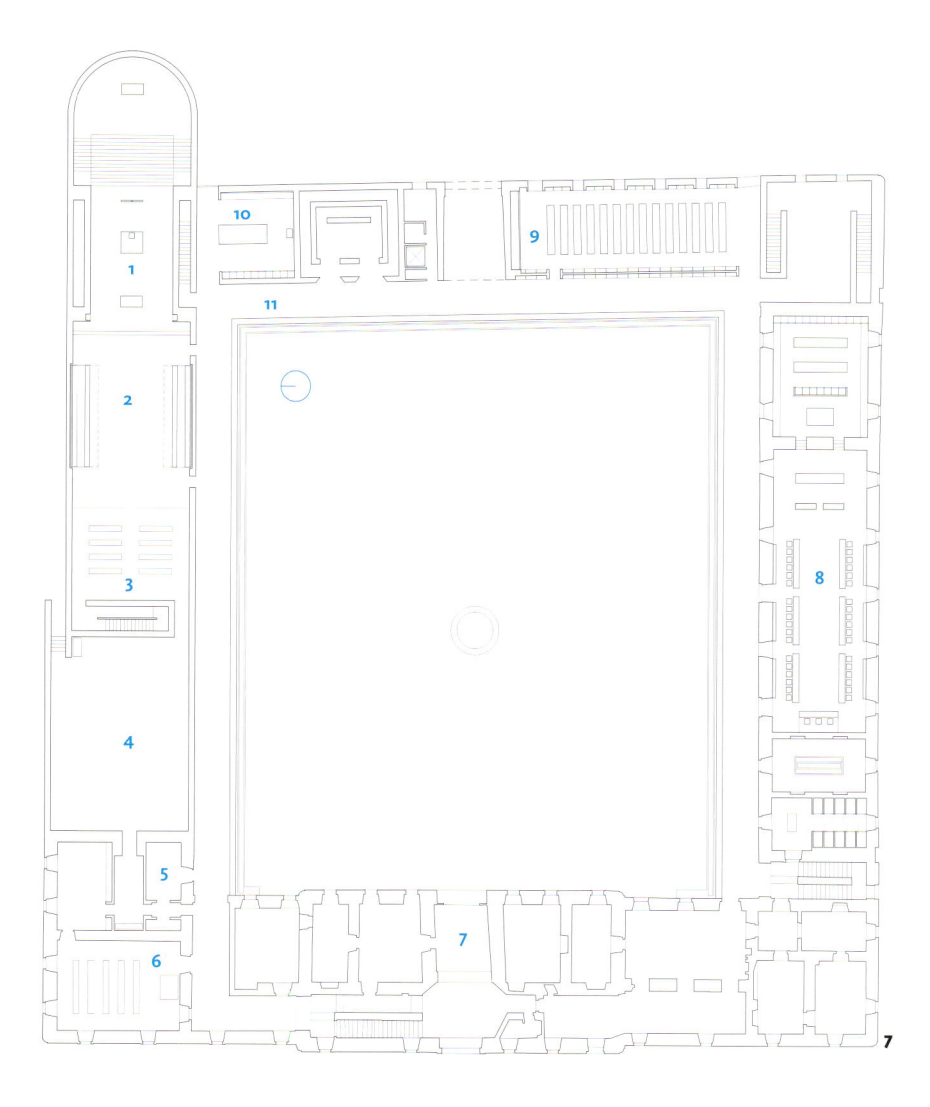

3.06

NIGHT PILGRIMAGE CHAPEL

LOCHERBODEN, AUSTRIA

GEROLD WIEDERIN

1997

'It's not a chapel in the common sense,' says architect Gerold Wiederin of his nocturnal chapel in the Tyrolean hills. 'I didn't want closed walls, it should be an open structure in the woods so you are invited to come sit there and to pray.' If there are still any doubts as to whether an organization like the Catholic Church can have the breadth of mind to encourage modern architecture, then Wiederin's design for this small, unenclosed chapel on the edge of a forest should go some way towards assuaging them. The one-time employee of groundbreaking Swiss firm Herzog and de Meuron even won the admiration of his former bosses with this unapologetically modern but gracefully formed chapel intended for participants in a pilgrimage to celebrate a miracle of the Virgin Mary which occurred in 1871. Six times a year pilgrims visit during the night, journeying through the forest by candlelight and then pausing at a clearing at the top of the mountain. This clearing is now defined with a modest concrete structure, a shelter for the officiating priest that looks out over a space sometimes occupied by 2,000 worshippers.

Though he is not religious, Wiederin admits that he was 'very much taken with the mood and mysticism of the place' and 'wanted to create a special mood and atmosphere'. That he has done by making an open structure, where people can come any time outside of the pilgrimage ceremonies to sit in contemplation or worship. The building, really a 'baldachine', Wiederin explains, since only the priest stands inside, is pure in its simplicity: four supports, one solid, cubic altar area and a braced roof with raised abstracted crosses on the ceiling and on the rooftop are all made of untreated, exposed concrete cast in situ. The altar, pulpit and priest's chair are of prefabricated exposed concrete. All of which could describe a cold concrete box, but inherent elements keep that epithet from applying here. The openness of the building combined with its lush, natural setting, creates a feeling of being in nature rather than retreating from it. With no walls to shield the interior, the lit chapel becomes a beacon in the night to the pilgrims emerging from the forest. The simplicity of the pure concrete gives precedence to the surroundings, and gives the chapel the delicate appeal of a folly when viewed against the backdrop of the thick forest and bare cliff face.

The interior is not without ornament; in fact, the chapel's one work of art is also greatly enhanced by the concrete frame. Helmut Federle's glasswork is set within the rear wall of the chapel in the space where you would expect to find a crucifix. It consists of loosely stacked lumps of rough-cut,

1 The flat roof features a cross motif that can be seen from the surrounding cliffs.

2 At night the chapel is a small beacon. Helmut Federle's sculpture – coloured glass pieces set within iron bars that represent boughs or flames – is the focal point of the chapel.

3–4 The elevation and side section show the exceedingly simple rectangular forms that make up the chapel.

5 The ceiling motif corresponds with that on the rooftop.

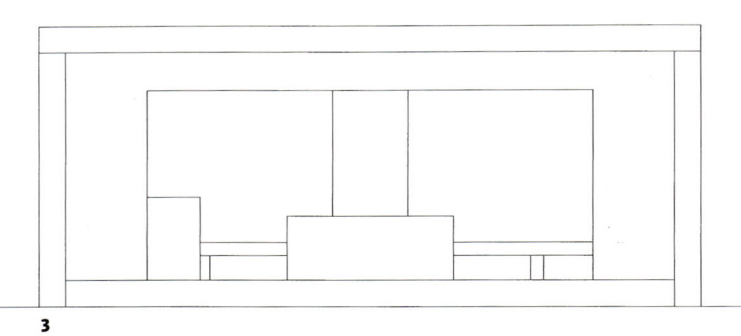

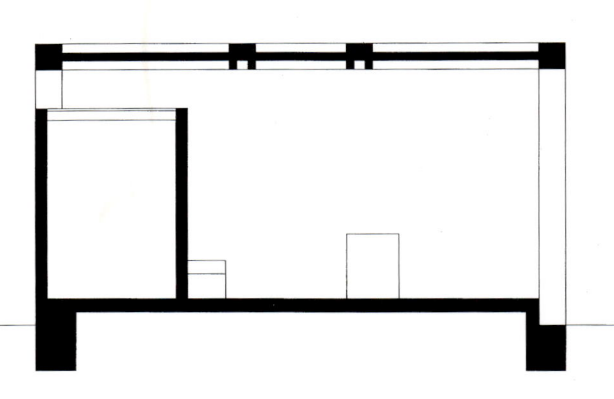

6 The interior of the cave in the rock face becomes a vanishing point through the chapel. The building's long, low form and concrete construction respond to the surrounding cave and rock.

coloured glass held in place, in the niche between two concrete slabs, by iron bars that angle and cross like tree branches. A stylized version of stained glass, the 'window' is illuminated from behind the wall in the sacristy but only on pilgrimage nights. The multi-coloured light contrasts with the bands of light emanating from the cross shapes in the ceiling, making the little chapel glow with colour and dimension.

Wiederin's departure from the traditional forms of chapel building were not wholly a single-minded pursuit of Modernism. There were two churches nearby, one from the turn of the nineteenth century and one that is 200 years old. 'I didn't want this to be just another chapel,' he says. One could hardly make such a statement about the finished structure. But for all of its unchapel-like qualities, the building's religious connotations were always meant to be clearly and easily read. The symbol of the Virgin Mary and the papal cross are engraved in the altar and are 'suggestive of the genius loci and of the nearby Benedictine cloister of Stams, to which a close relationship exists,' Wiederin explains. But perhaps the best summation of the spiritual and aesthetic aims of the project comes in his statement that: 'Here architecture provides the framework for a religious observance in the midst of unformed nature. It is a place of contemplation for the individual with the awareness that the miracle itself is to be found in its own specific environment.'

1 The new temple is located among traditional-style buildings in national parkland.

2 The site plan shows the temple's unintrusive form among the existing temple buildings and priests' quarters in the lakeside setting.

3 The Buddha is backlit by the glazed rear wall of the temple.

3.07

WHITE TEMPLE

KYOTO, JAPAN

TAKASHI YAMAGUCHI & ASSOCIATES

2000

White walls and ceilings and a distinctive box shape, Takashi Yamaguchi's shrine to maternal ancestors seems like the work of the minimalists' minimalist. But it is something beyond minimal. Like his Glass Temple (see p.44), the White Temple is near Kyoto, about two hours' journey from the city, and is similarly suffused with the purity of white light. Set in the natural beauty of parkland on the shore of a large lake, the temple is unusual in both form and purpose. In Japan, the architect explains, 'it has been customary to enshrine and pray only for the ancestors of the male line of descent. Even today, our national system of family registration is oriented to the male line, so one's maternal ancestors eventually fade from memory and never receive memorial services.' This project, he says, 'was born from a recognition of the necessity to give thanks to one's maternal as well as paternal ancestors'. As in other temples, Buddhist mortuary tablets inscribed with the names of the ancestors are kept here so that the priest can hold ceremonies for them.

The structure of the White Temple might aptly be described as a white box: it is a white, rectangular volume with an open entrance square matched by a frosted-glass end-wall. The interior is mostly taken up with a stepped white slab that is the altar. The slab descends from the back of the building toward the front, so that visitors confront the white steps going away from them with the Buddha placed near the top, facing forward. Memorial tablets are placed here. The statue of the Buddha reflects the light coming from behind it is tinged with gold, in a halo effect. The box is made of rein-

3

4 At dusk the temple becomes a lightbox, the white walls a backdrop for the natural landscape.

5, 8 The sections (this page) and elevations (opposite) show the utter simplicity of the design.

6 The glass-box protrusions at the rear of the temple are extensions of glazed rooflights.

7 The lighted temple at night. The architect wanted the interior to evoke 'a floating sensation'.

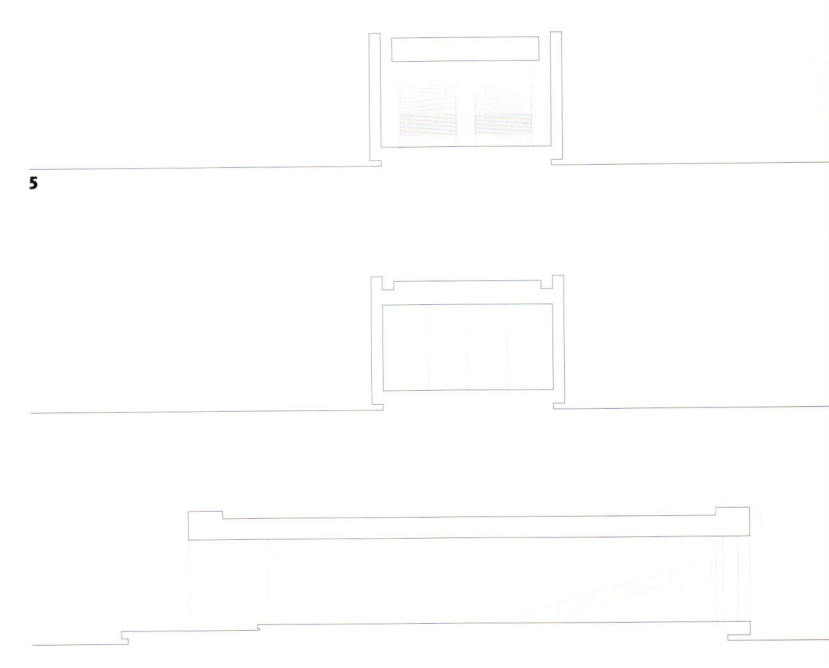

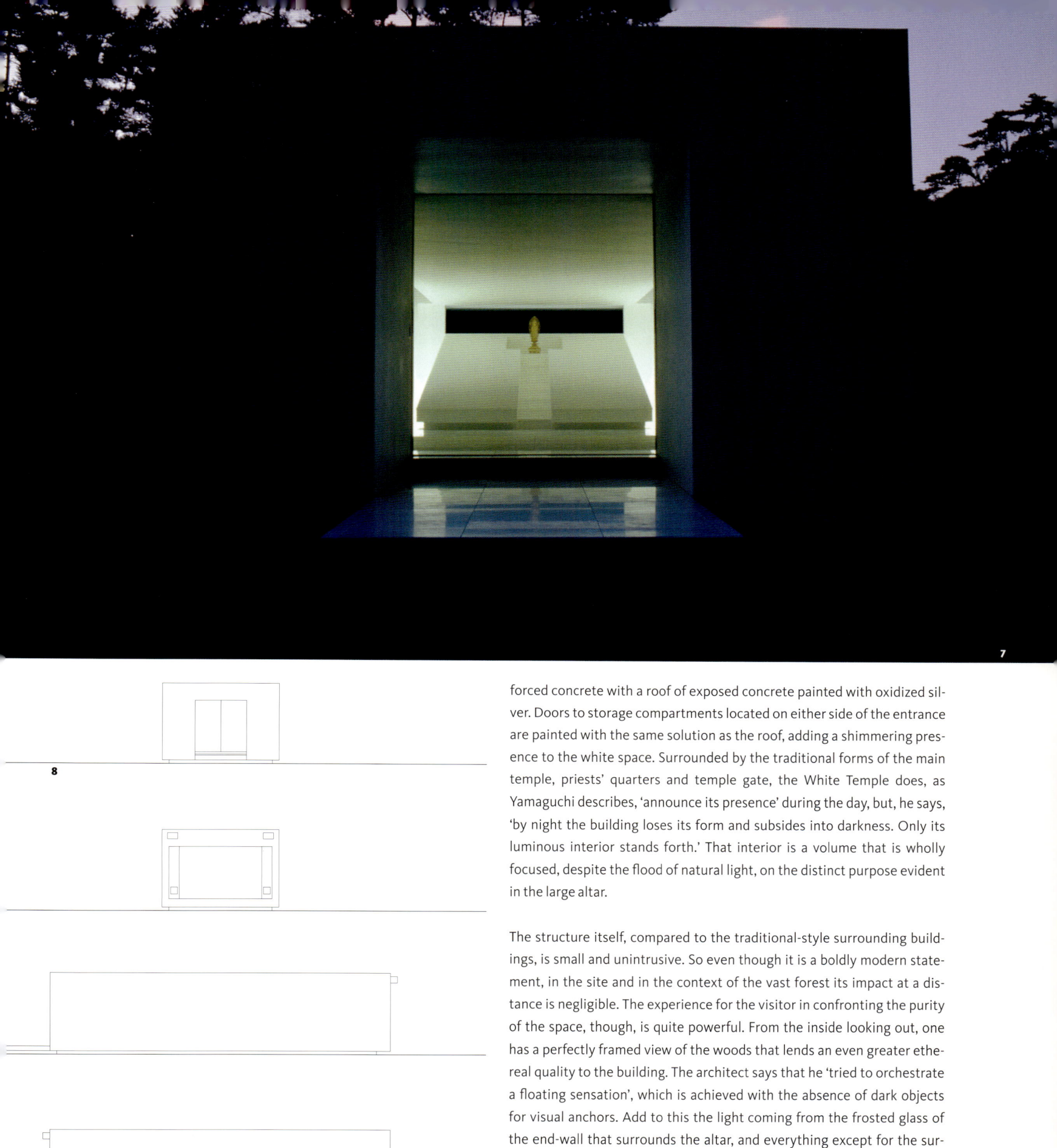

forced concrete with a roof of exposed concrete painted with oxidized silver. Doors to storage compartments located on either side of the entrance are painted with the same solution as the roof, adding a shimmering presence to the white space. Surrounded by the traditional forms of the main temple, priests' quarters and temple gate, the White Temple does, as Yamaguchi describes, 'announce its presence' during the day, but, he says, 'by night the building loses its form and subsides into darkness. Only its luminous interior stands forth.' That interior is a volume that is wholly focused, despite the flood of natural light, on the distinct purpose evident in the large altar.

The structure itself, compared to the traditional-style surrounding buildings, is small and unintrusive. So even though it is a boldly modern statement, in the site and in the context of the vast forest its impact at a distance is negligible. The experience for the visitor in confronting the purity of the space, though, is quite powerful. From the inside looking out, one has a perfectly framed view of the woods that lends an even greater ethereal quality to the building. The architect says that he 'tried to orchestrate a floating sensation', which is achieved with the absence of dark objects for visual anchors. Add to this the light coming from the frosted glass of the end-wall that surrounds the altar, and everything except for the surrounding forest and sky feels less substantial. With an approach that negates the physical in such a way, the perception of the metaphysical must become more possible.

1 The chapel is set back from the ornate gate and has its own cobbled, tree-lined path.

2 The extruding volume of the sacristy suggests an additional gateway to the chapel entrance.

3.08

SANTO OVIDIO ESTATE CHAPEL

DOURO, PORTUGAL

ÁLVARO SIZA

2001

When speaking of Álvaro Siza in a religious context it is hard not to refer to his great church at Marco de Canavezes (1996); its tall, white, fluted façade has become almost iconic in modern religious architecture. However, it is some measure of talent when an architect can adroitly turn his hand to the small as well as the grandiose, and Siza's little chapel for a renovated estate in a forested area of northern Portugal attests to his flexibility of scale.

Located less than 20 miles from his previous landmark ecclesiastical project, the Santo Ovidio estate once consisted of a manor house set on a large farm that profited from agricultural and forest produce. When Siza began work, the farm had become much reduced from its original size and contained a vineyard, the old house, a 'pleasure garden with belvedere' and Baroque-style fountain. To these the architect added a garage, tennis

2

3 The use of stone and whitewashed concrete refers to traditional rural buildings, though the shape is greatly simplified.

4 The plan shows the procession from the path (far right), up the steps to the raised porch (left) with sight lines demonstrating how the building is revealed as visitors progess up the path.

5 The spare interior recalls the primitive chapel that once occupied the site, but its purity of planes and angles is distinctly modern.

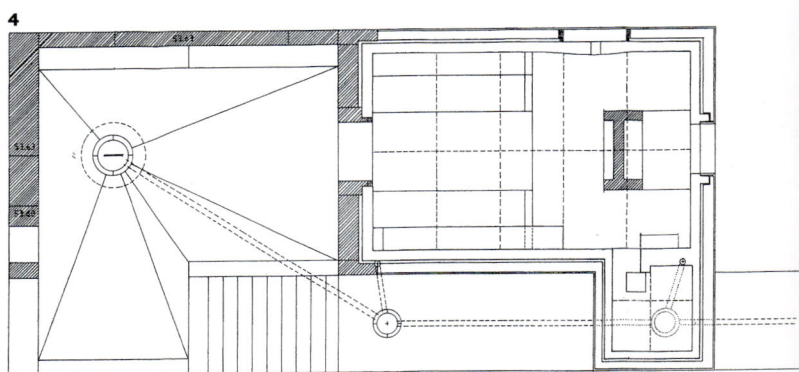

court, an indoor swimming pool – located in a former tenant's house – and a chapel. According to Siza, there had once been 'a primitive chapel dedicated to Santo Ovidio' but it was demolished by a previous owner.

The new chapel is an idyllic retreat within a modern, design-conscious collection of buildings, which Siza has carefully arranged and integrated. Viewed from the old scalloped, Baroque entrance gate, which has been retained, the chapel appears as a complementary whitewashed stone-and-concrete structure, similar in scale to the gatehouse, its half-moon apse window referring to the curves of the old portico. It is reached by a stone drive running beside the residence gate and, a few steps nearer, the cantilevered box of the sacristy becomes visible, forming a symbolic separate portico leading to the steps and, at a right angle, the tiny church entrance 'courtyard'. Though the entrance to the chapel is not enclosed, it is obscured by this reverse entry – an entry which is given prominence by being faced in stone, rather than the whitewashed concrete of the other three walls. The stone is carried up the path so that there is a steady processional flow of colour and texture from the gate to the steps, across the porch and up the wall of the façade.

Inside, the pure concrete interior inevitably recalls a monastic cell but, as with the exterior elements, its subtle details distinguish it as a space of aesthetic significance. A granite altar and floor slab align with the single half-moon-shape window, whose form relates to the interior volume of the sacristy. The half-moon window is carved out of the thickness of the concrete wall, as is a cross placed not behind the altar but to the left, opposite the sacristy in the north-east wall, and glazed with gold-veined marble. The granite altar and centre floor panel, along with the bulky wood benches, bespeak purity and solidity, material strength tinged with an awareness of material beauty.

This is a private chapel for the use of the family and is part of a larger residential complex, but it possesses its own integrity as a piece of thoughtful building, a quiet, spare sanctuary with intimations of grand design.

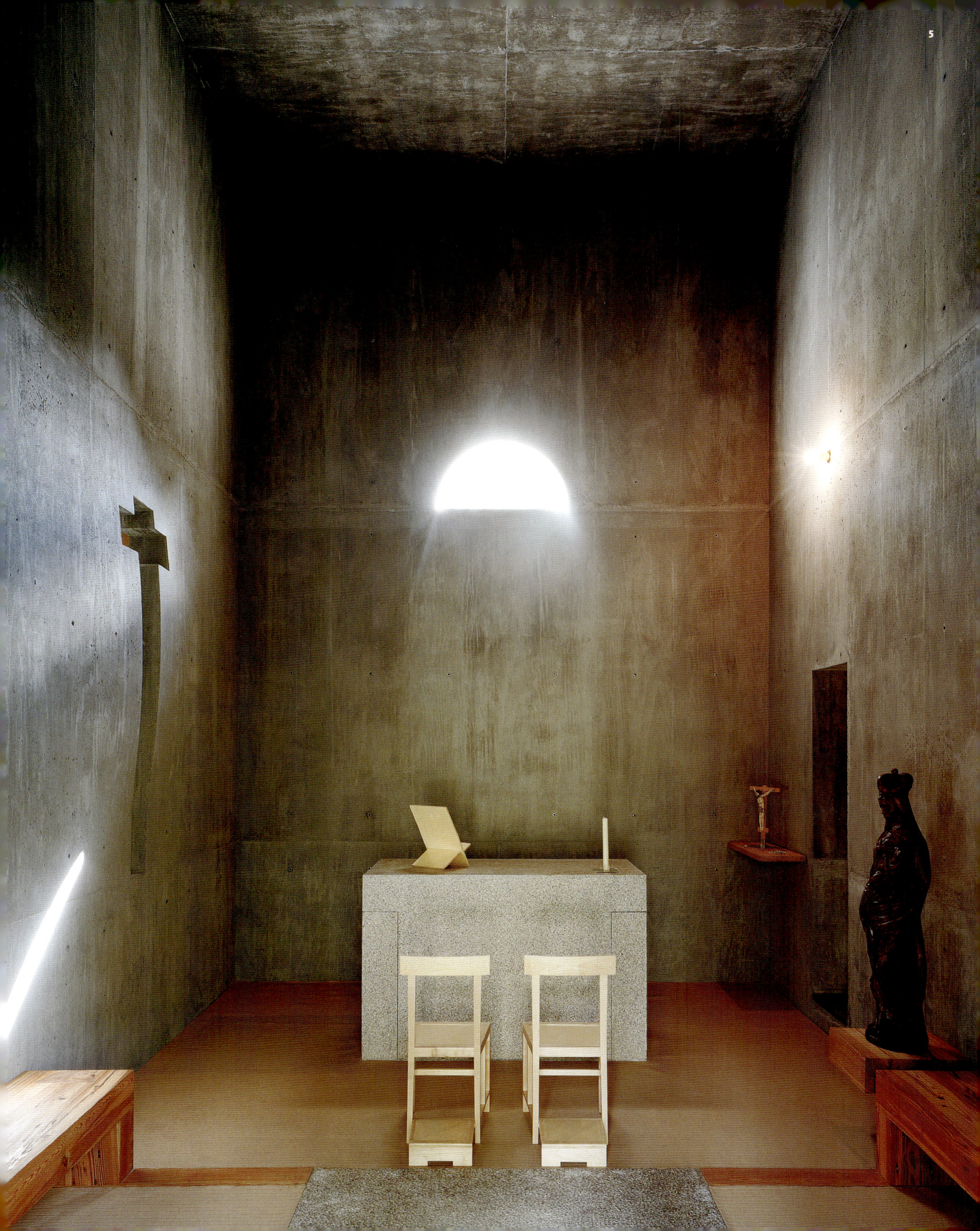

4 GRAND ICONS PRAYER AND WORSHIP ON A LARGE SCALE

Church of the Sacred Heart, Munich

Ecclesiastical buildings are often seen as monolithic, overpowering, awe-inspiring reminders of omnipotence. The great cathedrals of Europe, the great mosques at Mecca and elsewhere in the Middle East, have an overwhelming architecture to coincide with the infinite measure of God. Today both Christian and Muslim architecture continues the tradition of grandeur, of welcoming not just hundreds but thousands of worshippers into vast halls. This kind of building type is less prevalent among the synagogues of post-war Europe. And though certainly in Asia there are temples to compete with the grandest mosque or cathedral, they tend not to be built on such a scale in this century. Non-denominational or multi-faith spaces have always courted a quieter and less intrusive corner of the architectural spectrum. Consequently, the buildings that most approach monumentality tend to be cathedrals, churches and mosques, which, despite reports of an overall decline in religious commitment in Europe and the West, attract enough worshippers to justify their vast capacities.

However, the most successful of recent designs do not simply provide ever larger monuments but approach the task of accommodating large numbers with an up-to-date aesthetic wisdom and vision. Some projects are modest in size but can be opened up to include great numbers of people. The new Dresden synagogue doesn't have any such capacity but it carries a social-historical distinction that makes it a monument, in fact if not size, that very much reflects a twenty-first-century temperament.

Whatever their aesthetic impact, the cathedral of Our Lady of the Angels in Los Angeles and the church of San Giovanni Rotondo near Genoa are two of the most famed projects of religious architecture at the turn of this century. Built by renowned and internationally celebrated architects to house thousands of people each, they were destined for huge attention. But their achievements in design and engineering, and in responding to the demands of the community and existing landscape give them importance beyond size and moment.

The same is true of the first synagogue to be built in East Germany since reunification. The project was burdened with historic-emotional baggage but wears its distinction well, emerging as a dynamic symbol outside, and inside as a luminous sanctuary. The grandeur of Daniel Bonilla's school chapel in Bogotá is also somewhat hidden until its giant doors open to allow up to 1,000 people to worship in what is essentially a well-crafted church for 100.

In a climate seemingly less suited to outdoor worship, architects Allman Sattler and Wappner have created a work of similar flexibility. Their box, sheathed in thousands of panes of specially formulated glass, was also designed so that practically one entire façade can be opened to embrace larger crowds outside.

Abdelhalim I Abdelhalim's new mosque outside Riyadh is less obviously progressive, but it is a work of distinction in the way that it addresses the juxtaposition of ancient and modern in a refined, forward-looking design. In much different circumstances, the Dublin Islamic centre designed by Michael Collins Associates also contends with the challenges presented by strong traditional influences, which were complicated by the desire to fit comfortably into the existing, largely Catholic, neighbourhood.

The achievements of these modern reinterpretations of grand design are that they enrich their contexts without overpowering; that as necessarily imposing forms, they offer ideas as large as their volumes to contemporary society.

1, 3 The massive portals of the outer glazed shell open to allow the church's capacity to grow from 400 to thousands.

4.01

CHURCH OF THE SACRED HEART

MUNICH, GERMANY

ALLMANN SATTLER WAPPNER

2000

A glass box might seem like the ultimate Modernist statement, bold, sharp and distinctive, something we've become used to seeing as a luxury private residence or hi-tech corporate headquarters. The glass box has yet to make its way into church architecture, although Philip Johnson's Crystal Cathedral in California emphasized the grandeur possible with the material as well as the beauty in a spiritual context. In Munich, architects Allmann Sattler Wappner have recognized those possibilities but they have also concentrated on the ability of glass to shield and enhance something else and to act as a beacon. If we think of the practice of keeping valuables behind glass, we can see some of the thinking that produced this particular glass box, something beyond the Modernist icon.

Creating, as the architects explain, 'two diaphanous, concentric shells with contrasting material properties', highlights the sanctity of the interior by illuminating and revealing it. This method contradicts the practice of medieval builders, who hid the interior behind masses of stone with only small inlets of light. The stone massings served a purpose other than concealment, of course, but there is a precedent in churches, as in mosques, to maintain the privacy of the interior space by controlling the light and creating a protected inner sanctum. Here, the architects have thrown open the church interior through transparent structures set one inside the other: a louvred maple box within a glazed structure made from regular rectangular panes held in place by a gridded steel framework. The panes diminish in size down to a grid of squares at the south-east façade which is almost entirely taken up by a set of giant doors. These doors operate on a pivot mechanism and can be adjusted to different positions depending on the weather and on the type of celebration being conducted. When they are swung fully open they create an outstretched invitation to the exterior courtyard that confirms the sense of transparency of the great glass box, so that, as the architects put it, 'the vestibule and the churchyard are joined to form a continuum of space'. A pair of smaller doors set into the monumental glass portals allows for everyday use or private services.

Inside the glass shell, the maple interior structure is a piece in itself worthy of attention. The delicate but soaring feeling achieved using levels of thin maple slats is akin to the effect of Gothic vaulting, drawing the eye upwards. The space between the louvres increases horizontally as you approach the altar, expanding the amount of light filtering into the structure. Therefore, the culmination of natural light is at the presbytery and altar, much in the same way that a cathedral's dome or rose window would focus light in the same area. Behind the altar, the large Cross is made from a material, 'tombak', that is a mixture of copper and brass, which has been overlaid in a contrasting direction to achieve the appearance of the Cross. The religious iconography is subtle throughout. The glass panes on the portals have cruciform motifs, which, the architects explain 'are intended more to be perceived at second sight than as illustrations to focus the attention'. The furnishings are subdued as in most church buildings but

2 The thermally efficient glazed structure consists of an outer pane made from two layers of 8 mm (¼ inch) single-pane safety glass laminated together with PVB foil in between. Neutral heat-protective coating was applied between the panes, and the interpane space was filled with argon gas. The inner panes are 10 mm (¼ inch) thick safety glass with a low iron-oxide content.

4–5 The north elevation (left) shows the concentric structures, with the bell tower at right. The long section of the east façade (right) shows the rectangular form of the building.

6 The delicate transparency of the glazed outer shell belies its loadbearing capabilities and contrasts with the hardy wood interior, which is protected by the glass structure.

7 Slats of maple emphasize verticality.

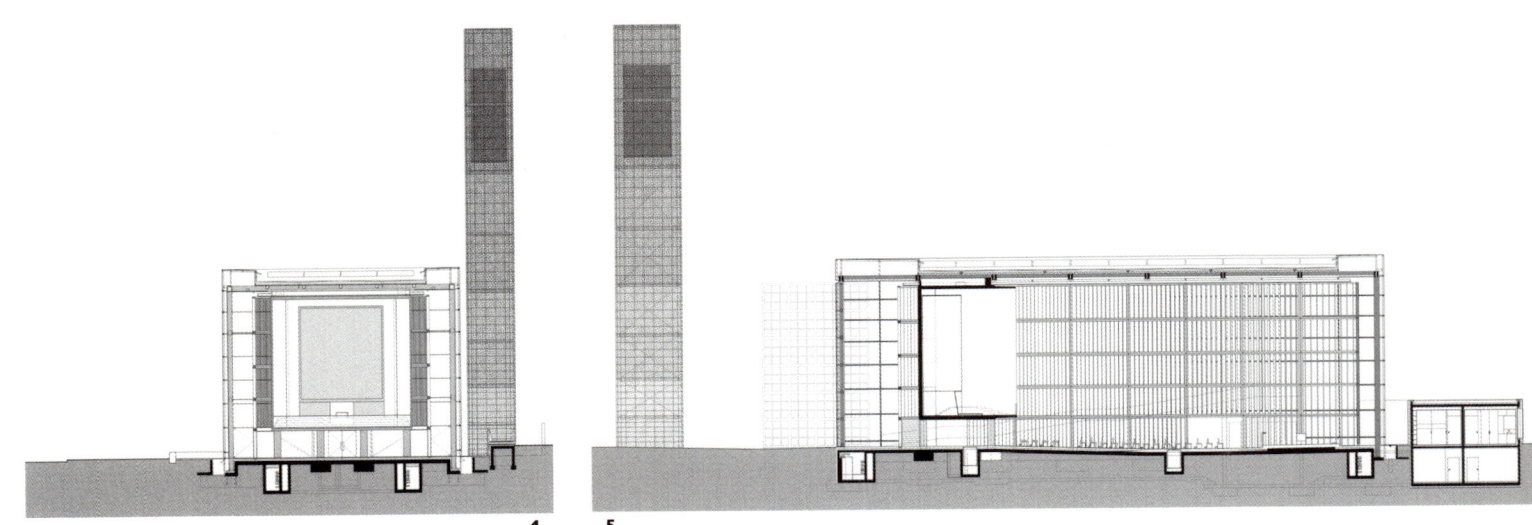

8 The rows of oak pews along with the angled slats focus attention on the altar.

9 The plan shows the plaza at the south entrance, and open space both between the two shells and within the maple core.

the architects' aesthetic can be seen in the modern oak benches with neatly folding backrests.

This is not the glass box that got religion, rather it is a highly refined system of transparency and concealment that produces what the architects call a 'crystalline materiality', with its specially conceived system of glass panels that are slightly opaque and that function at a high level of thermal efficiency. A system in which vertical glass strips take the weight of horizontal glass strips helps provide wind resistance and allowed the use of very slender steel supports, which increased the overall transparency. The end result leaves room for both reason and faith.

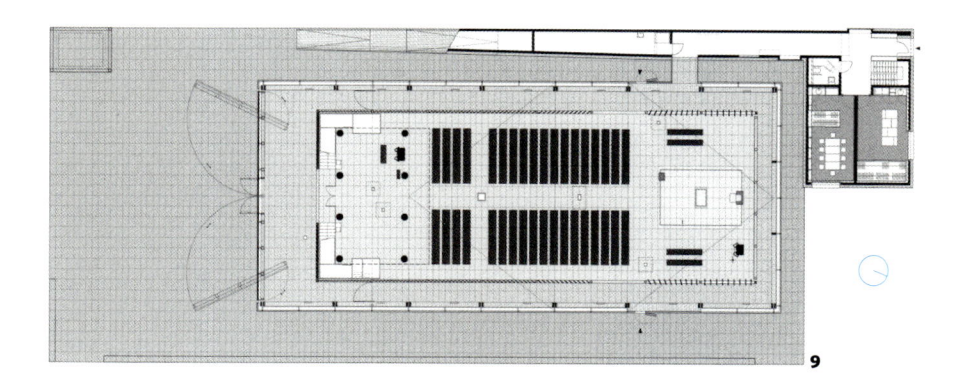

1 The mosque at night with the palm courtyard mimicking the lines of the colonnaded arches.

2 The mud stucco exterior recalls an ancient building tradition while the rectilinear forms create a more modern profile.

3 Site plan
1. mosque, 2. sarha, 3. housing, 4. library, 5. arrival plaza, 6. entrance plaza, 7. festival plaza, 8. old city wall, 9. valley gate

4 The entrance shows the architect's use of strict geometry in form and decoration.

4.02

IMAM MOHAMED IBN SAUD MOSQUE

RIYADH, SAUDI ARABIA

ABDELHALIM I ABDELHALIM

1998

The Imam Mohamed Ibn Saud Mosque is a grand oasis in the desert, meant to combine what the architect describes as the two main activities of Saudi life: 'prayer and el barr, which is the local term for picnicking and recreation in the desert.' This was one of a number of urban projects sponsored by the Saudi government to commemorate the one-hundredth birthday of their kingdom. Dr Abdelhalim I Abdelhalim's plan for a mosque-library-residential complex, known as a masjid al-jami, with space for 2,500–3,000 worshippers incorporated a large public square oriented around the old settlement of Addiriyyah, which is on the outskirts of Riyadh. Wishing to respect the history of the ancient city, Dr Abdelhalim devised a solution that incorporates the 400-year-old city wall into the scheme but places the mass of the complex outside the perimeter, where the majority of the population now live in modern buildings. The completed plan also acts as a transition between the man-made environment and the naturally verdant valley of Addiriyyah. Referred to in Arabic as the Wadi Hanifah, the valley is a drainage course for surface water and is extremely verdant in places, making it a popular recreation spot.

Set on a bare plateau that overlooks both the old city of Addiriyyah and the lush vegetation of the wadi, the new complex refers immediately to the old city with its sandstone and mud stucco exterior. However, its finely tuned rectilinear shape and neatly ordered profile harmonize with the modern residential and institutional buildings in the newer part of the city. Generous, but equally ordered, plantings of palm trees allow the new scheme to blend in with the greenery of the Wadi Hanifah, which is such an important focus for all of the area's inhabitants. A linear 'palm grove' on the north side of the site works as a buffer between the road and the entrance areas. Past the arrival plaza, a formal paved sarha – or open courtyard space – directly outside the mosque is planted with palms set on the same modular plan as the interior columns of the main prayer hall, thus creating a transition toward the ceremony of prayer. 'The space of the sarha was treated as an extension to the mosque,' the architect explains. Prayer and other activities take place in the outdoor spaces on festival days, and arcade walkways, along with the numerous planted palms, provide ample shaded spaces for prayer and rest.

Within the formalized walkways, the mosque sits as per tradition, at the centre of the complex. The dome structure, which signals the location of the mihrab, is quite a low-key version in comparison with the domes of the great mosques, and is set within a rectangular structure that protrudes

2

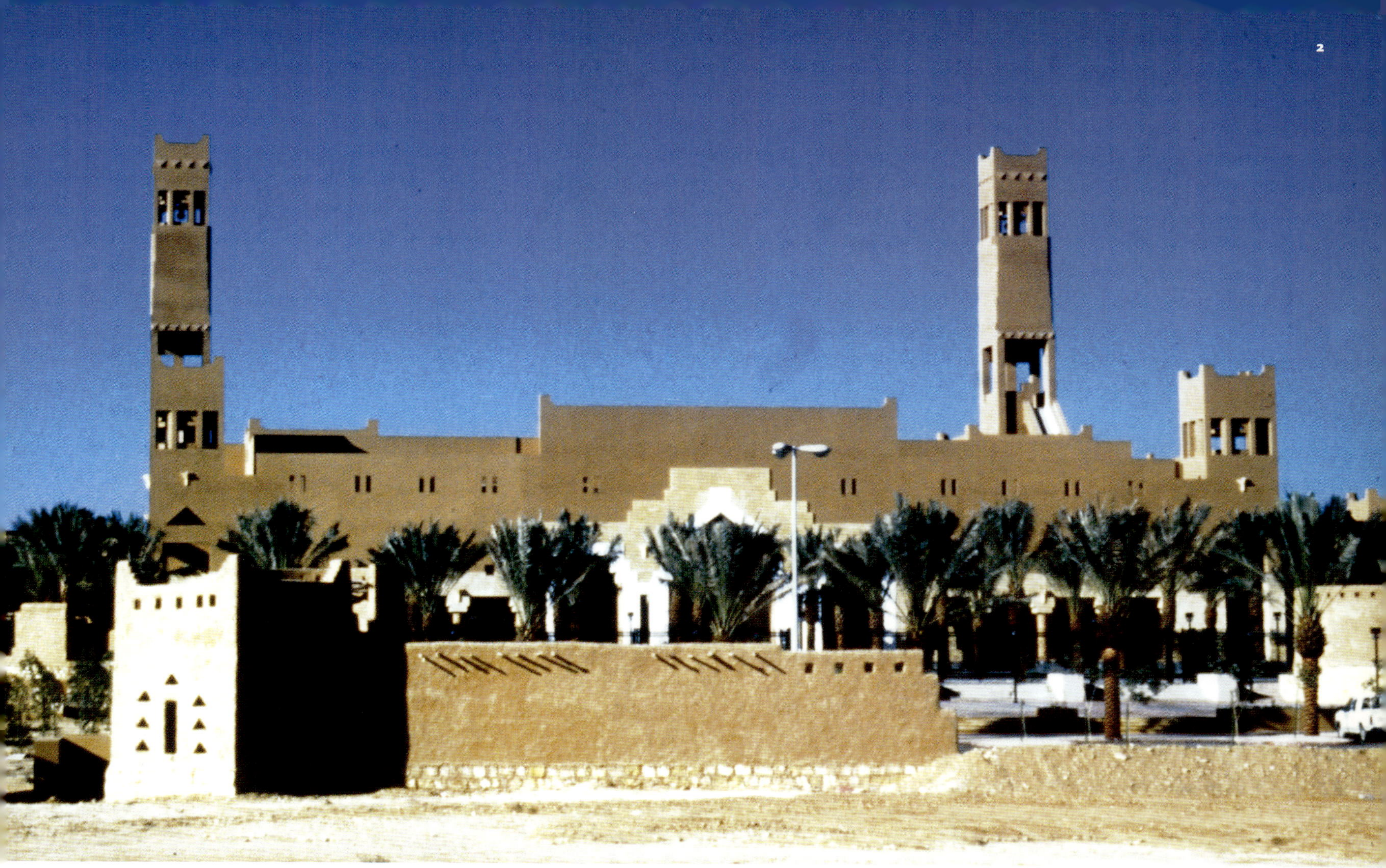

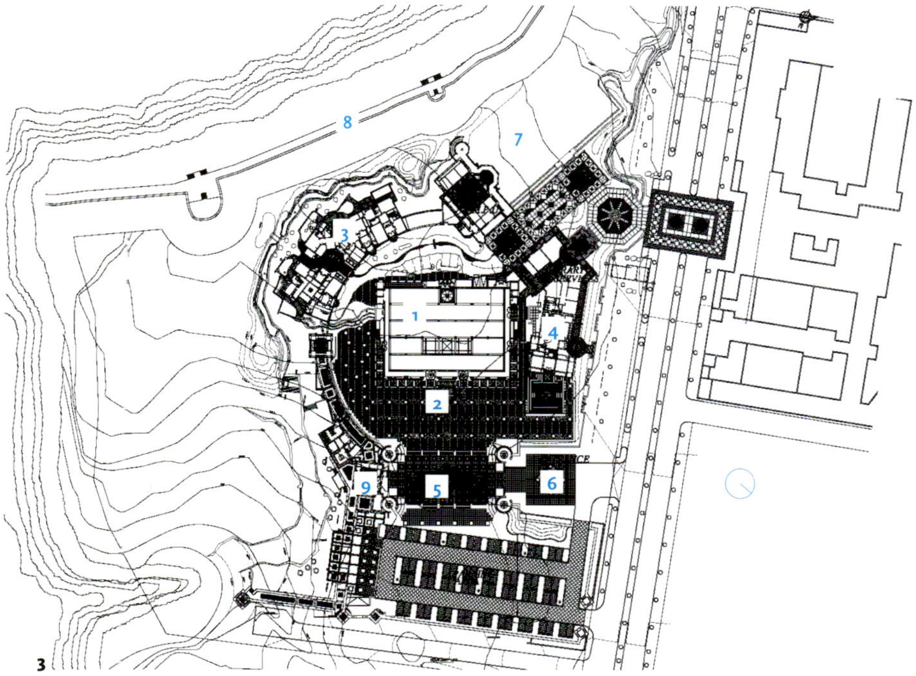

3

4

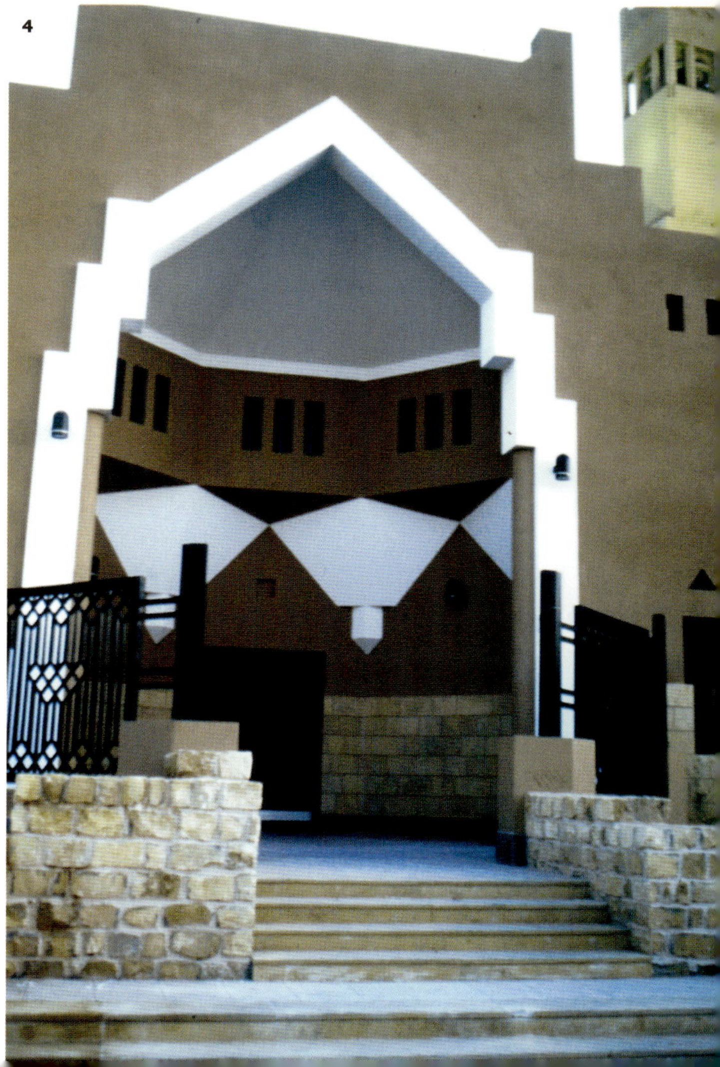

slightly from the lower bulk of the other buildings. Centred between two soaring minarets, however, the dome forms the unmistakable iconic combination. Inside, as the modular plan of the sarha continues, the highly developed system of skylights draws a surprising amount of natural light into the solid mass of the building, dissolving some of that solidity and, as the architect says, 'strengthening the relationship with the sky'. The mosque interior, while being supported in the traditional way by arcaded rows, reflects the overall bias of the architect for angular clarity. While he allows for rounded columns, the capitals are stepped and branch out in Y-shapes to form a series of linked chevrons. These patterns are repeated elsewhere in the galleried spaces and the dome of the mihrab, which has openings that filter light in a perfect pattern of triangles.

Abdelhalim says of the interior that 'all the forces affecting the design were combined and resolved to form the geometrical order of the building'. And the high degree of order is perhaps the most immediate aspect of the design. But there is more method than just aesthetic control, though in a project of this scale that kind of control is invaluable. Linking the changeable landscape of the desert with the backdrop of a historic city and the increasingly mundane appearance of urban design is no trick of simple geometry. It is an achievement that requires strength and sympathy, qualities the Imam Mohamed Ibn Saud Mosque embraces from the ground up.

5 The mihrab of the mosque is distinguished by a stepped skylight that creates a triangular light pattern beneath the arch.

6 Elsewhere, the white interior is sculpted with sharp angles and raised geometric elements.

7 The front, north-east elevation shows the highly regulated pattern of lines and angles and overall symmetry.

8 The main prayer space coheres to the crisp geometric order of the building.

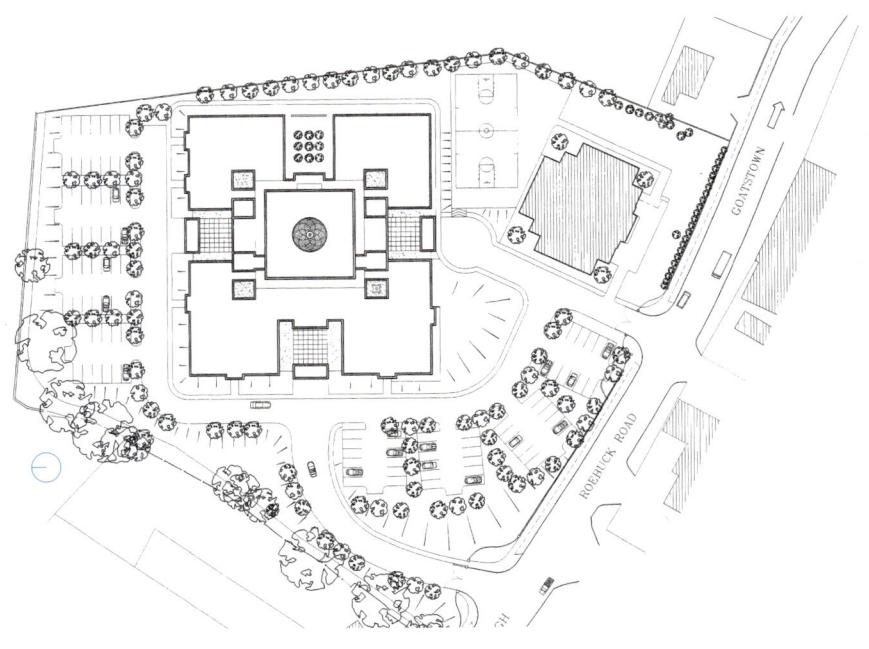

1 The site plan shows the complex with the mosque in the centre, parking in the northern and south-west corners, the existing school building in the south-east corner and the main road at right. The site has been planted on all sides.

2 The main, west, façade with the male entrance at left.

4.03

ISLAMIC CULTURAL CENTRE

DUBLIN, IRELAND

MICHAEL COLLINS ASSOCIATES

1996

3 The female entrance on the southern façade.

4 Plan: a family entrance allows families to enter the structure together and then circulate to separate mosque entrances inside.
1. main entrance, 2. administration, 3. female entrance, 4. classrooms, 5. courtyard, 6. mosque, 7. residential, 8. family entrance, 9. multi-purpose hall, 10. minaret

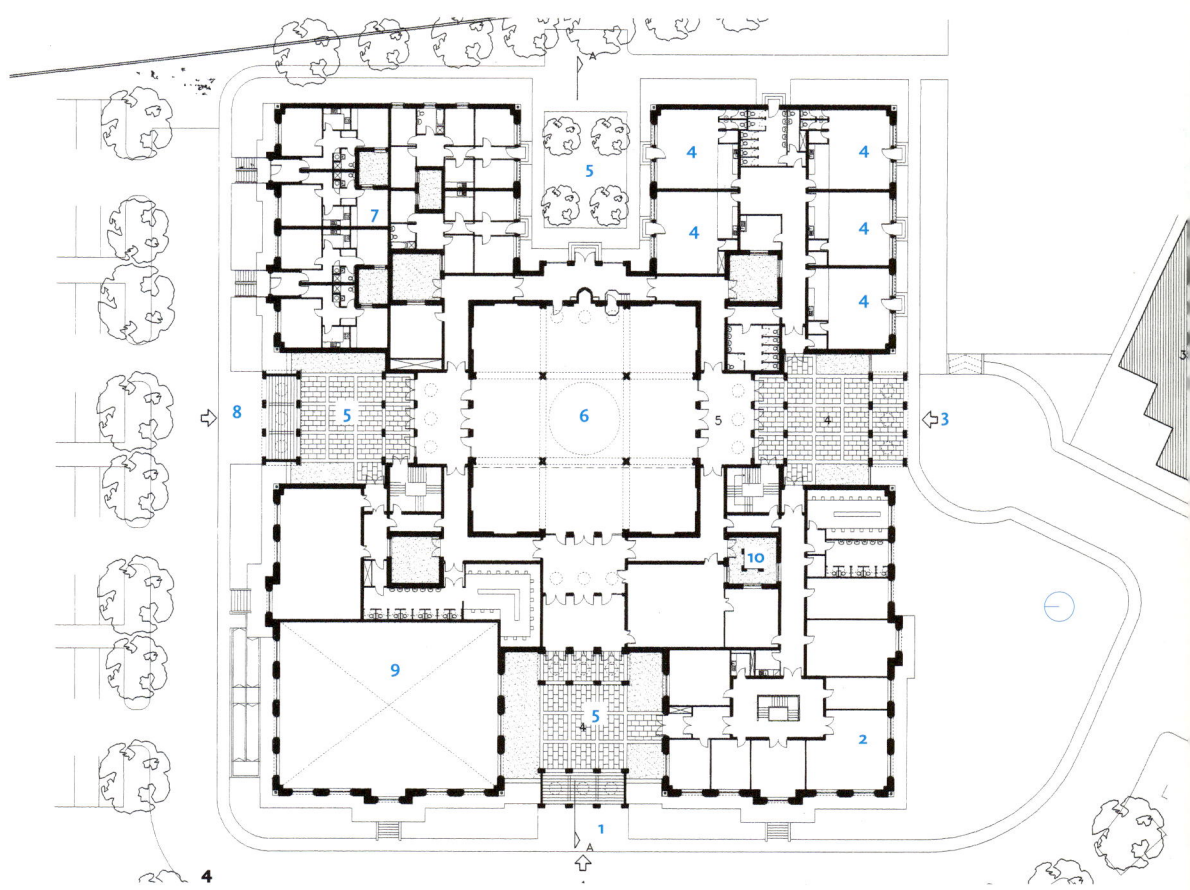

5 The delicate, stylized mushrabiyah allow much more natural light than their traditional counterparts while maintaining the delicate geometric pattern in laser-cut stainless steel.

Ireland does not seem like the most likely place for a major Islamic facility but it is, in fact, home to around 20,000 Muslims according to the Islamic Foundation of Ireland. A large majority of these people live in or near Dublin, a fact that helped to convince the Maktoum family of Dubai to sponsor a new facility in the city. This was to be a congregational mosque, or masjid-i jami, and so would include various community services and would require space for a range of activities. The project brief included the central mosque as well as daily prayer halls, a five-room school, sports hall, shop, restaurant, library, meeting rooms, apartments and administrative offices. The architects were chosen by a member of the family with whom they had worked on previous projects, and who expressed the wish that the traditional aspects of Islamic architecture would be successfully reconciled with Western interpretations. The actual design requirements were few: the architects were asked to include a dome, minaret and natural stone entrance.

Architecture is all about interpretative gestures and Michael Collins, along with project architect Brian Murphy, rose to the specific demands while also inventing a building that would sit well in its residential setting. 'The clients were and are very concerned that the cultural centre be seen as a part of the existing community,' Murphy explains. 'They were very conscious of fitting into that community.'

The building first strikes the viewer with its low profile, which does in fact help it to blend, distinctive as it is, into the landscape. The protruding dome and minaret rise out of the rectilinear façade with some delicacy; there is no looming form nor are there great shadows cast. Because of a slope that gently rises as you move toward the building, it is not immediately perceptible that the mosque structure itself also rises above the surrounding buildings. The plan, though it encompasses a range of facilities, is simple: based on 'a square divided into nine smaller squares with the

6 The granite portal combines simple rectangular openings with a series of small domes that create contrast in shape and colour.

7–8 The west and south elevations show subtle signs of asymmetry within the tightly controlled geometry.

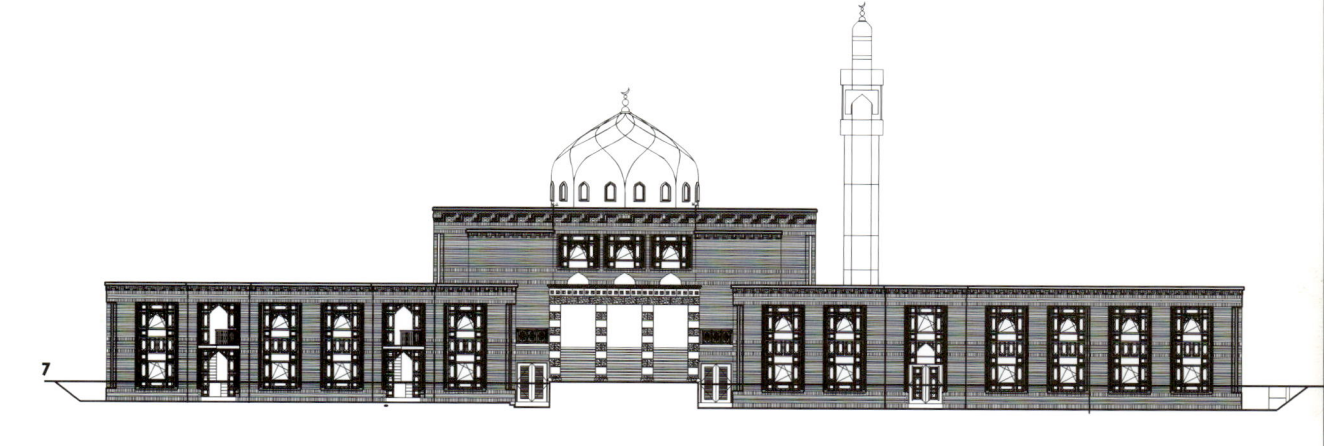

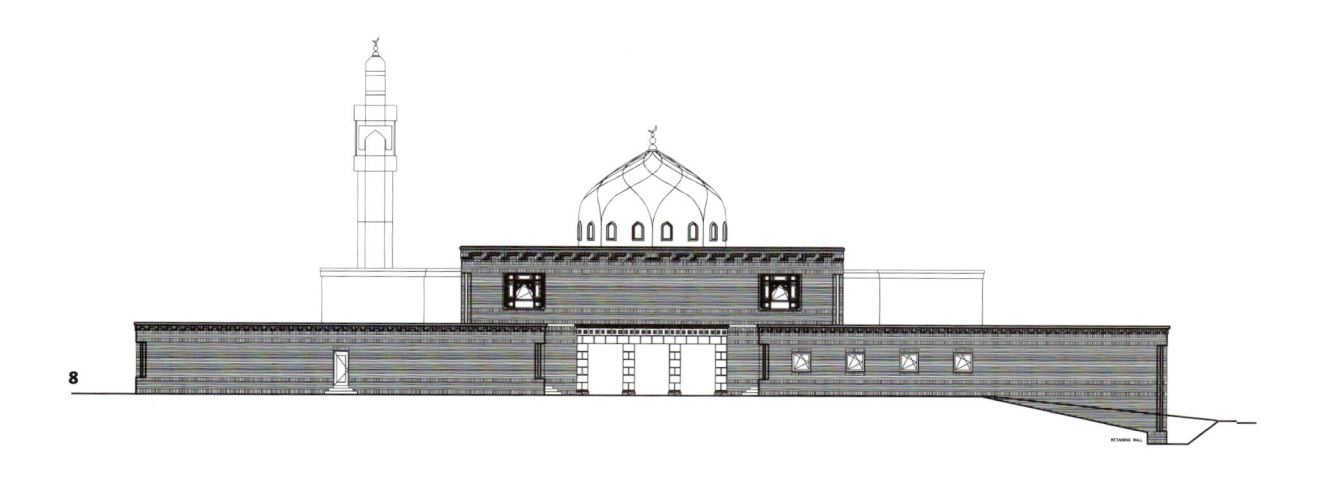

9 The single minaret is a microcosm of the design's materials and patterning.

mosque placed in the centre'. This model was used throughout, even in the design of the window screens, the breakup of the windows and the arrangement of rooflights. In addition, all of the rooms, as well as the mosque, are facing directly toward Mecca, an orientation that was achieved through numerous calculations and expert consultation.

Other elements that helped the building settle into its Western context were materials like the brick, chosen to reflect the local buildings but used in a soft buff colour rather than red, and the blue, engineered brick chosen to match the blue granite of the entrance portico. The granite complies with the request for natural stone but the blue-grey colour feels appropriate to the Irish climate. Instead of actual crenellation at the roofline, the blue brick is used in geometric motifs to suggest the modelled rooflines of Islamic buildings as well as the different building levels. Instead of the heavily worked wooden mushrabiyah used in hot climates to filter the strong sunlight and give privacy, the architects have created more delicate laser-cut stainless-steel screens that frame and highlight the fenestration but allow the much-desired sunlight in. Within such a highly regular pattern and use of materials the dome stands out, as it was indeed meant to do.

What might seem at first like a modern, Western restraint on Islamic tradition is actually a graceful tribute to Islamic style presented in a Western language that is itself adaptive. 'The centre has proved extremely popular,' says Brian Murphy, 'both with the Islamic community and with the students of the University.' The restaurant and shop are well-used by the community at large. It is a success story that is a triumph of the community spirit but also of design that tempers tradition with logic and presents a peaceful reverence for both.

10 The main worship space is a spare room of light geometric detailing. A single large dome with three smaller domes designating the mihrab are set within the grid of the coffered ceiling.

11–12 The sections show the block of the mosque building within the complex. Below, the mihrab is surrounded by near-perfect symmetry.

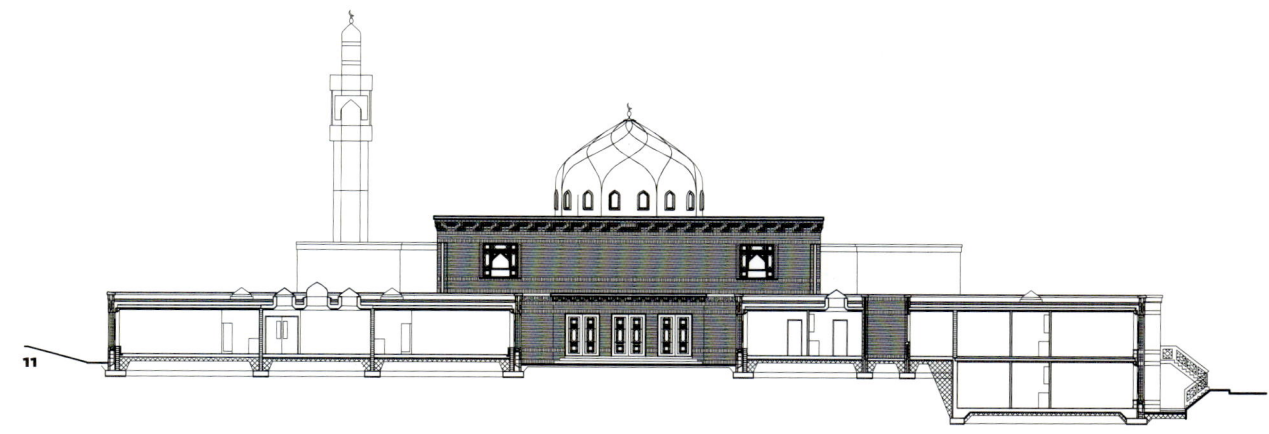

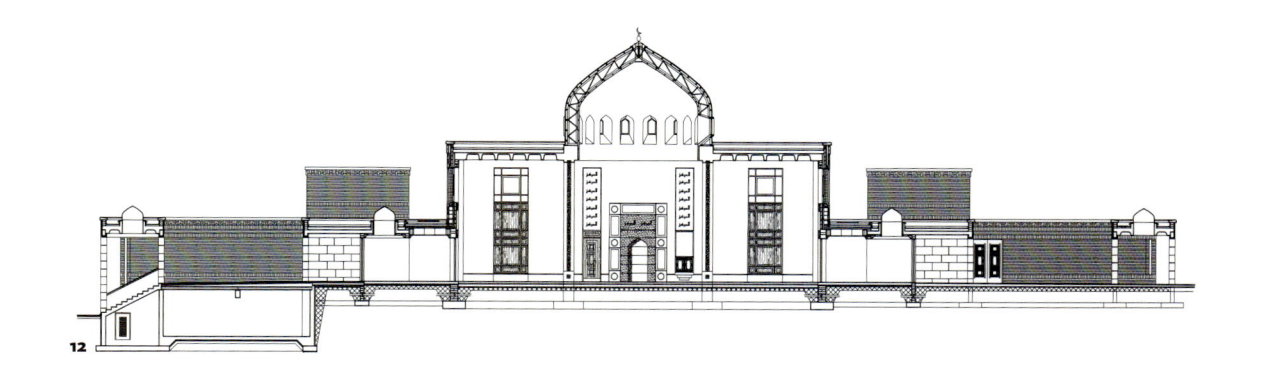

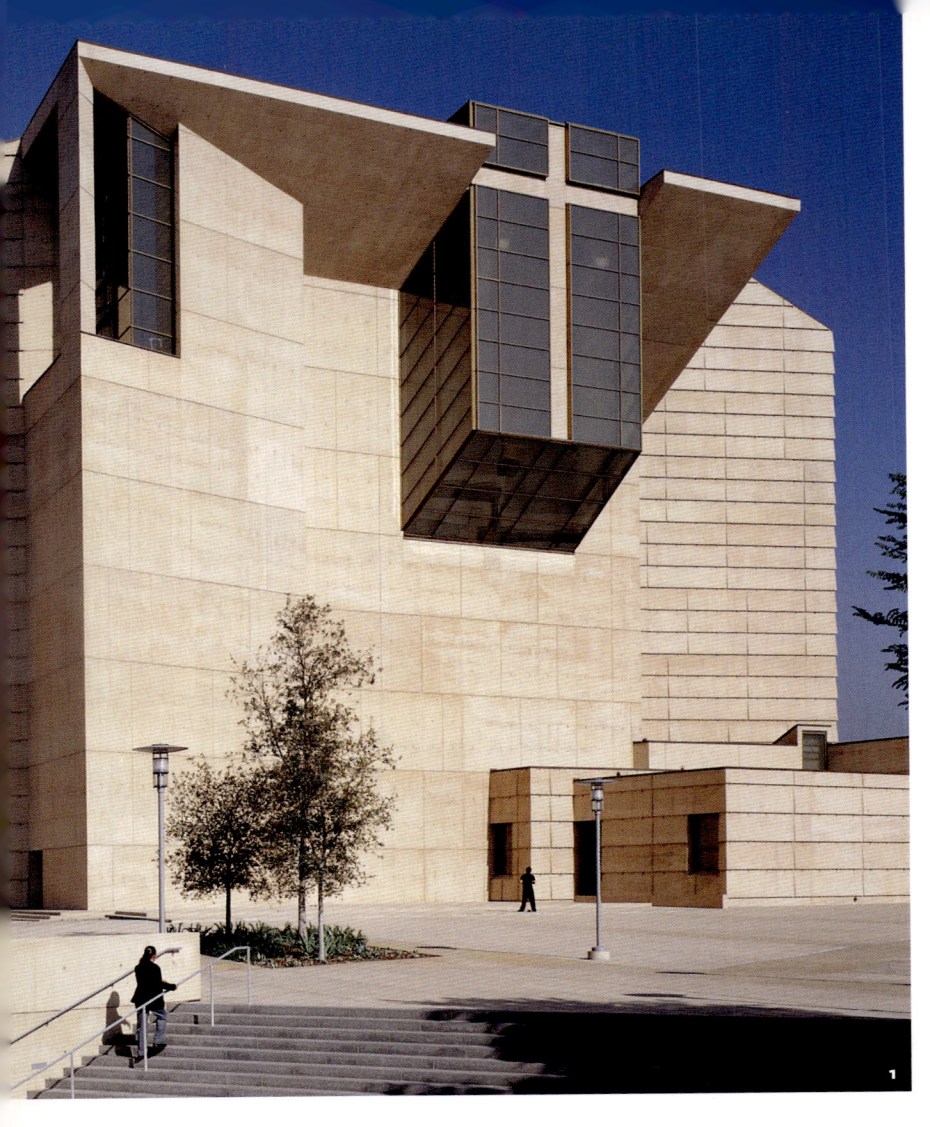

1 The mass of the building is broken down with projecting elements and by laying some of the concrete cladding in a shingle style. The concrete is an aggregate that was specially formulated to achieve the warm colour.

4.04

CATHEDRAL CHURCH OF OUR LADY OF THE ANGELS

LOS ANGELES, CALIFORNIA, USA

RAFAEL MONEO

2002

The building of the first cathedral in the United States in over 25 years happened rather fittingly in Los Angeles, one of 21 settlements founded by Franciscan missionaries who in the eighteenth century travelled from Spain to what became California. They claimed both the land and the indigenous people for the king and the god of Spain, and constructed missionary churches in each settlement. Los Angeles' later nineteenth-century cathedral, Saint Vibiana, was deemed irreparable after a series of earthquakes, so the precedent existed for a large Catholic centre though it had not been addressed for many years. With the legacy of the Franciscan fathers, it seemed also appropriate that a Spanish architect was chosen to create this new structure, which would be a landmark in many respects – bringing together the Catholic community's long-held desire for a spiritual centre and the regeneration of the downtown Los Angeles area, which has long lacked coherence.

Rafael Moneo's inspiration for the design of Our Lady of the Angels came from a range of sources far removed from the California missionary heritage, but the faceted, golden-hued concrete (with pozzolanic-dust additives) is not entirely out of touch with the squat, eighteenth-century mission buildings. He cites Erik Bryggman and Le Corbusier as well as Byzantine and Baroque ideas. The finished building shares qualities of light and form with Bryggman's funeral chapel in Turku, Finland, as well as Le Corbusier's minimalist, planar tendencies. The Byzantine influence also has to do with light and the way the architect used alabaster panels to produce a diffuse effect in a similar way to stained glass. He sees Baroque references in his 'architectonic' approach to the Cross which, rather than being a bare presence, is encased in a projecting box that is fully clad in alabaster and so brings light pouring into the nave, in what the architect describes as 'a mystical metaphor for God's presence'. It is indeed dra-

2 The site plan illustrates the dynamic shape of the structure bordered by the Hollywood Freeway to the north and major streets on all sides. The wide plaza area provides a much-needed place of quiet.

3 The cathedral occupies a corner in a busy intersection of downtown Los Angeles. The glass boxes protect and illuminate the alabaster panels on the interior.

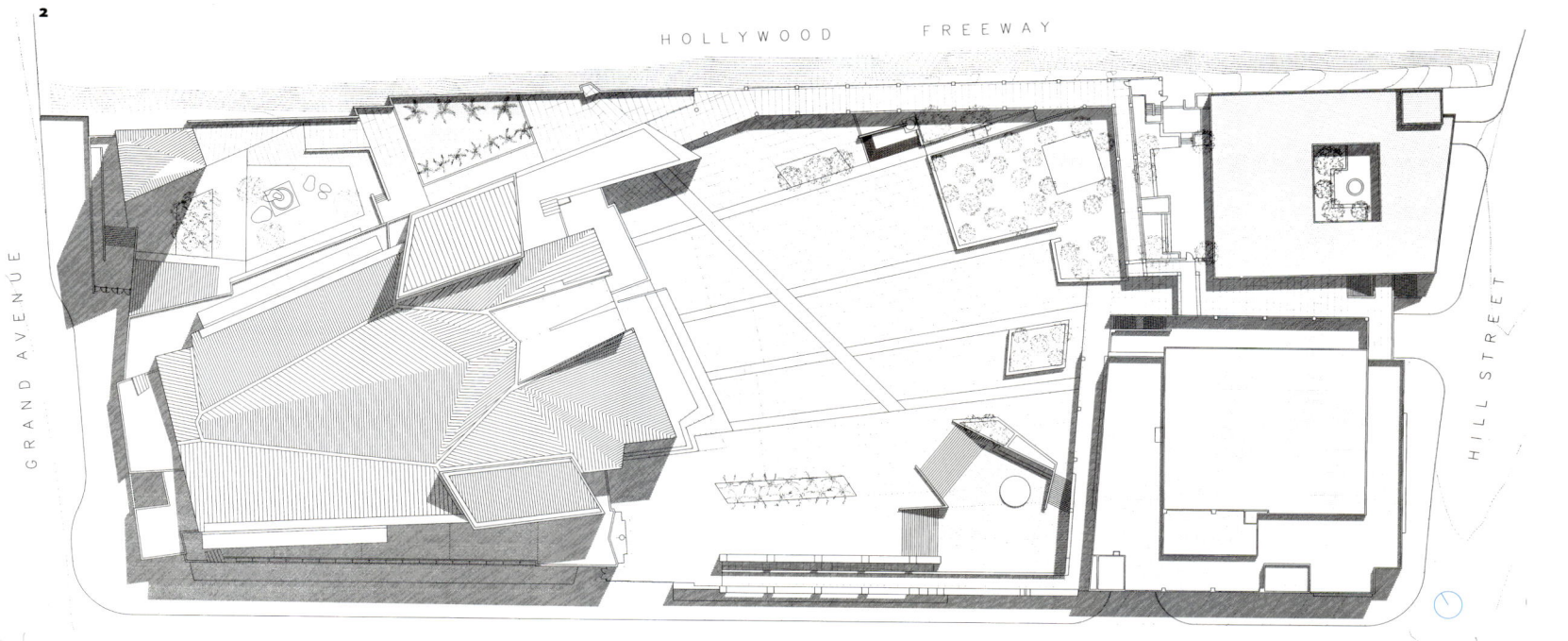

4 The portal that lines the street and gives entrance to the large plaza is reminiscent of the California Mission style and makes the complex accessible to pedestrians in an area dominated by road traffic.

5 The north elevation of the complex along the Hollywood Freeway.

5

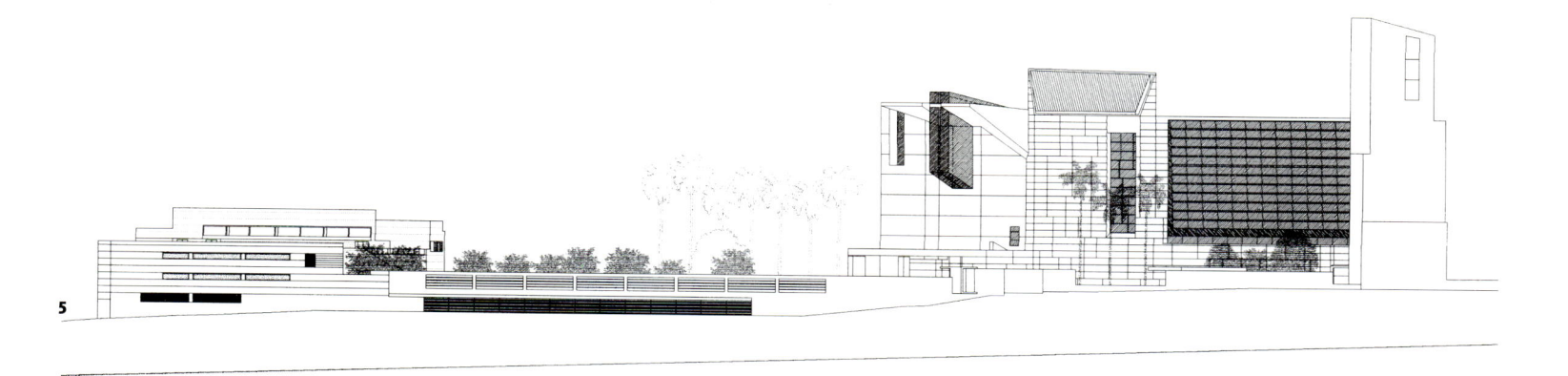

4

6–7 The sections show the seismic isolators underneath the building which will help to minimize movement in the event of an earthquake. The front section, bottom, shows the wing-like projections, the V of the roofline and the symmetrical shingling on either side.

8 The alabaster panels create a soft, glowing light in the side chapels. Approximately 2,500 square metres (27,000 square feet) of alabaster panels were used.

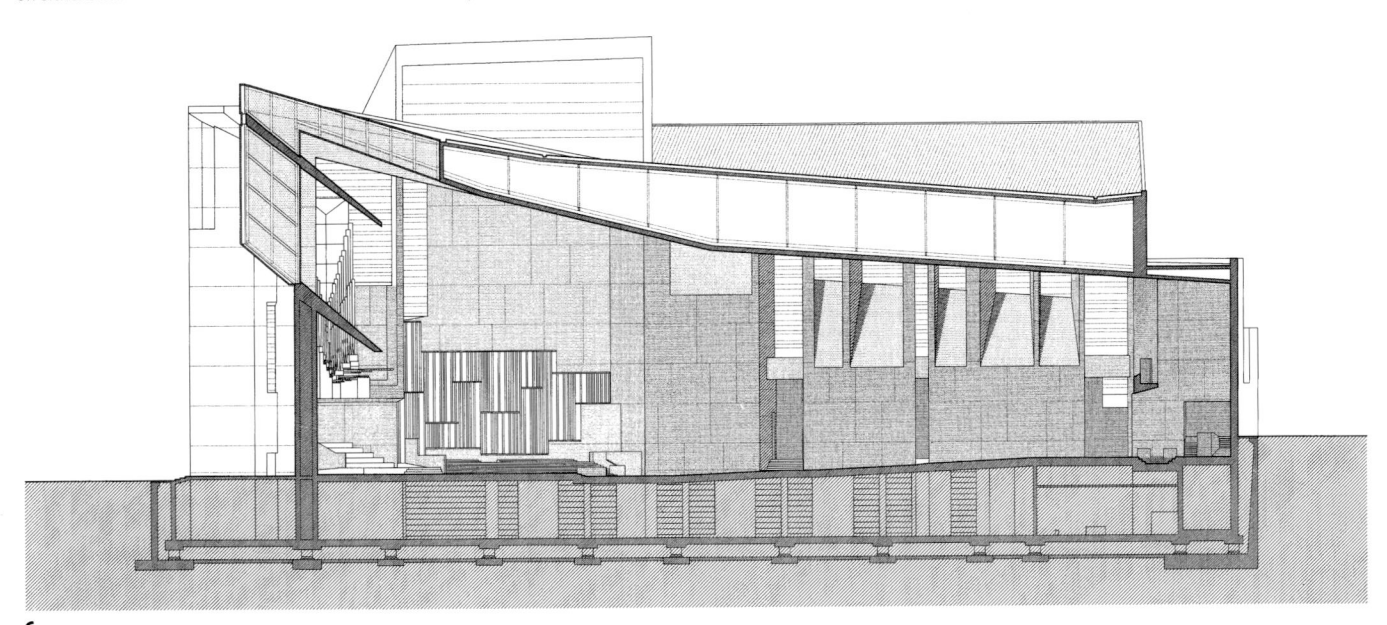

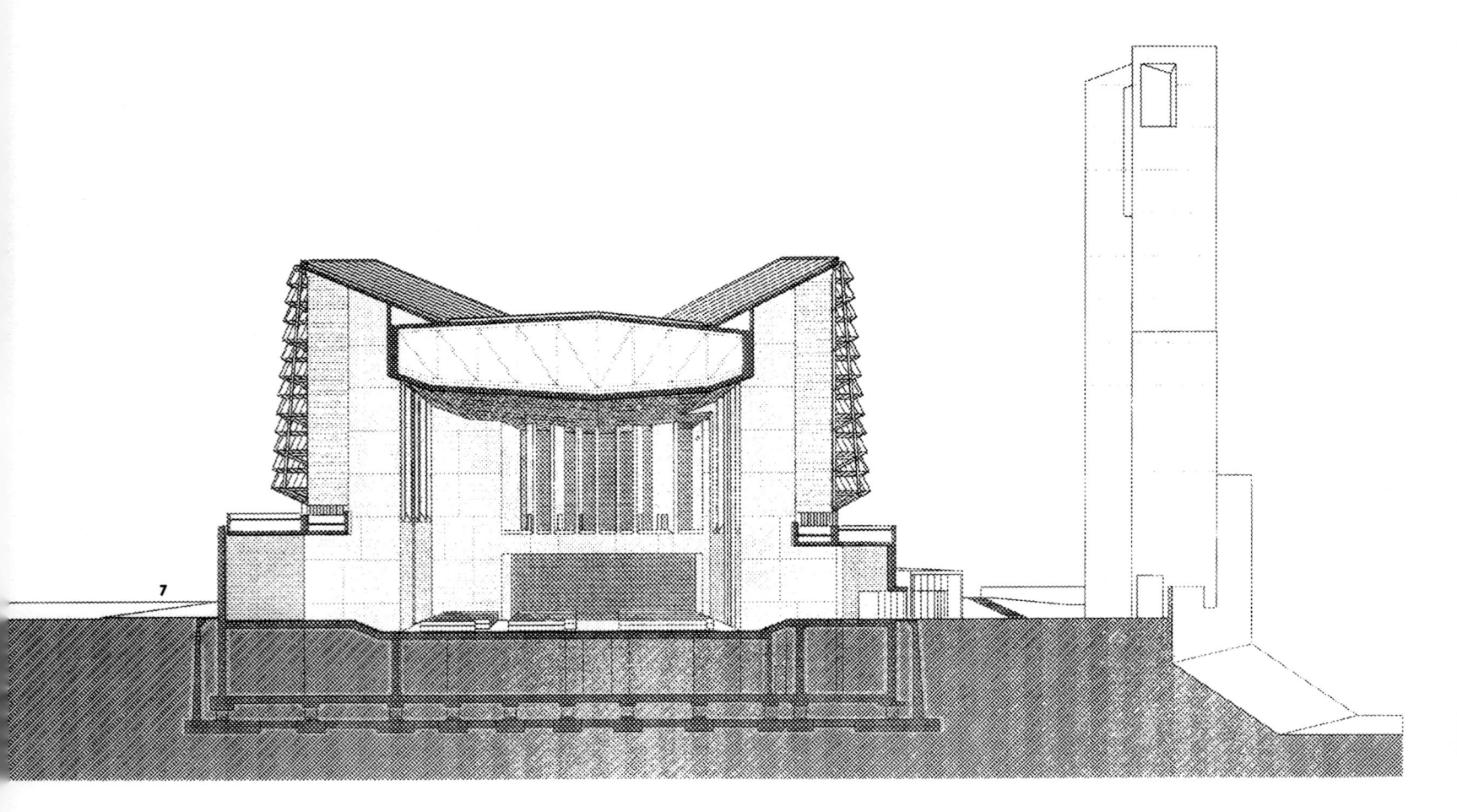

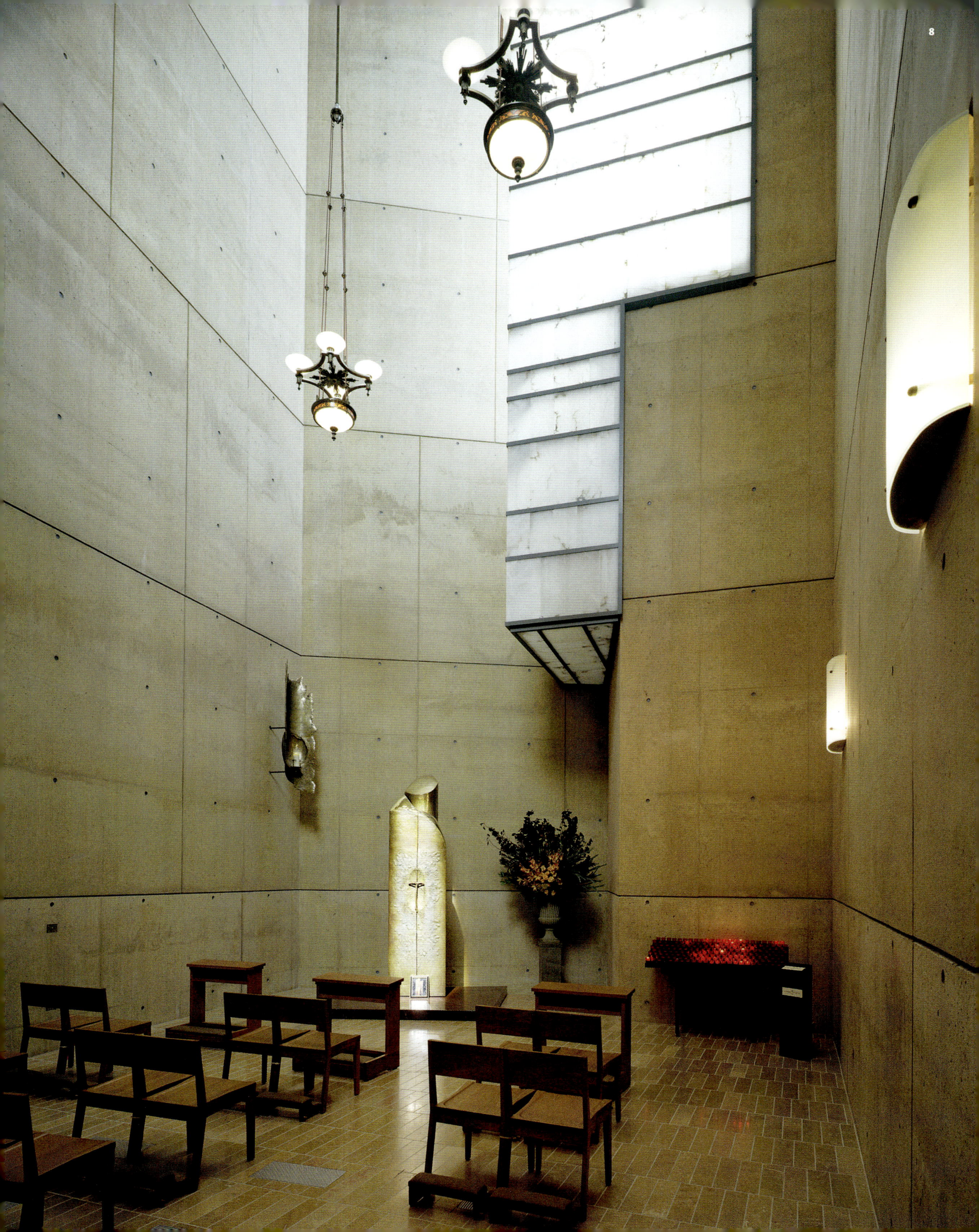

9 The plan shows the unconventional entrance to the side of the altar (bottom right) and into the ambulatory, which leads past the chapels to the bottom of the nave (left). The altar is at the widest point of the building.
1. entrance, 2. ambulatory, 3. nave, 4. altar, 5. sacristy, 6. chapels, 7. choir, 8. garden, 9. bell tower, 10. plaza entrance

10 The interior of the main space is a spare volume articulated by subtle patterns in the ceiling woodwork and the alabaster fenestration.

11 Light, softly filtered through the alabaster panels, enters the side chapels and illuminates the main space through an interior clerestory.

matic but the overriding sense of the space is more spare than ornamented, more quiet than riotous Baroque or even Byzantine qualities would imply.

There is an element of soaring Gothic in the way the concrete walls are broken into columns, with the horizontal segments of alabaster stretching up between them. The orthogonal planes are countered by diagonally laid cedar and fir ceiling panels that help maintain a sense of movement in the large, airy space. And it is large. The nave has the capacity for 2,000 and is over 100 metres (330 feet) long. The building rises 11 storeys from its elevated site between the downtown streets and the Hollywood Freeway. Moneo likens the freeway to a river and says that, as many European cathedrals are sited on rivers, this appropriately is sited on a 'river of transportation'. Those who have spent time on the freeway may find the reality quite a bit less poetic, so it might simply be a case of making a virtue of a less-than-beauteous site.

With the arrangement of the plaza and gardens, as well as the unorthodox entry (through the ambulatory that is separated from the nave), the architect explains that he was trying to separate public and worship space and 'something else, what it is that people seek when they go to church'. This is a more private sort of experience. The separated entry means that people can visit the chapels without disturbing the service in the main space or those at prayer. Surrounding the church too are several 'buffering, intermediating spaces': the wide plaza raised above the street level, the paved stairs and the planted palms. These help to join the cathedral to the community with public space but also to enshrine the church itself as a public space for private contemplation.

With the staggered, soaring ceiling heights, thousands of alabaster panels, glowing stone, and the presentation of the building across a wide courtyard with palm trees and a buffering window-wall along the freeway side, the building bespeaks grandiosity without actually claiming it. Perhaps this is to do with the spare interior and the exterior's Modernist assemblage of boxes that divert attention to separate spaces rather than focusing on a single image. For in Moneo's new cathedral, and not unlike much of the western US, the strongest sense is of the space in which to divine one's own belief.

1 The roof is made of staggered, overlapping panels of prepatinated copper.

4.05

CHURCH OF SAN GIOVANNI ROTONDO

FOGGIA, ITALY

RENZO PIANO BUILDING WORKSHOP

2004

It is a project that started with a negative: the architect's decision not to accept a commission from the Capuchin monks of San Giovanni Rotondo to create a new, much larger church to accommodate the ever-increasing number of pilgrims to the spot where Padre Pio once delivered his sermons. But the result is an exultant affirmative. Not only did Renzo Piano eventually agree to take on the project, he made it a testament to the fruitful combination of age-old building material and modern technology.

Padre Pio (born Francesco Forgione in 1887) was considered a saint even during his lifetime and drew crowds that packed out the little church at San Giovanni Rotondo, where he is said to have first 'received the stigmata' during Mass in 1918. It is also claimed that he had the power of prophecy and that his image 'appeared' to Allied bomber pilots during the Second World War imploring them not to attack his parish. Half a century on, it is throngs of his devotees, not enemy aircraft, that have rendered his church obsolete.

It was during the process of Pio's consideration for canonization that the Franciscans determined the need for a larger venue. Padre Gerardo, the Capuchin monk in charge of the province that includes San Giovanni Rotondo, approached the architect renowned for his groundbreaking public buildings (perhaps most notably the Centre Georges Pompidou in Paris). However, the architect declined, finding the project 'too intimidating', but the monk persevered, sending daily faxed prayers: 'In your patience possess ye your souls' (Luke 11:19).

The challenge of the project, states Piano, 'lies in the use of local stone as a structural material'. The final loud affirmative is made manifest in the 50 metre (160 foot) stone arch, possibly the longest supporting arch ever built in stone. This, Piano insists, was not a record-setting venture but rather a way to probe the possibilities of working with stone today, 'almost a thousand years after the Gothic cathedrals were built'. So the calculations were all achieved through the use of high-tech computer systems

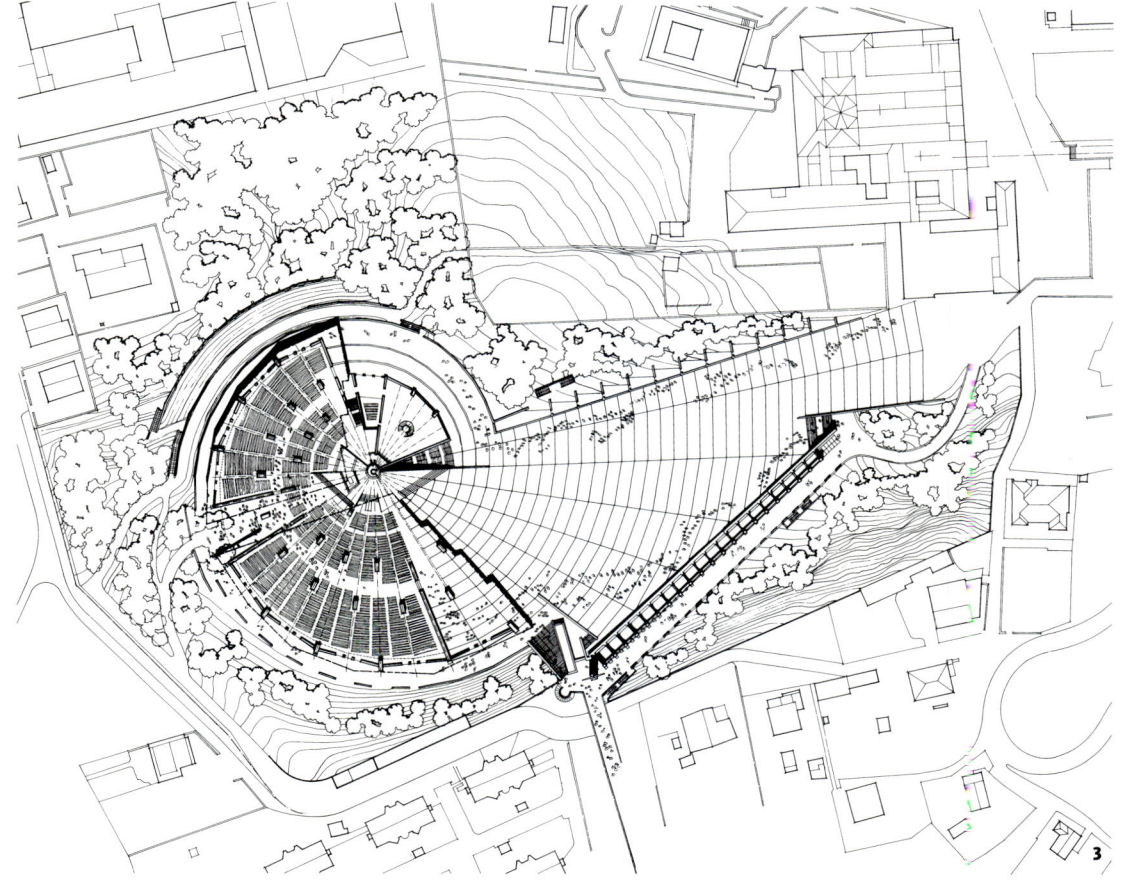

2 Stone arches, designed in collaboration with engineer Peter Rice, are constructed in segments, using computer programming to determine the precise size of, and to cut, each piece.

3 The radial plan settles the building within the slope of the hillside above the town; numerous new trees will be planted all around.

4 The monumental stone arches raise the building to a height of 16 metres (52½ feet) at the parvis.

5 The construction framework.

6 The elevation with the old church and monastery at right and the new structure sitting at a slightly lower level at left. The central column forms a core below ground level that continues up through the main space.

7 The dramatic span of the arches creates an interior that is both vast and accessible, with the elegant form of the structure clearly visible.

172–173

put to work in aid of 'the oldest construction material of all' to create a structure of ribbed vaulting that is startling in both its smooth modernity and its obvious relationship to Gothic building type – in which the delicate-seeming ribs appear to burst upwards, throwing the stone up and out, defying its fantastic weight with the illusion of lightness.

It is a marriage of humility and grandeur as well as of past and cutting-edge present. Despite having a capacity for 6,000 inside and room for another 30,000 in the paved open courtyard, the building is meant to sit quietly and comfortably, and only really present itself once visitors have mounted the end of the new approach road. This will be partly due to a shielding wall, which is 25 metres (80 feet) high at one point and carries the 12 giant bells that will announce the hour of Mass. In contrast, the spiral-shaped dome is less obvious 'and surrounded by trees', says Piano, so it will not be visible 'until the visitor is close to the parvis'. The façade will be 'simply a glass front' he explains, instead of something monumental, that will not 'intimidate the faithful but invite them to approach'. So while the grandiloquent statement is there in all its glory, the feeling is not of a building reaching up and beyond its parishioners, but of one held down, pinned to its roots but signifying great heights.

That said, the effect inside is perhaps as awe-inspiring as any high-reaching Gothicism. The radial design of the dome is furthered in the plan of the interior and in the rather surprising curvature of the floor into a concave element that mirrors the shape of the dome. Where the dome peaks, above the parvis, roof openings allow direct sunlight to penetrate the otherwise semi-dark space and dramatically illuminate the altar, 'concentrating attention on the focal point of the religious ceremony,' the architect explains, showing no hesitation in using the full splendour of his architectural vision to enhance and affirm the power of the liturgy.

8
Below ground level, the vaulting for the floor support springs from the central column.

9
A skylight cut into the roof above the altar adds to the drama of the radiating interior.

1 The synagogue and community centre face each other across a plaza, the site of the former building which was destroyed.

2 Clad in the same stone, the community centre (right), with its smooth, regular surface, helps accentuate the unique shape of the synagogue building (left).

3 Small, low-level windows line the street façade and correspond to similar openings in the community centre.

4.06

NEW SYNAGOGUE

DRESDEN, GERMANY

WANDEL, HOEFER, LORCH + HIRSCH

2001

Of all the names of towns and cities that bring almost instant recognition of the terrible havoc of the Second World War, Dresden must be among those most evocative. In the violence of Kristallnacht, November 1938, its synagogue, the first built in the region of Saxony and completed by Gottfried Semper in 1840, was desecrated and destroyed. The Allied bombing of 1945 took care of the rest of the historic city, including other buildings by Semper: the opera house, the palace and the Frauenkirche. In the post-war rebuilding of Dresden these buildings were somehow salvaged and rebuilt, but the synagogue was only addressed in 1990, more than half a century after it was destroyed. Here, the architects say, the idea of continuity became 'questionable'.

Apart from the challenge inherent in creating a sacred space, and in addition to confronting the troubled past, the architects Wandel, Hoefer, Lorch and Hirsch had some looming historical milestones to contend with: the rebuilding of the first synagogue in Dresden, and in Saxony, would consti-

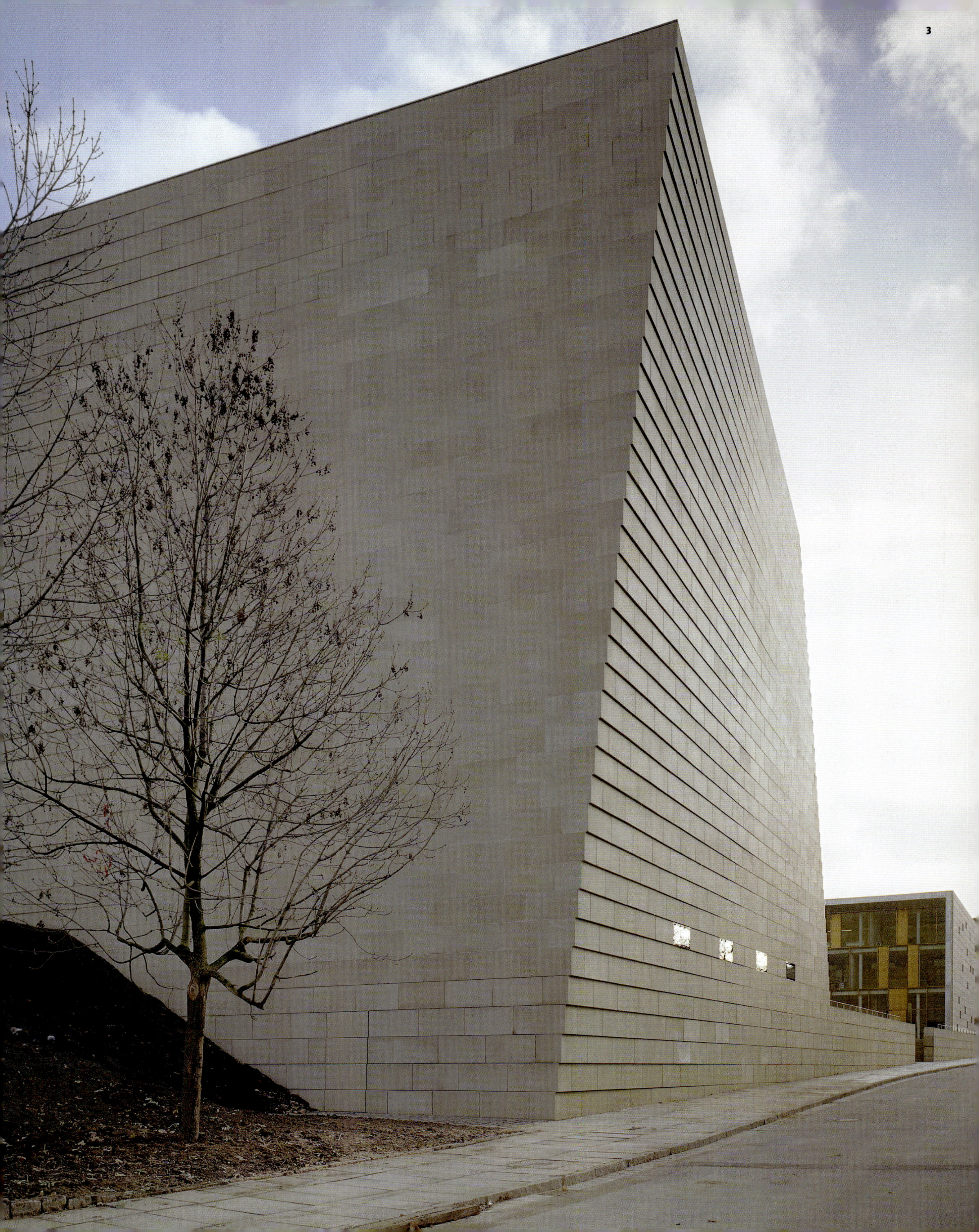

3

4 The section shows the outline of the prayer space within the larger volume.

5 The brass curtain creates a corridor between the stone structure and the prayer space.

6 A wood platform and backdrop emphasize the portable elements of worship.

7 The elevation shows the simple basic forms that complement each other at either end of the site.

8 The plan shows the synagogue (left), with planted trees in the central courtyard, and the outline of the former synagogue next to the community centre.

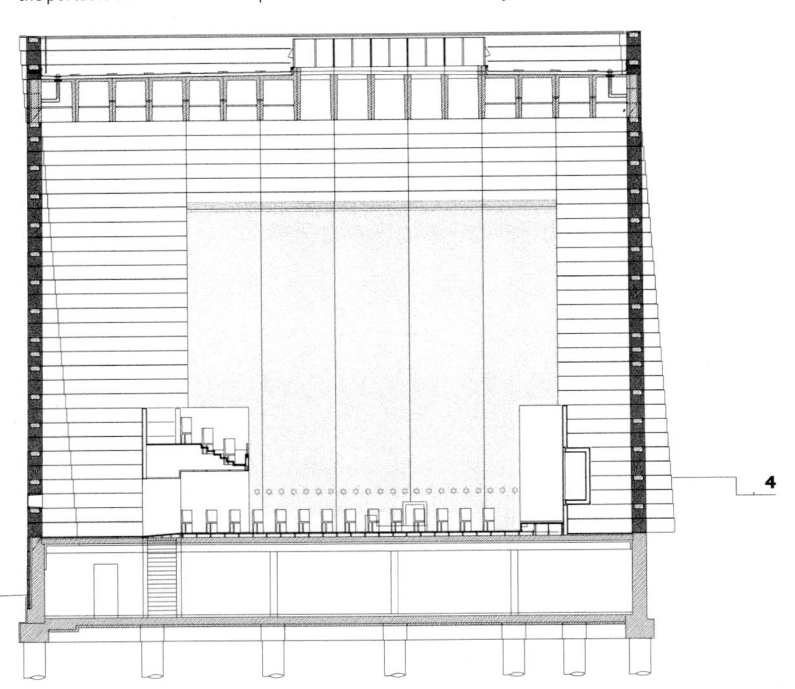

tute the first synagogue to be built in the former East Germany following reunification in 1990. It was to be a place of community, a centre for social and cultural life as well as religious tradition. And while it would be a building intended for use mainly by the Jewish community of Dresden, which by 1990 had dwindled to a mere 50 or so but has grown sharply since, it would also be a place where the non-Jewish inhabitants of the city would be invited for special events.

The answer to this imposing brief is a complex that is both forceful and delicate, modern and mindful of the past. Two stone block buildings, the synagogue and community centre, face each other across an open courtyard on a rectangular site perpendicular to the river Elbe. The space once occupied by the former synagogue has been left eerily empty in remembrance, a paved courtyard which is joined by a planted area of roughly the same size between the two buildings, softening the hard reality of the past with the hope of new growth. The synagogue's block structure twists slightly off its axis, both in its shape and in relation to the other building. This was done in order to reconcile the site with the desired eastern orientation but it also adds a startling dynamism to the stone. Through a 'gradual shifting of orthogonal layers', blocks of specially mixed concrete with sand aggregates, the architects produced a skewed shingle effect that means the building does not appear static. From some angles in fact it looks as if it is struggling upwards out of its earthly foundations, a spiritual striving in block form.

Inside the 41 concrete layers that make up this disaligned box, another shape is created to form an interior of surprising delicacy, intimacy and calm. The main space of worship is enshrouded in a diaphanous brass mesh curtain with a band of pattern formed by a repeated Star of David. This curtain is meant to be 'reminiscent of the tabernacle as a portable "House of God",' say the architects. 'Figurative representations have been excluded so that particular significance is attached to ornamentation' rather than icons. With knowledge of what had been destroyed, it is hard not to see this as an attempt at permanence, though, in the words of the architects, 'the new synagogue symbolizes the conflict between stability and fragility, between the permanent and the provisional, the temple and the tabernacle'. Whereas the temple is immovable, in the past the ark could be taken anywhere so that worship was not confined to a limited context.

Light flows down from the opening above the bimah and is diffused through the mesh curtain, creating a golden glow that transcends the solidity of the surrounding stone and the dictates of history.

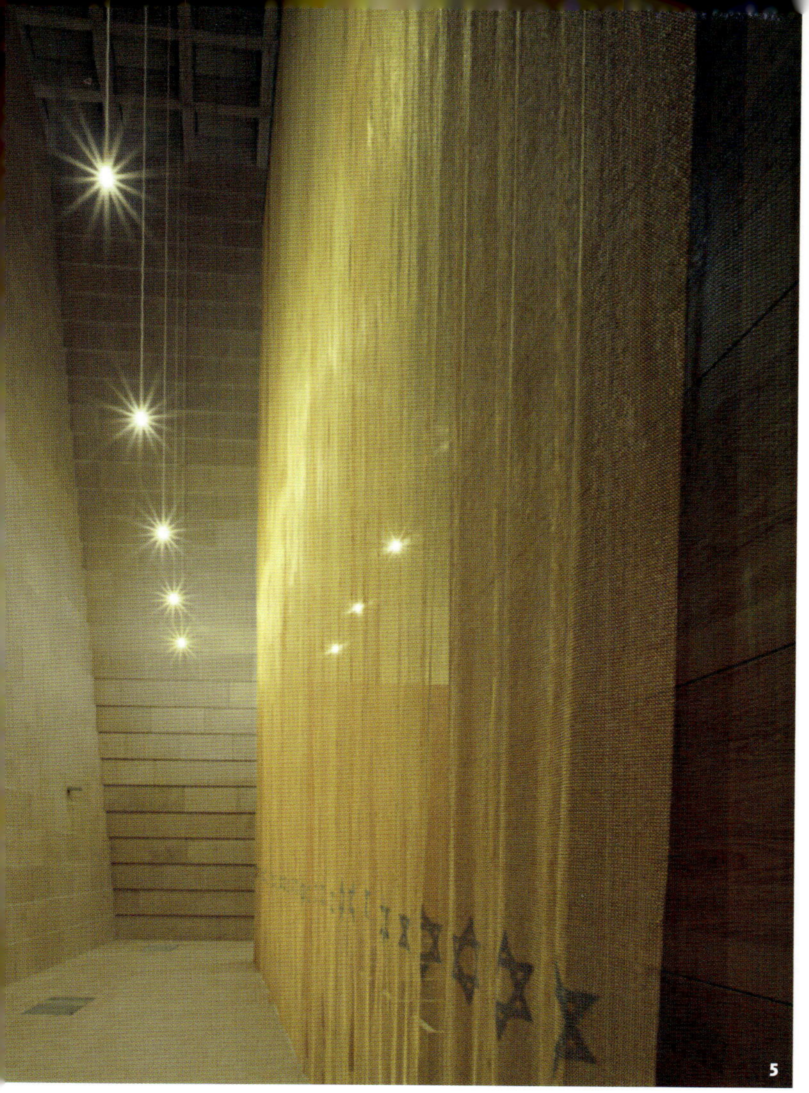
5

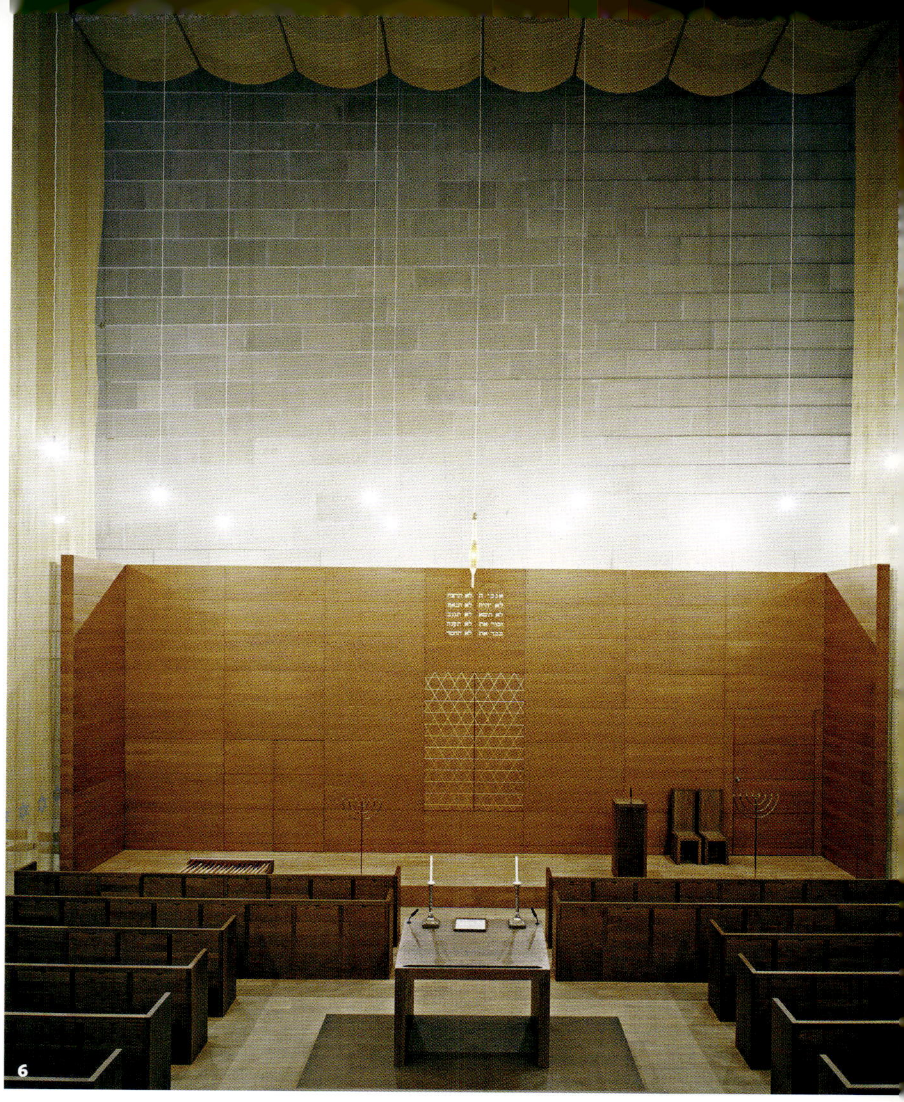
6

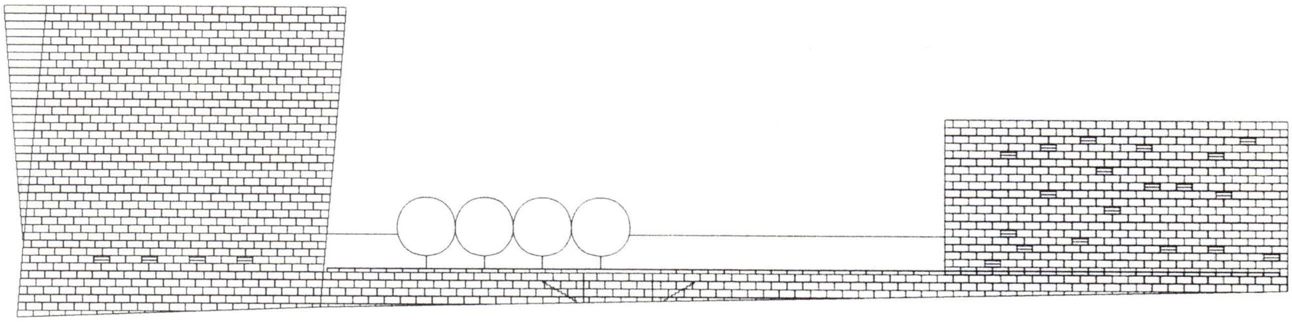
7

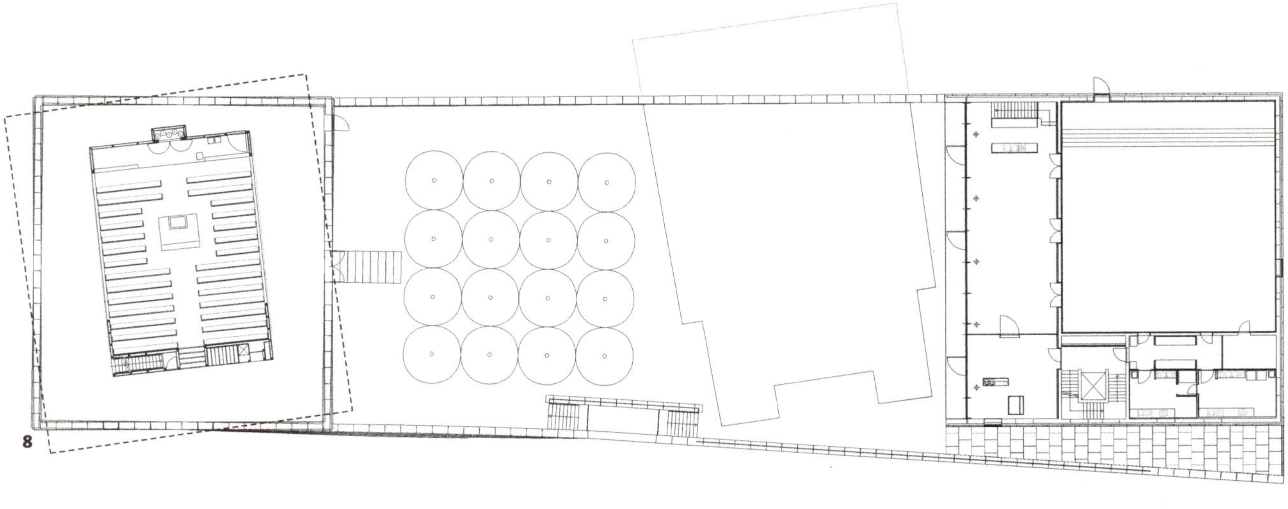
8

1 The enclosed chapel as a small, Modernist 'prism'.

2 Site plan
1. entrance, 2. pool, 3. office, 4. sacristy,
5. nave, 6. north-east ambo

4.07

LOS NOGALES SCHOOL CHAPEL

BOGOTÁ, COLOMBIA

DANIEL BONILLA ARQUITECTOS

2002

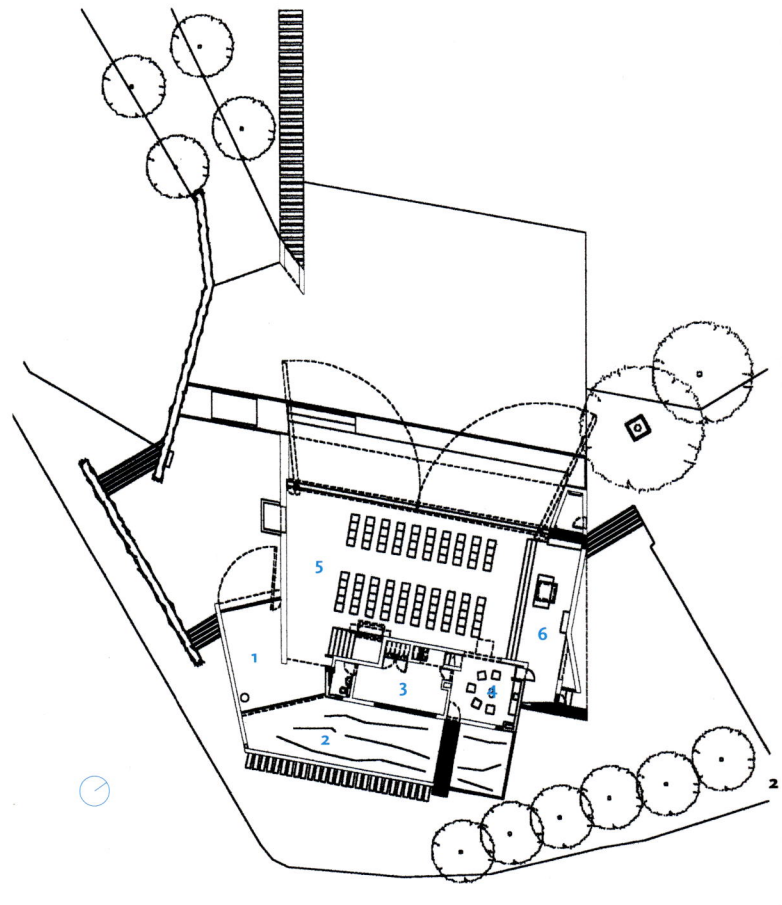

The architects conceived this chapel attached to a primary and secondary school in Bogotá on poetic terms. Based on 'life's dualities', the building, they say is 'a pure and elemental prism [that] represents purity, essence and harmony'. There is a purity in the white concrete and local hardwood, and in the opening up of the box so that the inner sanctuary becomes accessible to all. For what makes this building rather grand, in its own rather modest way, is its ability to accommodate from 100 to 1,000 people through the swing of its massive wood portals. Then the priest moves from the altar in the north-east ambo to the choir dais at the eastern side to face the crowd that congregates outdoors, only slightly below floor level. In this expanded state the nave stretches far beyond the shelter of the small white box and the church sits in open embrace.

The theme of a 'prism' altered by 'various volumes and cracks' is carried through in the use of solid planes in wood and concrete that have been pierced or inset with panels. Windows in the doors, walls and ceilings are small and patterned, leaving the surfaces nearly intact. Out of the flat roof

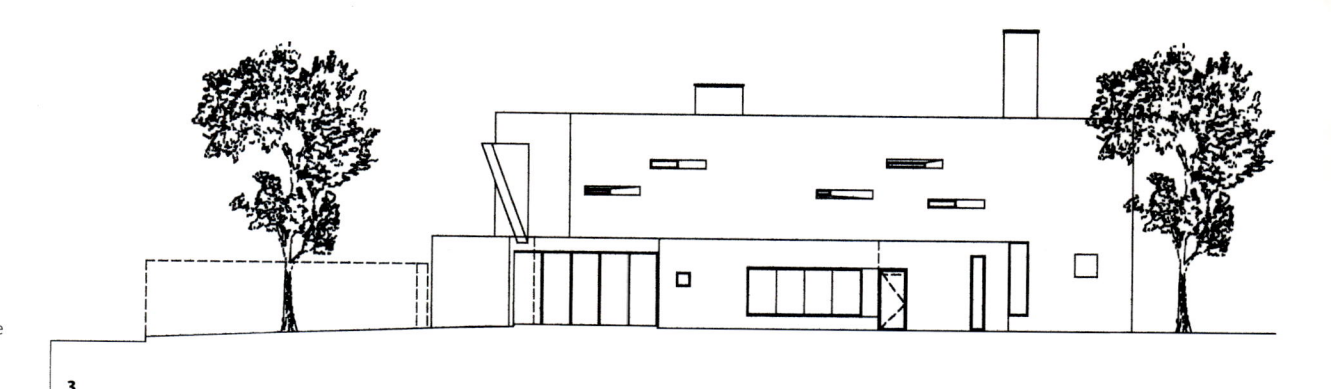

3 A discreet linear volume appears in the elevation (east façade).

4 With the pivoting doors swung open, the church becomes a congregation place for 1,000.

5 Looking toward the south-west façade, the chapel is a pure white form.

6 The bridge leads to the entrance of the priest's office and sacristy.

7 The pool and barrier wall create a peaceful enclosure.

8 Cross-section looking north-east

9 Long section looking east.

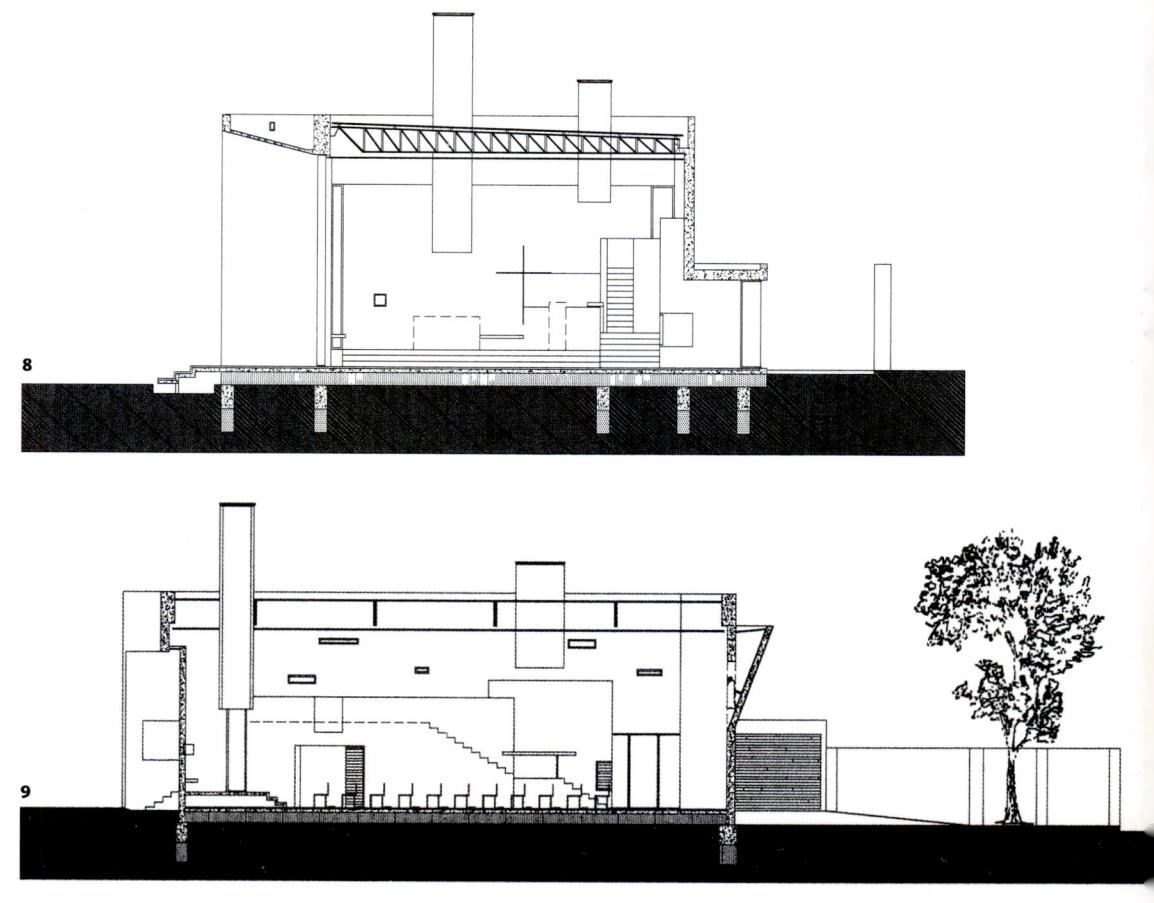

10 The enclosed interior receives light from above and through the portal openings.

11 The Cross set in the pool is visible at the back of the nave.

12 When the great doors are open, the platform at right becomes the altar dais.

and south wall, boxed light wells that are sculptural protrusions in the concrete rather than separate elements project, and with the great doors set back well inside the roofline, the box retains its integrity even while framing the tremendous wooden wall. As with a prism, those elements that have been allowed to break up the purity become enhanced by their contact with it.

Further to their stated aim, the architects have made a virtue of coordinated details to ensure that 'harmony' is not merely a poetic term but a physical presence. The planes of the doors contrast warmly with the white planes of concrete, which form the two main walls and appear in layers on the east wall with stairs for the choir sandwiched in between. The narrow rectangular apertures in the walls and ceilings correspond with striations in the wood and concrete. The small openings allow in a limited amount of light, so that when the doors are closed the interior has the intimacy of a small chapel. The light stone floor interspersed with patches of marbling mirrors the juxtaposition of concrete and wood: the marbling on the floor is almost directly reflected in the ceiling lights. Materials are pure and consistent, even down to the benches modelled on a Greek key-shape and fabricated in compressed wood strips. Many linked components produce a smooth whole, so that while the interior has a perceptible aesthetic it is not one that jars when the doors are open. Flow is facilitated by this simplicity and harmony.

While the doors are the most imposing feature of the design, the many details make a composition that would be noteworthy even without this defining gesture. The crisp shape of the concrete form, most appreciable from the south-east, demonstrates the purity which the architects sought, and which is emphasized by the reflecting pool that helps to create a boundary between the sacred space and the other school buildings. Entering through the small door at the west, visitors can see, through the glazed portion of the eastern wall, both the water and a heavy, rough-hewn wood Cross that sits in the still water of the pool against the illuminating backdrop of another concrete plane. It is an achievement to produce a building that is so well tuned to sight lines and detail, and quite another to make it accessible and appreciable on both a small and large scale. Dualities aside, it is a fine thing to see, through the clarity of the prism, such multifarious possibilities for beauty.

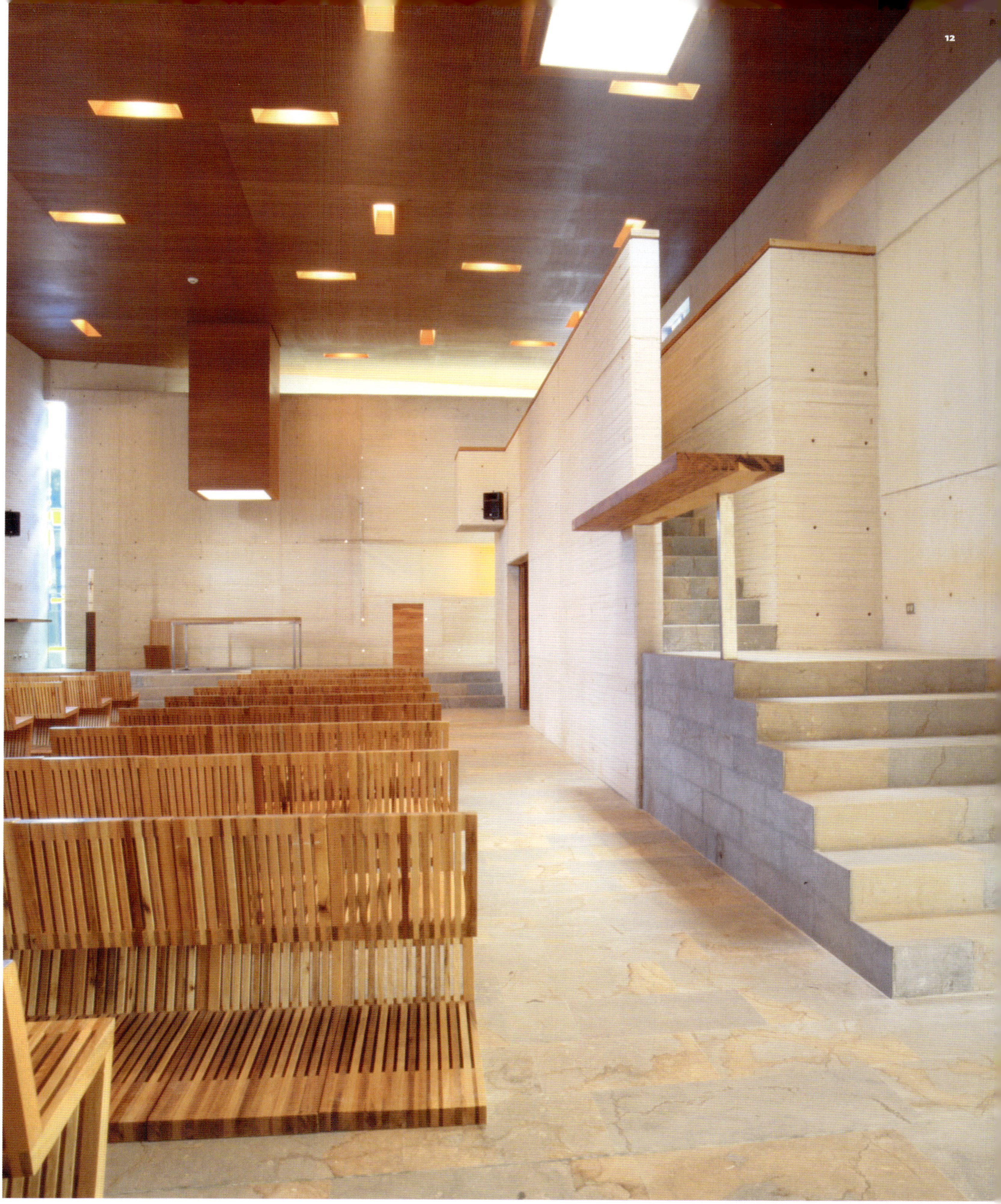

5 MODEST MAGNIFICENCE HIGH IDEALS AND HUMBLE MATERIALS

Antioch Baptist Church, Alabama

An often overlooked kind of religious building is one constructed with small means or in challenging circumstances, yet such a building possesses an elemental integrity and, at least in the examples in following projects, a high degree of architectural ingenuity. As a result, they become very affecting demi-monuments. When communities invest their own time and precious, comparatively meagre, resources in a building they have a great stake in its success. And when architects are forced to look beyond conventional building practices by the very real pressures of cost, they often find it to be a surprisingly creative process. In these situations, when the building does succeed economically, aesthetically, spiritually, the rewards seem greater than when vast sums are spent. This may go some way toward explaining why these low-budget sacred spaces provide such a great sense of satisfaction, and why architects who could be producing much more lucrative designs continue to take on the challenge.

The old adage about necessity being the mother of invention is particualrly apt in describing the work of many of the architects here. Whether it is a need that comes from an impoverished community seeking a new space for worship, as in the projects created by Sam Mockbee's Rural Studio, or a condition that has arisen from a disaster such as the Kobe earthquake of 1995, the drive to make something for almost nothing has brought some lasting developments.

Both the Yancey Chapel and Antioch Baptist Church by Rural Studio are testimony to the possibilities of recycled building materials. Though the materials are more obvious in the Yancey Chapel's automobile-tyre walls, the Antioch church wears it re-claimed beams and metal sheeting just as proudly. Jae Cha's church/community meeting house in Bolivia was not built using recycled materials, as the prevailing construction material in the village is earth used to build mud huts. But her polycarbonate and wood building makes a significant contribution for a minimum cost, using a simple form that is elegant, well-suited to the climate and easily maintained by local inhabitants.

Similar requirements seem to have influenced Shigeru Ban's Paper Church, built in the wake of the Kobe earthquake. Ban applied his research and developments in structural paper tubes to make a building that was not only low-cost and aesthetically pleasing but that could be constructed, taken down and reassembled by a relatively unskilled group of volunteers. The paper-tube method was also successfully applied to temporary housing structures.

The chapel by Antonio Ruíz Barbarín in Spain and Jensen and Skodvin's hilltop church in Norway are less obviously low cost but were built for far less than the average public or residential project would command. Attached to a Jesuit retreat, Barbarín's chapel makes an elegant complement to it from unspectacular materials. Jensen and Skodvin limited their range of materials to accommodate existing trees and boulders, which are allowed to puncture the floor of the building and courtyards. According to the architects, the tight budget forced them to search outside the standard structural solutions, a valuable exercise for any building. Whether it is for a chapel, a mosque or a housing complex, designs that produce good, efficient buildings for the least possible cost are as much in demand now as ever, and architects who take on the task of producing them will be at the forefront of larger and much-needed advances.

1 The partially submerged chapel appears as a long, low barn or shed structure through the trees.

2 A grand entrance made up of humble recycled parts.

5.01

YANCEY CHAPEL

SAWYERVILLE, ALABAMA, USA

SAMUEL MOCKBEE AND RURAL STUDIO

1996

It is difficult to stop short of hagiography when writing about the late Samuel Mockbee, who founded the Rural Studio architecture programme through Auburn University in 1992. Working in his own architectural practice in the 1980s, Mockbee once described how he could not get away from the advice of Leon Battista Alberti to 'choose between fortune and virtue'.[1] Though he would have been the first to question his own heroism, it seems, from all that we know, that Mockbee chose the latter. Together with D K Ruth, head of the architecture programme at Auburn University, Mockbee decried the teaching of 'paper architecture' that neglected real building experience. With the Rural Studio, Mockbee aimed to give architecture students valuable hands-on building work while also trying to address the needs of the rural poor in Hale County, Alabama.

Rural Studio began building houses for poor families in 1992, using donations of money, materials and labour. Their first project was a house made of hay bales with a corrugated plastic roof. In 1995 Rural Studio's fifth-year architecture students began working on larger, community projects. The first of these was the Yancey Chapel, often called the 'tyre chapel' because its walls are made of discarded tyres that were donated by a local scrapyard, which had been ordered to get rid of them. The chapel grew as the thesis project of fifth-year students Ruard Veltman, Steve Durden and Thomas Tretheway. A local dairy farmer offered the land and Mockbee offered the suggestion of a chapel. The tyres, numbering around 1,000, had to be hand-packed with soil before being put in place and then sealed with stucco. The pine roof-beams that create such a soaring, pictur-

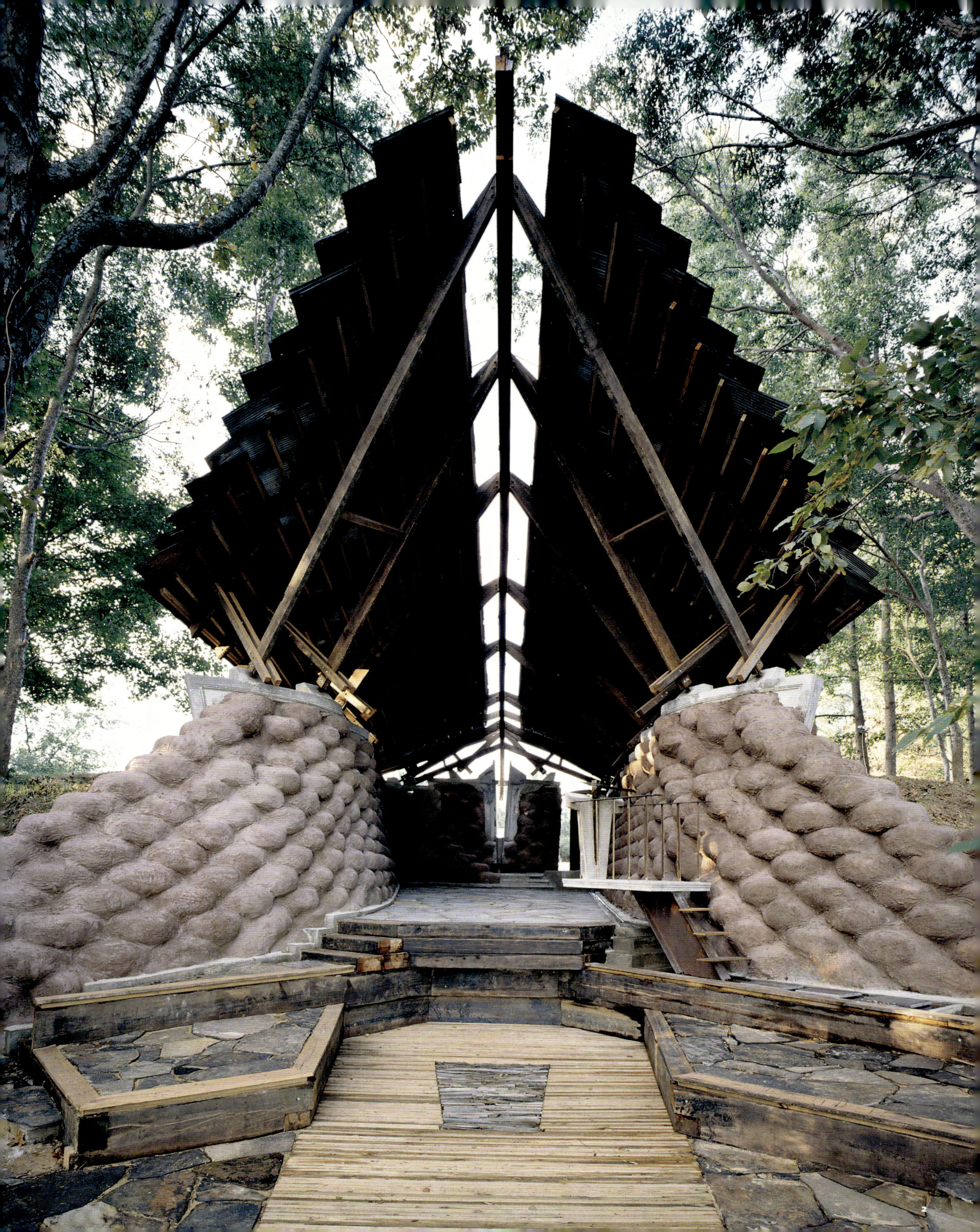

3

3 Inside, the ceiling timberwork recalls traditional church structures.

4 Concrete detailing adds a touch of refinement.

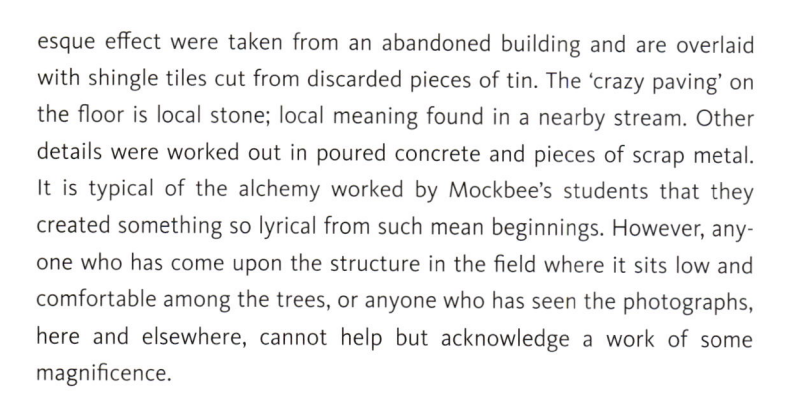

esque effect were taken from an abandoned building and are overlaid with shingle tiles cut from discarded pieces of tin. The 'crazy paving' on the floor is local stone; local meaning found in a nearby stream. Other details were worked out in poured concrete and pieces of scrap metal. It is typical of the alchemy worked by Mockbee's students that they created something so lyrical from such mean beginnings. However, anyone who has come upon the structure in the field where it sits low and comfortable among the trees, or anyone who has seen the photographs, here and elsewhere, cannot help but acknowledge a work of some magnificence.

Some people find that part of the magic of the building becomes lost when the materials become recognizable. Others find the metamorphosis even more compelling when they comprehend its entirety. There are some elements inherent to the building that another architect would be tempted to emulate, but here they come from necessity. The gloriously steep pitch of the roof comes not from an aesthetic or even an architecturally historical gesture but from the fact that the area is reputed to receive 2,000 millimetres (80 inches) of rain a year. The narrow, tunnel-like interior set partly below ground level is dictated by the shape of a narrow trench, formerly the space for a cattle trough, but it provides an even more dramatic shape as the building rises out of the little hill into its sweeping roofline. A stream runs past the chapel and is bridged by a metal grille, lending its calming noise to the peaceful repose of the building. With their developing skills, perseverance and ingenuity the students managed to complete the chapel at a cost of $15,000 (£10,000), hardly enough to get you a water feature for a standard new-build project, let alone a chapel to set next to it.

Mockbee's abiding belief was that all people, rich or poor, shared the desire for 'a shelter for the soul'. Veltman, Durden and Tretheway's chapel is a model for such a democratic philosophy, demonstrating that such a shelter can be much more than the sum of its parts.

1 When the church is illuminated at night the varying degrees of opacity are visible.

5.02

CHURCH AND COMMUNITY CENTRE

URUBO, BOLIVIA

JAE CHA

2000

Circles are potent symbols of unity, of congregation and of faith. A structure created to provide a sheltered venue for public meetings and communal activities, as well as a space for Christian worship and prayer, this circular enclosure also highlights the virtue of simplicity. It is the design of Jae Cha and was completed just a year after her graduation from the Yale School of Architecture. Cha is the founder of LIGHT, which she describes as 'a non-governmental, non-profit organization dedicated to creating public spaces that provide the physical foundation for economically diverse, self-supporting and self-guided communities'. Simply put, Cha continues, 'the goal is to provide small-scale civic architecture in developing areas'. It is a youthful idealism that has proved itself in a small Bolivian village where donations helped to build this modest but inspired meeting house.

The village is made up of a collection of 'traditional mud huts', Cha says, and, 'as there is no economy in the village, the men work in remote cities for weeks at a time and women are the predominant presence in the village'. Because of these circumstances, the church 'evolved into a community centre for women and children'. Its uses have expanded to daycare centre, kindergarten, market place and vaccination centre, with multiple uses possible due to the open plan and lack of designated furnishings and iconography.

Cha's use of the name 'LIGHT' for her organization is an apt one: though it no doubt refers to enlightenment and to the light of hope that it endeavours to provide to impoverished communities, it also describes the overall physical quality of this early triumph in her career. Though economy of materials was dictated by the minimal budget, the architect's choice and use of materials is both artful and bold without being an overwhelming or prideful statement. Two circles formed with local wood supports and corrugated polycarbonate sheeting are set on a basic concrete foundation. A corridor is created between the two circles, with entrances between them staggered so that the space retains a sense of mystery. The polycarbonate sheets appear in a pattern of panels that leaves spaces open to the elements and adds interest and dimension to the design. The viewer sees a

2 Simple corrugated metal and wood-beam construction is refined through the use of cut-outs and patterning.

3 The plan shows the entry points on the circle, with the staggered openings on the inner circle.

4 Elevation.

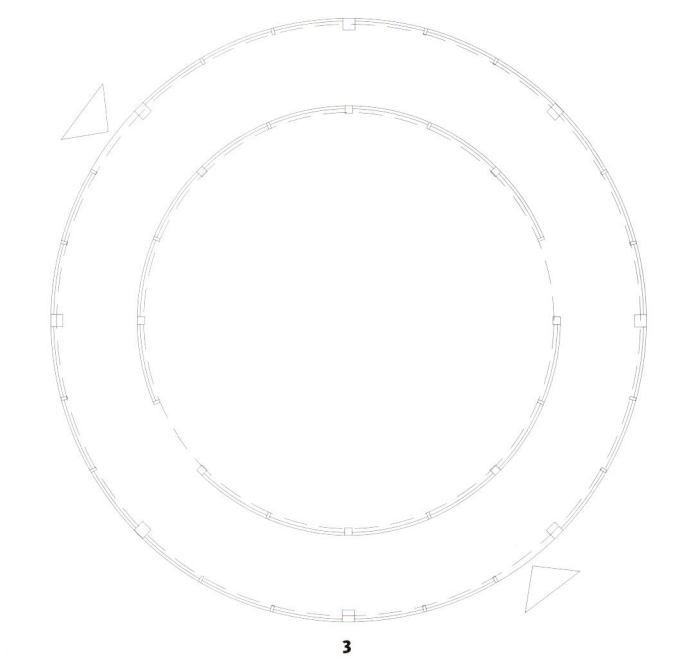

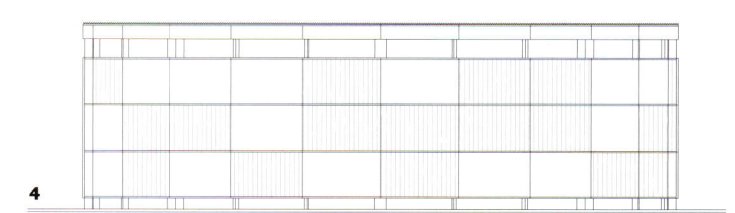

5 The corridor between the outer shell and inner wall.

6 The bare interior is awash with the box pattern created by the light.

complete, circular building but the sides are a patchwork of opened and closed spaces that reveal more opened and closed spaces in the inner wall. Therefore, the simple develops an unexpected visual complexity, a complexity that is enhanced by the differing degrees of transparency within and without the walls.

Inside, an open space is criss-crossed with light and shadow in patterns reminiscent of a Mondrian painting in black and white. In some spaces, the trees and sky are clearly visible, in others, a sheet of plastic makes the view more obscured and in still others, where the polycarbonate sheets on the inner and outer wall overlap, the light becomes more obscured but never fully blocked. The unglazed sections allow for much-needed ventilation, while the solid roof keeps out the heavy rains. 'Flexible public spaces can provide the physical foundation for economically diverse, self-supported and self-guided communities,' says Jae Cha. But she demonstrates that they can provide something beyond those highly laudable, practical goals: something of beauty, which must surely be good for the soul.

1 The entrance plaza of the church where mature trees have been left untouched by the construction.

2 The section shows the glass wall at ground level topped by the drystone wall.

5.03

CHURCH

MORTENSRUD, OSLO, NORWAY

JENSEN & SKODVIN

2002

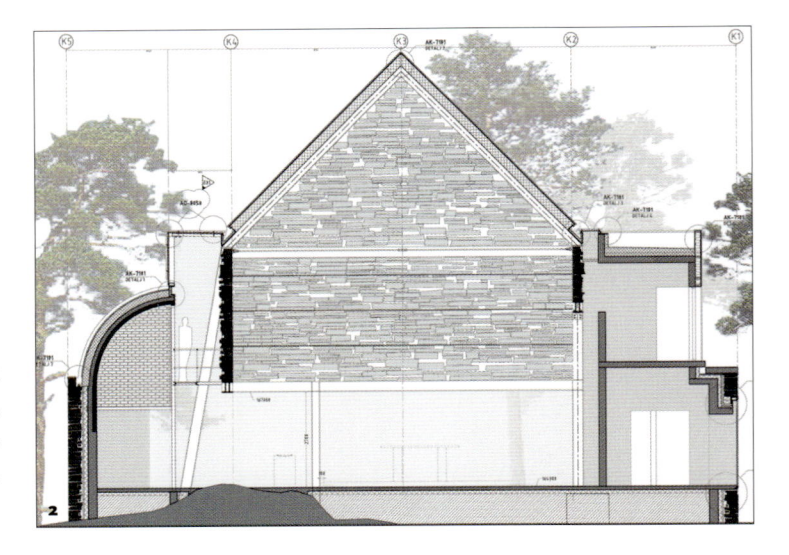

The last decades of the twentieth century saw the development of undeveloping, that is the theory of deconstruction as applied to architecture which, together with the practice of post-Modern approaches, brought about the fragmentation of elements that could be considered in isolation from one another. This was not always successful, in theory or practice, in producing a cohesive aesthetic result. Here, in a church designed as part of a parish complex near Oslo in Norway, a fragmented approach has been taken, not as the manifestation of theoretical statements but from a source in direct opposition to abstract philosophy: the physical landscape. On a dramatic crest of a small hill in an area formed by glacial movement and amid a forest of mature pine trees, Norwegian architects Jensen & Skodvin chose the landscape as their starting point and very decidedly worked with it and around it, incorporating the natural setting into every possible aspect.

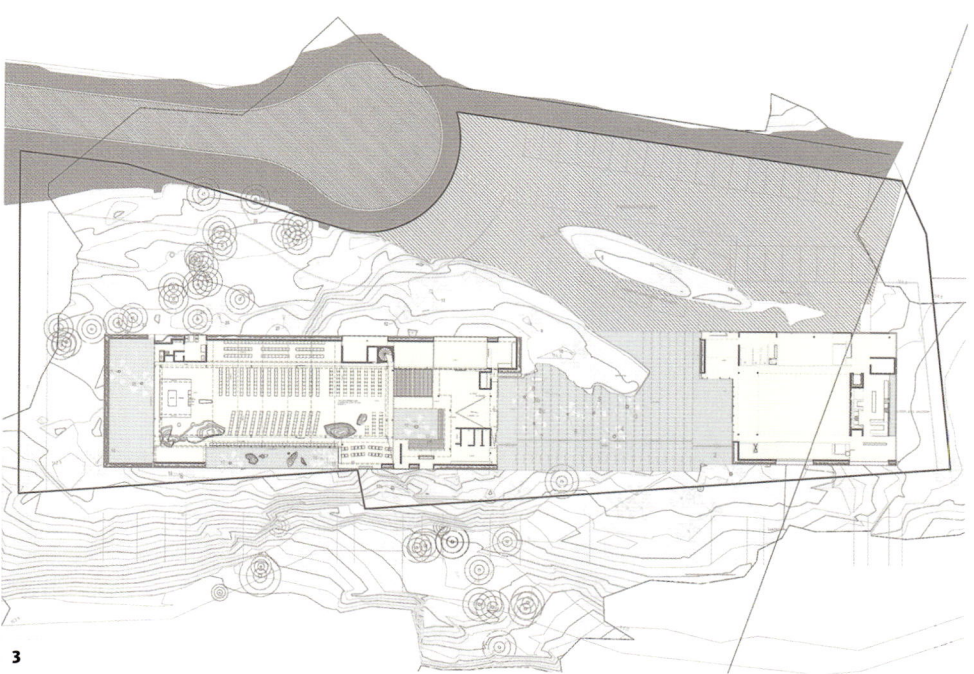

3 The site plan shows the dramatic topography of the location. The church is at the left end and the community centre at the right.

4 The eastern façade. The mix of glass, drystone and metal construction blends well with the rocky, tree-lined setting.

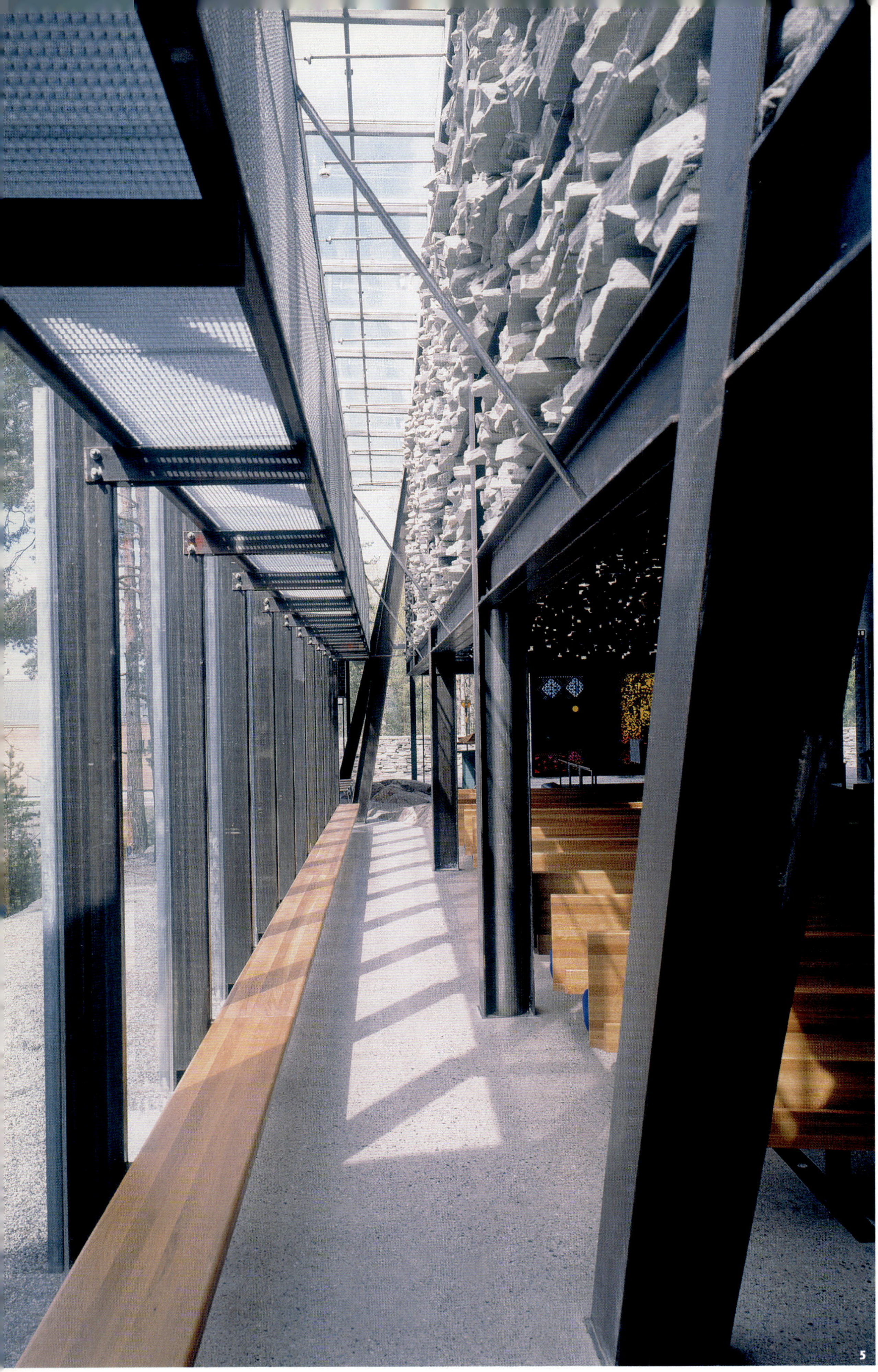

5

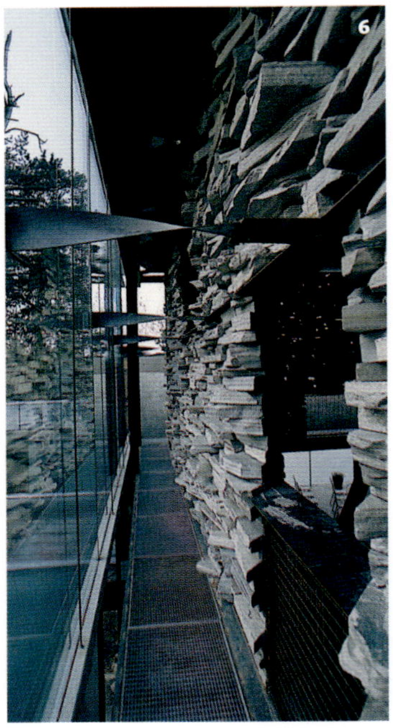

6

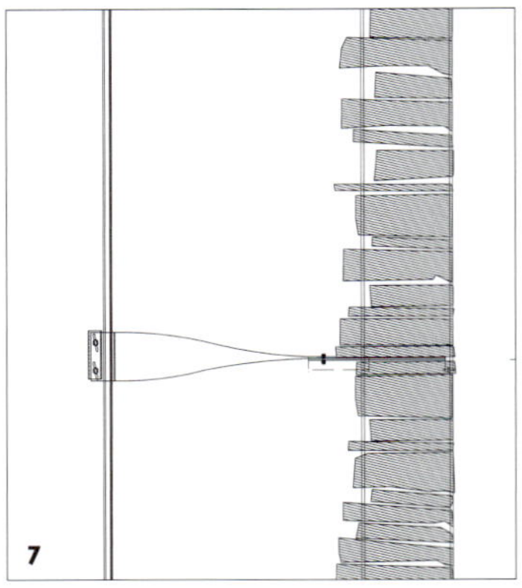

7

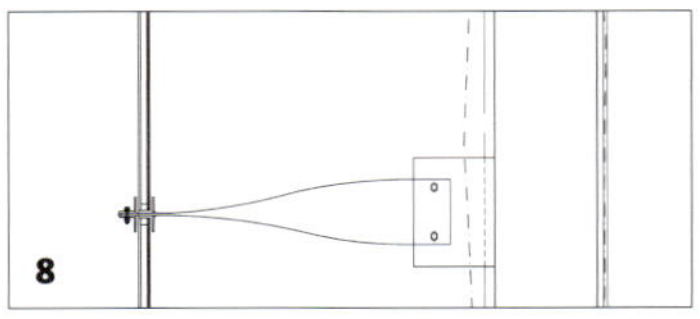

8

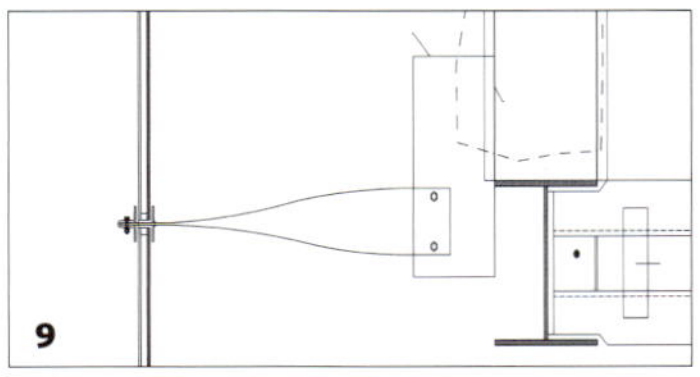

9

5 The I-beam supports carry the drystone wall at the second-storey level.

6 The 'propeller' supports run from the steel framework of the drystone wall to the glazing supports at the upper level.

7–9 Details of the propeller construction.

10 Dappled sunlight filters through the stone wall, while the ground floor glazing provides a view of the dramatic natural setting.

Rocks and trees spring out of the built landscape much as they did before human intervention on the site. The architects report that, in fact, 'the church takes its major divisions from elements already on the site,' so that 'trees are preserved in atriums within the enclosure and rock formations emerge like islands in the concrete floor of the church, between the congregation and choir' and elsewhere in the paved courtyards. The architects even took this a step further, creating drystone walls constructed in the traditional manner except that the walls begin at the second storey level, being supported by steel troughs resting on I-beam vertical supports. Double-height glazing creates transparency at ground-floor level, and a protective outer layer for the stone at the second level which still allows light to come through the small gaps between the stonework. This dappled lighting is reminiscent of old stone churches and of the light that flows through stained glass. The result is that, standing in the nave, the interior feels very traditional and atmospheric, and the fact that this is a building largely made of steel, glass and concrete is rather like those Byzantine engineering feats, artfully de-emphasized in the face of a more wondrous creation.

11 The west court with the existing trees.

12 The eastern section shows how the church and the parish centre, at the lower end of the site, negotiate the hilly terrain.

13 The linearity of glass and steel is broken by the natural imperfections of the stone.

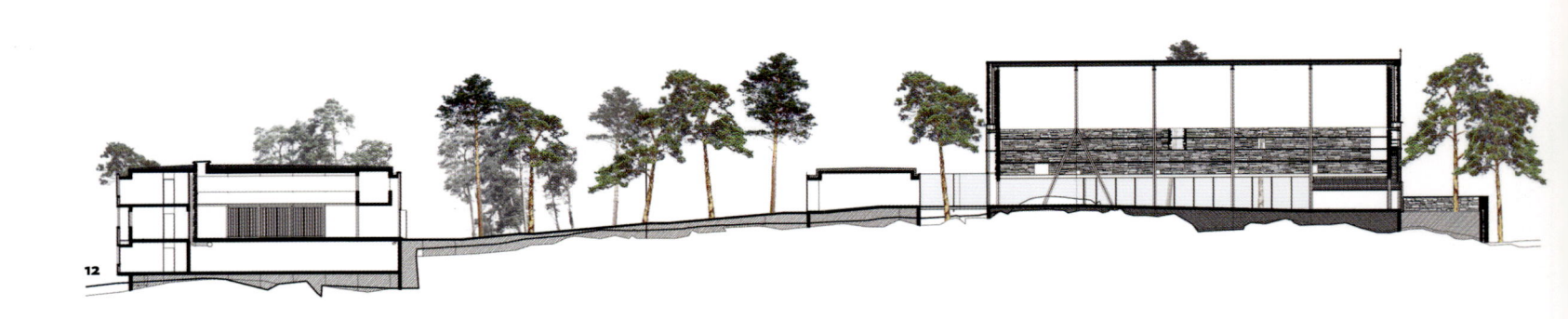

With drystone behind glass, glacial rock rising out of the floor and pavement and trees enshrined in courtyards, the architects have created what feels like a centre for native ecology in a new building whose budget could have easily dictated something far less innovative and certainly less appealing. Working around the various elements has resulted in a building that achieves coherence through a multitude of solutions. The main structure is, in fact, a steel framework. The drystone walls sitting on their steel trough beams are 'stiffened' by horizontal steel plates that run between the columns at one metre (three foot) intervals and derive their strength from the actual weight of the stone. These steel plates, strengthened by the stone, help to anchor the glazed façade by way of twisted 'propeller' bands of steel that tie the plates to the vertical steel glazing joints. The roof is then carried by the stone wall. These are some of the 'basic methods and techniques' that the architects used to meet budget demands. However, they say that in seeking out these simple but unconventional means they found solutions that were not only cheaper, but 'also gave us greater architectural freedom'. This freedom enabled them to embrace 'the tension between the wish to create a "silent", self-referring room and a variety of obstacles limiting this possibility'.

Simple ideas often require complex methodology. No blasting of the site and no excavation was necessary for the design, only a 'thin layer of soil' was removed for the building to take place. This no doubt avoided cost and preserved a beautiful landscape, but it set up problems that had to be resolved in terms of negotiating levels and building around natural elements. Part of the success of this scheme is the multiple ways that it reaches out to its environment and celebrates the natural setting without seeming a jumble of ideas. The architects themselves say that what emerged was a building of 'fragmented and complex character', but here fragmented just means that there are many parts to the unified whole.

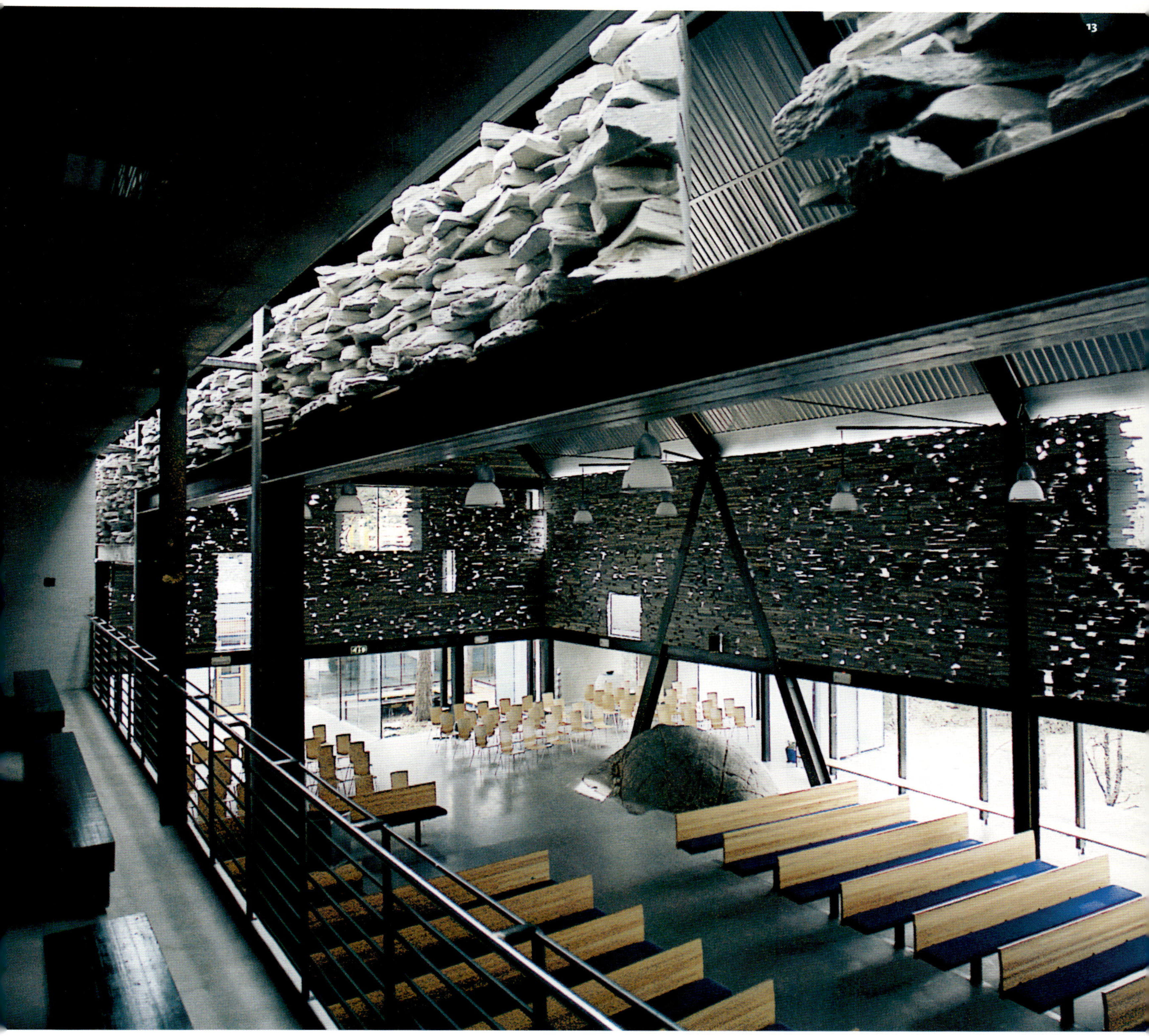

13

1 The mean construction materials are not immediately apparent in the welcoming, illuminated church.

5.04

PAPER CHURCH

KOBE, JAPAN

SHIGERU BAN ARCHITECT

1995

Out of disaster hope can spring, and so can innovation. Just before 6 a.m. local time on 17 January 1995 the south-central regions of Osaka and Kobe in Japan were hit by an earthquake measuring a staggering 7.2 magnitude on the Richter scale. Bringing devastation to an area 100 kilometres (62 miles) in radius, the quake was responsible for around 5,500 deaths, 35,000 injuries and the destruction of an estimated 180,000 buildings. The evening after the disaster, probably 300,000 people were homeless.[1] These areas are the second most populated in Japan, so great swathes of housing, transportation lines and general infrastructure were laid waste.

In the Nagata area of Kobe, a community composed largely of Vietnamese refugees had lost their homes and their church and community centre. Architect Shigeru Ban, who had been experimenting with his unique paper tube structure (PTS) since the late 1980s, was able to address these losses with highly practical, economical solutions. Working with 160 volunteers, Ban built 30 paper log-houses as temporary shelter, and the now-famous Paper Church to replace the Takatori church which was destroyed by a fire caused by the earthquake.

Ban, known for his 'Curtain Wall House' and other elegant minimal private residences, first made a temporary pavilion of paper tubes in 1989; he then moved on to a small library interior in which the paper tubes were fitted with reinforcing rods in the centre and used as trusses. In 1993 the Japanese Minister of Construction authorized the PTS as a material for permanent building structures. Most recently, the paper tubes have reappeared in the undulating form of the Japanese Pavilion at the Hanover Expo of 2000. However, it was in Kobe that this method really showed itself as the highly flexible, effective building technique that it is. For the architect the need was not only to build cheaply and effectively, but also to build simply – not just to satisfy minimalist aesthetics, but 'because the construction of the church had to happen within a very short time frame' and 'assembly had to be easy enough for volunteers to carry out without the use of heavy machinery'. The structure also had to be easily disassembled for relocation, should that be necessary. So the PTS system was the ideal method to satisfy a host of practical requirements.

The church is made up of 58 paper tubes, each of which is five metres (16 feet) high and 330 millimetres (13 inches) in diameter and 15 millimetres (half an inch) thick. They are arranged in an elliptical shape with the tubes along one side set more closely together 'to form a backdrop behind the altar as well as providing storage'. The other tubes are set more widely to facilitate the flow between the interior and exterior. Light enters through

2 The drawing shows the generous overhang of the roof which allows for a surrounding porch-like shelter, or minimized narthex.

3 Wooden joints secure the paper tubes to the ground and to the plywood sill-plate at the top that connects all the tubes.

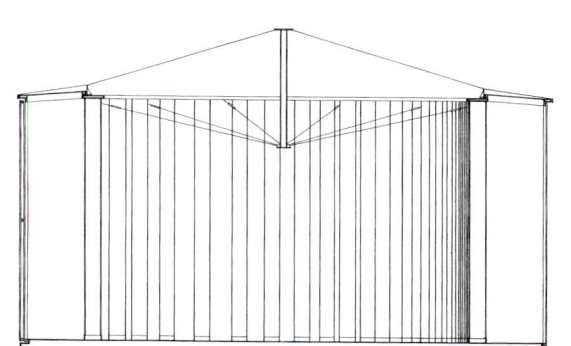

4 The plan shows the elliptical worship space within the square of the outer steel-frame structure which holds the polycarbonate doors.

5 A crowd comes for Mass, spilling out easily between the entry columns.

6 The rhythm of the nine pairs of doors echoes that of the paper-tube columns within.

7 The exploded axonometric reveals the component outer frame and inner ellipsis.

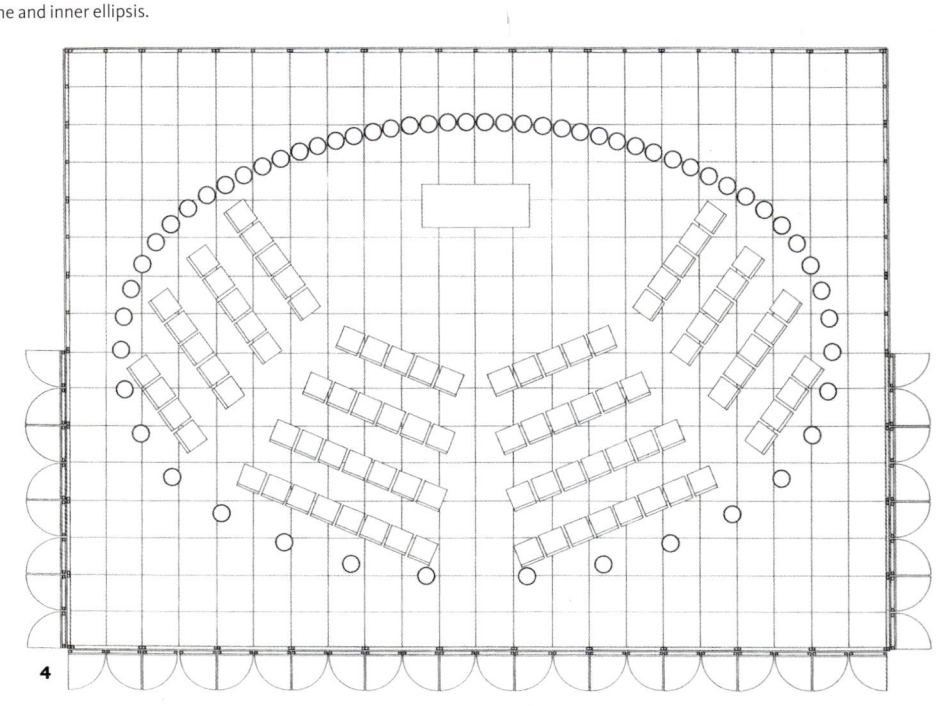

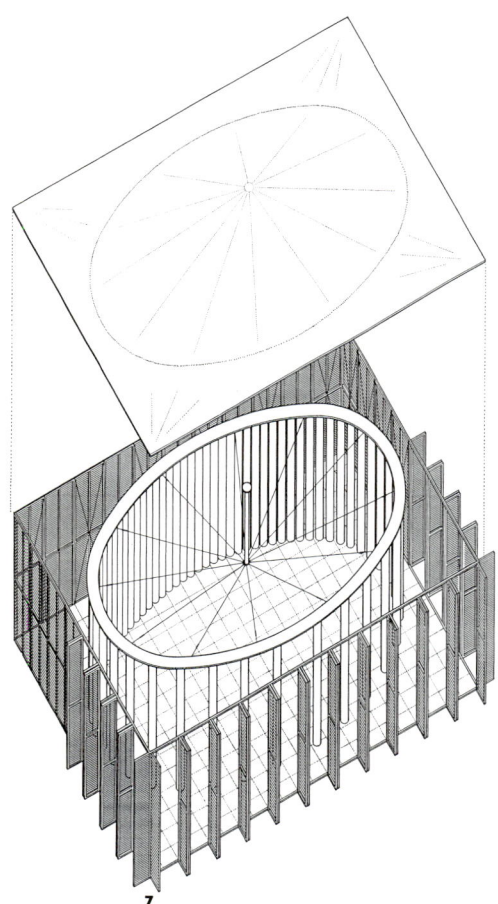

the PVC membrane used for the roof, and through the spaced paper columns. The interior can be closed off using 19 pairs of doors inset with polycarbonate panels set in a steel outer frame.

While the many post-disaster practicalities were being addressed the architect did not leave aesthetic requirements behind. The elliptical shape and the rhythm of the paper-tube columns make the small building, which measures 10 by 15 metres (33 by 50 feet), a graceful presence in the ruined street. The architect himself was very concerned with achieving a feeling of some grandeur even in such a modest construction and conceived this 'dynamic oval in the spirit of the seventeenth-century Baroque architect Giovanni Lorenzo Bernini'. Comparisons with the creator of extravagant interior decoration and the piazza of St Peter's in Rome may seem like a stretch, but too often constraints of time and money bring vision down instead of up where it should be. Ban at least is satisfied: 'The experience in this small temporary building is in no way inferior to that in a large, magnificent cathedral,' he says. And for some, belief is all that is needed.

1 The south-east façade with the extruding plywood box containing the restroom facilities and preacher's room.

5.05

ANTIOCH BAPTIST CHURCH

PERRY COUNTY, ALABAMA, USA

RURAL STUDIO

2002

The Rural Studio architecture programme of Auburn University in Alabama continues after the death of its founder, Samuel Mockbee, to produce remarkable, innovative and cost-effective buildings for disadvantaged rural communities. In 2001 students Gabe Michaud, Jared Fulton, Marion McElroy and Bill Nauck undertook as their thesis project the rebuilding of a church for a small congregation (a mere four families) in a forested area just outside Hale County, where Rural Studio is based. The task was to restore or replace a small existing church that had no baptismal font or restroom facilities and suffered severe weaknesses in its foundation. As a result of its failing frame, it was losing its place in the community.

The team decided it was necessary to build a new structure but insisted on reusing as much of the material from the old church as was possible. Since recycling and salvage are practically a matter of course for Rural Studio projects, the students were very efficient in remaking the old and inadequate into the newly adapted. Much of the wood wall panelling, floor and roof joists, and corrugated metal sheeting was taken from the old building. We have grown so accustomed to seeing plywood and corrugated metal in avant-garde gallery structures and follies that we might forget that these materials are as cheap as they are effective. However, the students of Rural Studio are well aware of the virtues of using common materials, particularly the second time around.

The viewer's first impression is of a new, modern, architect-designed little gem of a structure. The recycled building is a bright, sharply turned out shape in the landscape. Plywood extrudes from the integrated boxes of metal to make a curious but controlled construction. The architects describe it as 'two interlocking wrapping forms'. One is on the north–south axis and contains the high south wall, a roof of hand-built metal-and-wood trusses and a horizontal glass wall running the length of the room and

2 Existing headstones dot the green on the north side. The altar is located in the projecting wood structure at right.

3 The overlapping fold of the north–south structure creates space for an entrance corridor.

4 The long north window wall and glazed areas between the roof and wall sections provide ample light and openness in the small interior.

overlooking the cemetery. The other form 'runs east–west and forms the baptistery at the west and preacher's room and restroom facilities at the east entrance'.

The east–west block slots neatly into the wrapping skin of the north–south structure, but a play of angles adds complexity to the fit. Along the south wall, the east and west sections come together at a gentle angle. The roof is a lopsided V-shape with one long slope along the length of the nave and a short, sharp rise at the east entrance. As visitors approach the church, they are met by the heightened east façade and a side wall that ascends steeply to the roofline to enclose a porch/entrance hall, both of which provide a degree of ceremony and drama to the building. The vertical lines of the 'galvalum' – a highly weatherproof aluminium and zinc alloy – and the narrow wood panels also emphasize the significant ceiling height of the little church. Next to the entrance, a wood-panelled block containing the preacher's room and restroom facilities sits well below the roofline, leaving space for a glass clerestory above that admits the eastern light.

The simplicity of the materials and block form belie many subtle and thoughtful details that the architects brought to a very basic project. Behind small gestures are sometimes grand ideas. Samuel Mockbee once said that small projects such as these 'have in them the architectural essence to enchant us, to inspire us, and ultimately, to elevate our profession." The students who designed the Antioch chapel prove this is still true.

4

5.06

JESUIT RETREAT CHAPEL

NAVAS DEL MARQUÉS, ÁVILA, SPAIN

RUÍZ BARBARÍN ARQUITECTOS

2000

In a forested area outside Ávila a form resembling a polished black vessel appears to be heading out of the trees, its curved shape rising up to a glazed prow topped by the unmistakeable icon of Christianity. It is an unexpected but pleasing discovery that navigates the landscape between a rural setting and a restored building while addressing a modern brief. The inspiration for its design is also somewhat unexpected.

Commissioned to renovate a long slate-and-stone building from the 1970s which had been used as a prayer space and activity centre by its Jesuit congregation, Antonio and Javier Ruíz Barbarín were asked to make the interior more practical, adding accommodation, kitchen and dining space as well as shop and storage facilities, and to create a separate structure for prayer, worship and group meetings. For this structure they were inspired by Baroque churches, particularly the church of Santa Andrea al Quirinale in Rome. The Quirinale, designed in the late seventeenth century by Bernini, took the form of an ellipse, with the entrance on the shorter axis.[1]

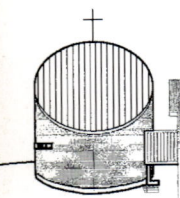

1 The black slate cladding adds gravity to the new structure.

2 The elevation shows the porch that attaches the church to the main building.

3 The interior is a dramatic meeting of light and dark, linear and curved.

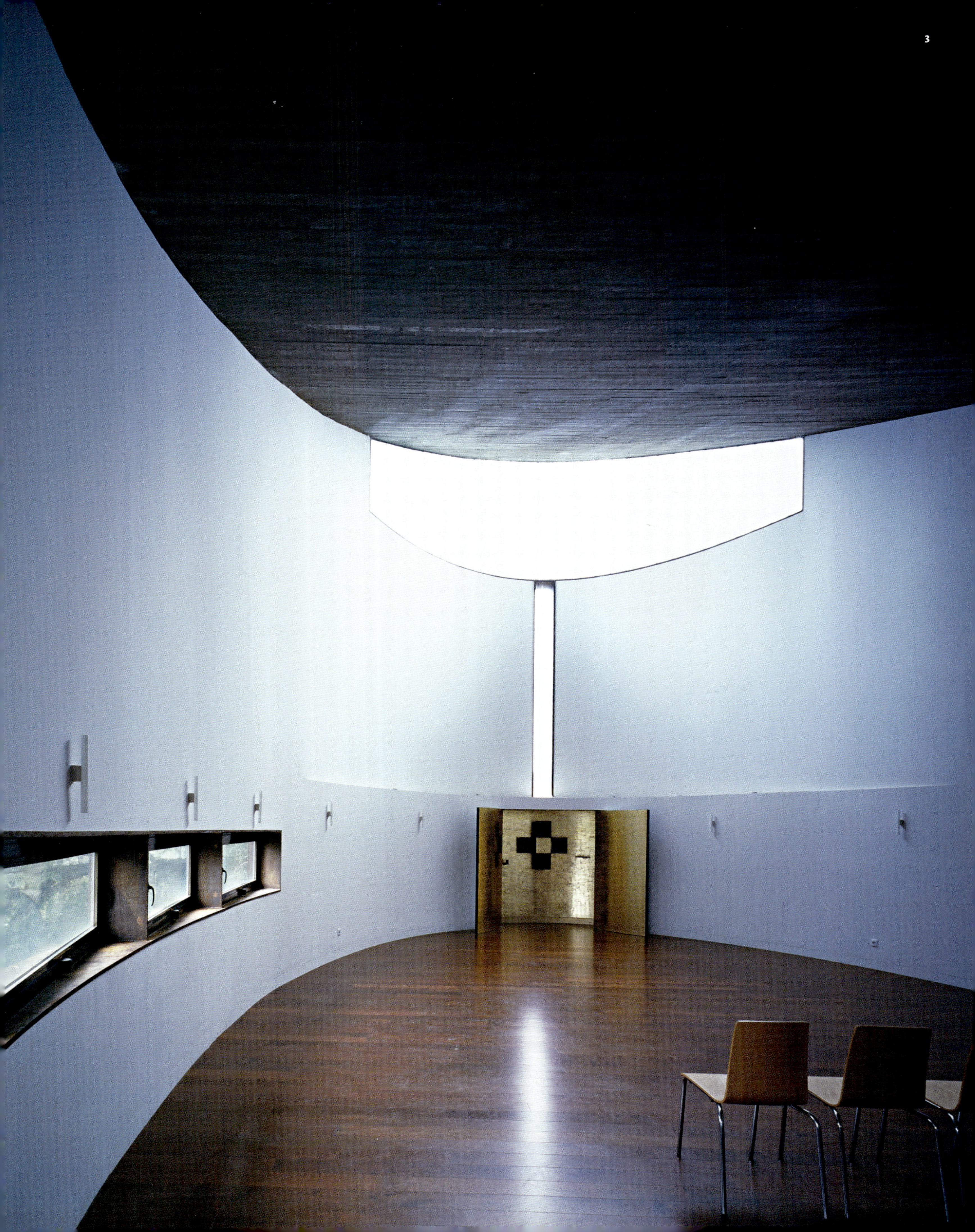

4

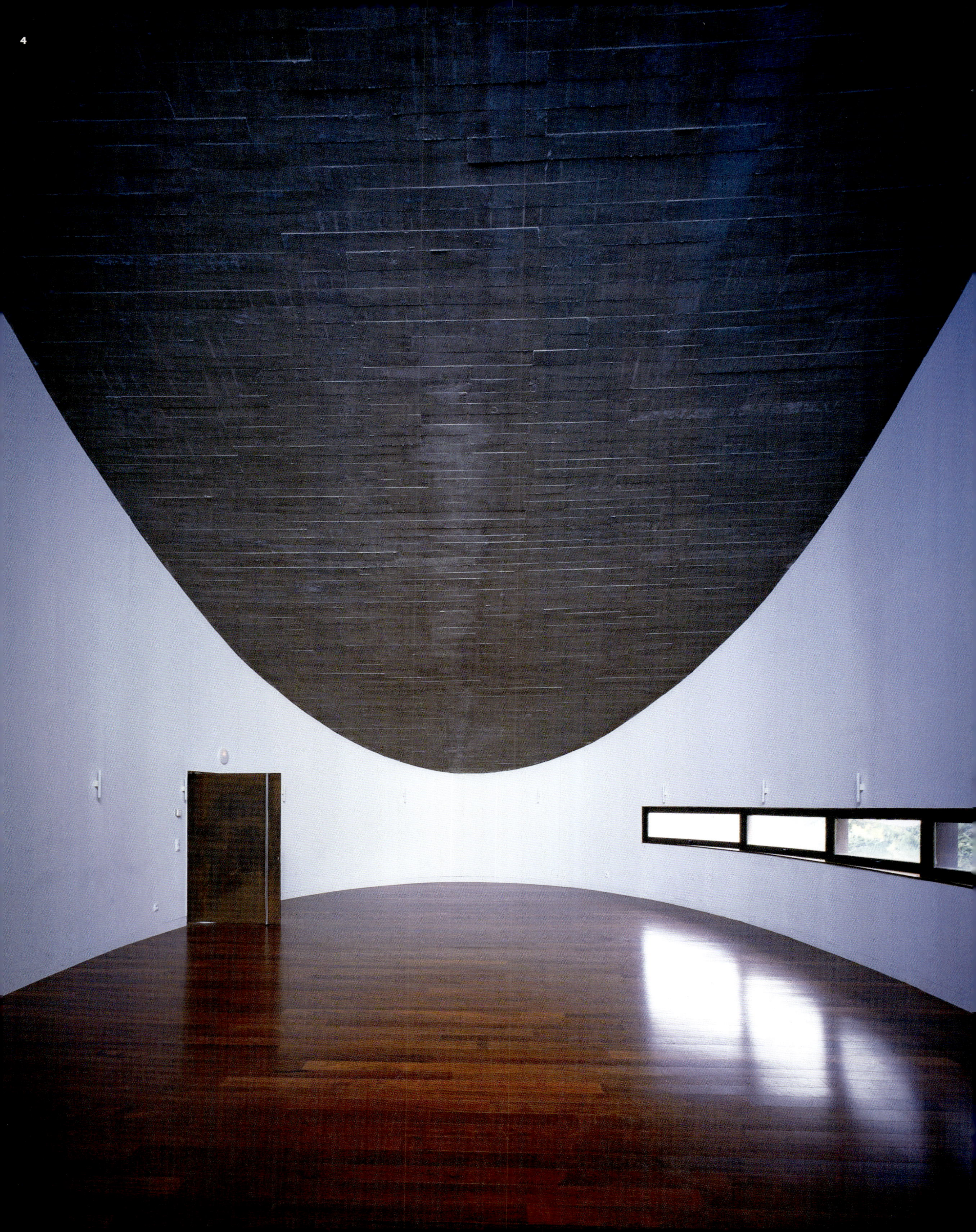

4 The impact of the slanted roof and elliptical form is accentuated by the use of matching wood on the floor and celing.

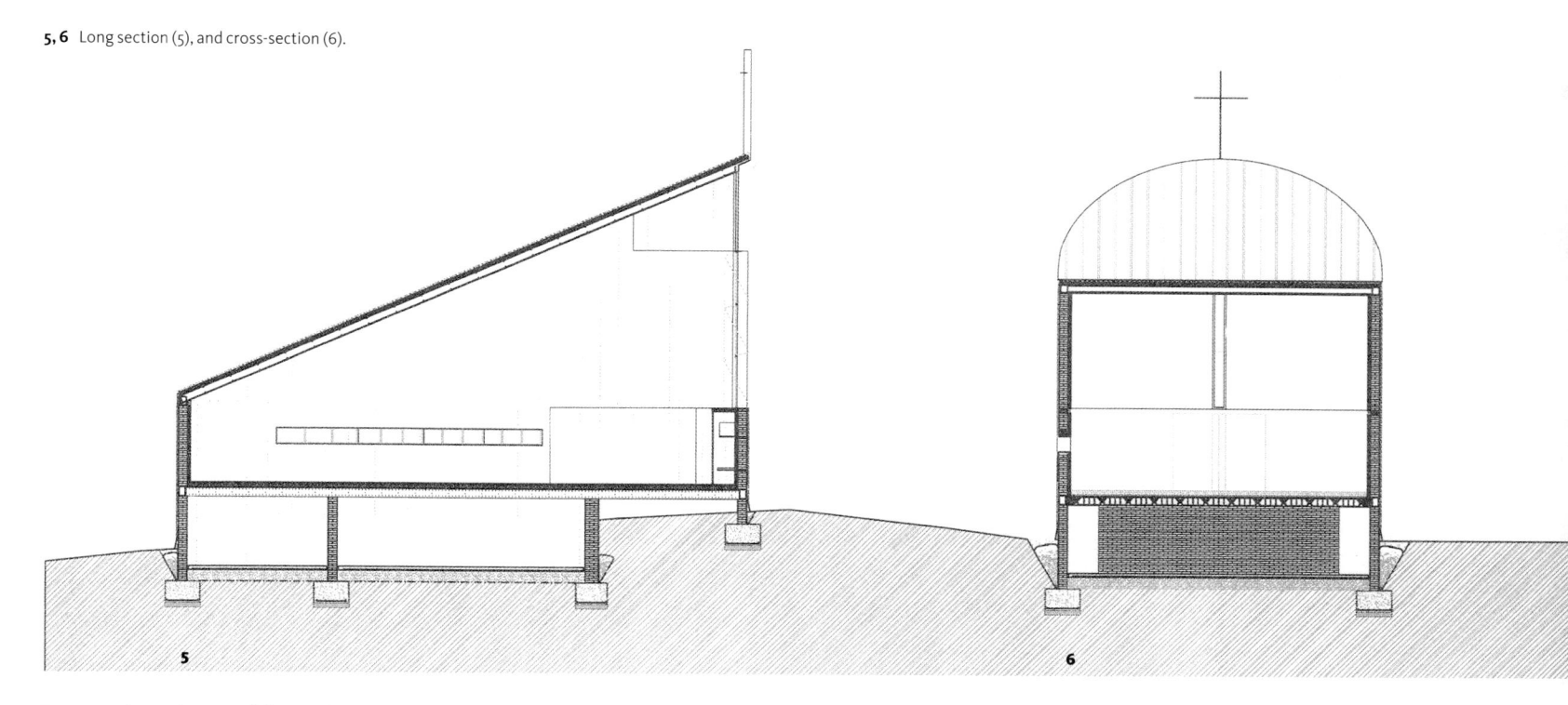

5, 6 Long section (5), and cross-section (6).

Despite their choice of form, the architects sought to present the new building 'as an enlargement of the old house', but with its own aesthetic appeal. The brick walls are faced in the same black slate as was used on the roof of the existing building but here, in the sweep of the walls, the slate has a more singular character. The oval volume has been cut at the same 25-degree slant as the old building's roof but on the elliptical volume it creates a dramatic slope down from the apse, where the high point above an arcing clerestory is crowned with a simple Cross. On the west side a narrow horizontal window set low in the wall allows the late afternoon sun to penetrate the space; while on the east side of the building is a small corridor, which the architects describe as 'an umbilical cord' connecting the space to the porch of the 1970s structure.

In such a small and pared-down design the refined use of materials, even structural materials, becomes, if not Baroque, then certainly more ornamental than one might expect. Cor-ten steel on the roof and window-surrounds strengthens the lines and impact of those elements. The yawning glazed section at the apex – a reference, in its top-lighting aspect, to a traditional dome over the presbytery – is achieved with vertical sections of U-glass, a material which is also used for the connecting corridor. The shape of the clerestory allows a wide swathe of natural light to enter the clean, white interior while the vertical treatment raises the perceived height of the roof angle. A thin, glazed opening runs down from the apse window, creating a near-cruciform shape and casting a path of light along the middle of the nave. With dark merbau flooring and a small, lit backdrop behind the altar, the inside is warm and intimate, enveloping the visitor in its curved caress pointing toward the light.

As the space is meant to be used for secular as well as religious purposes, the architects devised a foldable reredos, a triptych set within a niche in the northern point of the ellipse, to be used for services. When the doors are opened they reveal a gold interior and hold a box, used for the objects of the holy rites, also made of Cor-ten steel, in the form of a Cross – taking the consistency of materials through even to the sanctum sanctorum. However, the Barbaríns seem to know instinctively how to use consistency to create reference points rather than rules, thus freeing themselves to reach further than matching new with old, and achieving greater heights.

NOTES

INTRODUCTION

1 H. W. Janson, *History of Art*, Thames and Hudson, 1995, p. 462.
2 Carol Herselle Krinsky, *Synagogues of Europe, Architecture, History, Meaning*, Architectural History Foundation, 1985, p. 21.
3 Krinsky, p. 24.
4 Renata Holod and Hasan-Uddin Khan, *The Mosque and the Modern World*, Thames and Hudson, 1997, p. 13.
5 Holod and Khan, p. 29.
6 Holod and Khan, p. 13.
7 James Steele, in Ismail Serageldin, ed., *Architecture of the Contemporary Mosque*, Academy Editions, 1996, p.46.

CHAPTER 2

INTRODUCTION

1 Renata Holod and Hasan-Uddin Khan, *The Mosque and the Modern World*, p. 64.

CHAPTER 3

MONASTERY OF NOVY DVUR

1 Book of Saints.
2 Honour and Fleming, *A World History of Art*, p. 385.
3 Panofsky, ed. and trans., *Abbot Suger on the Abbey Church of St. Denis*.
4 Alison Morris, 'The Monastery of Nový Dvur'.

CHAPTER 5

YANCEY CHAPEL

1 Andrea Oppenheimer Dean and Timothy Hursley, *Rural Studio, Samuel Mockbee and an Architecture of Decency*, Princeton Architectural Press, 2002

PAPER CHURCH

1 eqe.com/publications/kobe/introduc.htm

ANTIOCH BAPTIST CHURCH

1 ruralstudio.com/sambomemorial.htm

JESUIT RETREAT CHAPEL

1 *Sir Banister Fletcher's A History of Architecture*, p. 904

GLOSSARY

AMBO
raised pulpit from which the Gospel or the Epistles are read in a Christian church

BIMAH
a table on a raised platform from which the Torah is read

BUTSUDEN
main hall of a Buddhist temple

ISMAILI
member of the group of Shia muslims who follow the Aga Khan as their spiritual leader

JAMAT KHANA
Ismaili congregational/prayer space

MASJID-I JAMI
congregation mosque, usually a complex that contains various community services, such as library, offices, classrooms and meeting rooms as well as a main prayer space

MENORAH
the candelabrum used in Jewish worship containing seven or nine candles

MINYAN
in Jewish worship, the miminum number of ten males required to have a congregation or recite particular prayers

MIHRAB
the niche in the qibla wall of a mosque that indicates the direction of Mecca

MINBAR
pulpit used by the imam (one who leads prayers) in a mosque to address the congregation, usually set to the right of the mihrab

MISRACH
Hebrew, meaning 'east', used to refer to the wall of the synagogue that contains the Torah shrine

MUSHRABIYAH
in Islamic buildings, an ornamental screen, usually of carved wood, used on windows to modulate light and provide privacy

NARTHEX
the vesibule or portico leading to the nave of a church

PARVIS
an enclosed space or portico at the entrance to a church

QIBLA
the direction of prayer, towards Mecca, usually used to denote the wall in a mosque that faces in that direction

REREDOS
ornamental screen or partition behind the altar of a church

SAGRATO
churchyard

TORAH
the five books of Moses constituting the Pentateuch, which is the basis of Jewish Scripture. Often contained on a leather or parchment scroll and kept in an ornamental shrine which is the focal point of the synagogue prayer space.

ZALIJ
Moroccan-style mosaic technique using traditional ceramic tiles

Thanks to Renata Holod and Hasan-Uddin Khan, *The Mosque and the Modern World* and Carole Hershelle Krinsky, *Synagogues of Europe*

BIBLIOGRAPHY

BENEDICTINE Monks of St Augustine's Abbey, Ramsgate, compiled, *The Book of Saints, A Dictionary of Servants of God Canonised by the Catholic Church: Extracted from the Roman and Other Martyrologies*, Adam and Charles Black, London, 1942

BOECKL Matthias, 'A Spiritual Assertion, Roman Catholic Church in the Donau-City, Vienna, Austria', in *Architektur Aktuell*, May 2001, pp. 54, 64–65

CAIRD George B., *Our Dialogue with Rome: The Second Vatican Council and After, the Congregational Lectures 1966*, Oxford University Press, 1967

CROSBIE Michael, *Architecture for the Gods: Recent Religious Architecture in the Americas*, Images Publishing Group Pty Ltd, Mulgrave, 1999

CRUICKSHANK Dan, ed., *Sir Banister Fletcher's A History of Architecture*, Twentieth Edition, Architectural Press, London, 1996

DEAN Andrea Oppenheimer and Timothy Hursley, *Rural Studio, Samuel Mockbee and an Architecture of Decency*, Princeton Architectural Press, New York, 2002

HEATHCOTE Edwin and Iona Spens, *Church Builders*, Academy Editions, London, 1997

HECKER Zvi, 'Architecture – an Act of Magic', in *Architektur Aktuell*, 246/247, October 2000

HOLOD Renata and Hasan-Uddin Khan, *The Mosque and the Modern World, Architects, Patrons and Designs since the 1950s*, Thames and Hudson, London, 1997

HONOUR Hugh and John Fleming, *A World History of Art*, Laurence King Publishing, London, 1999

ISMAIL Dr. Muhammad Kamal, et al., *The Architecture of the Holy Mosque Makkah*, Hazar Publishing Ltd, London, 1998

ISMAIL Dr. Muhammad Kamal, et al., *The Architecture of the Prophet's Holy Mosque Al Madinah*, Hazar Publishing Limited, London, 1998

JANSON H.W., *History of Art*, revised and expanded by Anthony F. Janson, Thames and Hudson, London, 1995

KRINSKY Carol Herselle, *Synagogues of Europe, Architecture, History, Meaning*, The Architectural History Foundation (New York), MIT Press (Cambridge, MA, and London), 1985

MORRIS Alison, 'The Monastery of Nový Dvur', unpublished paper, May 2003

PANOFSKY Erwin, ed. and trans., *Abbot Suger on the Abbey Church of St-Denis and its Art Treasures*, Princeton University Press, 1946

SERAGELDIN Ismail, ed. with James Steele, *Architecture of the Contemporary Mosque*, Academy Editions, London, 1996

STEELE James, *Architecture and Computers: Action and Reaction in the Digital Design Revolution*, Laurence King Publishing, London, 2001

WIEDERIN Gerold, *Gerold Wiederin, Helmut Federle, Nachtwallfahrtskapelle Locherboden*, Kunsthaus Bregenz, Hatje, 1997

WEBSITES

PAPER CHURCH
eqe.com/publications/kobe/introduc.htm

ANTIOCH BAPTIST CHURCH
ruralstudio.com/sambomemorial.htm

PROJECT CREDITS
In alphabetical order by architect

IMAM MOHAMED IBN SAUD MOSQUE AND SQUARE RIYADH
CLIENT Arriyadh Development Authority, Riyadh, Saudi Arabia
ARCHITECT Abdelhalim I. Abdelhalim, PhD
61 Mohy Eddin Aboul Ezz St., Dokki
Giza, Egypt
T 202 34 74 272
halim@access.com.eg
CONTRACTOR World Center for Trade and Construction
ELECTRO MECHANICAL DESIGN Saud Consult
CDC DESIGN TEAM Mohammad Saeed, Architect, Ayman El Gohary, Archictect, Khaled El Badry, Architect
LANDSCAPE CONCEPT Bodecker

JAMAT KHANA UNIVERSITY OF NATAL
CLIENT University of Natal Jamat Khana Trust
ARCHITECTS Architects' Collaborative, P.O. Box 17181
Congella, South Africa, 4013
T 00 2731 2061591
F 00 2731 2061590
E ac@dbn.lia.net
DESIGN TEAM Kevin Maccarey, Yusuf Patel
STRUCTURAL ENGINEER Abdul Satharia
QUANTITY SURVEYOR Imtiaz Tayob
CONTRACTOR Mike Lawton
CRAFTSMEN Mohamed Kanar and team, Morocco

CHURCH OF THE SACRED HEART MUNICH
CLIENT Catholic Parish Foundation of the Sacred Heart
ARCHITECTS Allmann Sattler Wappner Architekten, BDA
Bothmerstrasse 14, 80634 Munich, Germany
T 49 (0)89 165 615
F 49 (0)89 169 263
E info@allmannsattlerwappner.de
www.allmansattlerwappner.de
PROJECT ARCHITECT Karin Hengher;
DESIGN TEAM Susanne Rath, Annette Gall, Michael Frank
LANDSCAPE ARCHITECTS Realgrün
STRUCTURAL ENGINEER Ingenieur-gesellschaft mbH Hagl; façade engineer: Ingenieurbüro für Fassadentechnik R+R Fuchs
ARTISTS glass entrance door, Alexander Beleschenko; curtain behind altar, Lutzenberger & Lutzenberger; Five Wounds, M+M; 14 Stations of the Cross, Matthias Wähner

KOMYO-JI TEMPLE SAIJO
ARCHITECT Tadao Ando Architect & Associates
5-23 Toyosaki 2-chome Kita-ku
Osaka 531-0072 Japan
T 81 6 6375 1148
F 81 6 6374 6240

OUR LADY OF THE ARK OF THE COVENANT PARIS
CLIENT Diocese of Paris
ARCHITECTS Architecture Studio

CALTEX TERMINAL MOSQUE KARACHI
CLIENT Caltex Oil Pakistan Ltd
ARCHITECT Mirza Abdulkader Baig
B-14, Belle View, Block-7, Clifton, Karachi, Pakistan
T 92 21 586 9435
F 92 21 586 9435
E archiplus@hotmail.com, baig@e-architect.com
GENERAL CONTRACTOR Ancon Engineers
FIBERGLASS DOME Sharp Fiberglass Co.
SPECIAL FINISHES Al-Khidmat Traders

PAPER CHURCH KOBE
ARCHITECT Shigeru Ban Architects
5-2-4 Matsubara, Setagaya-ku, Tokyo, Japan
T 81 3 3324 6760
F 81 3 3324 6789
E SBA@tokyo.email.ne.jp
www.dnp.co.jp/millennium/SB/VAN.html
PROJECT TEAM Shigeru Ban, Shigeru Hiraki
STRUCTURAL ENGINEERS Gengo Matsui, Shuichi Hoshino, Architect & Engineer, TSP Taiyo-Mihoko Uchida
GENERAL CONTRACTORS volunteers

JESUIT RETREAT CHAPEL NAVAS DEL MARQUÉS
CLIENT Jesuit Congregation of Toledo
ARCHITECT Ruíz Barbarín Arquitectos
C/ Julio Caro Baroja 142 bajo derecha
28050 Madrid, Spain
www.ruizbarbarinarquitectos.com
PROJECT TEAM Antonio Ruíz Barbarín, Javier Ruíz Barbarín
COLLABORATORS Antonio Balguerias Chico de Guzmán architect; Beatriz Martín (gold altar); Antonio Rosado (quantity surveyor)
CONTRACTOR Construcciones Santamaría

LOS NOGALES SCHOOL CHAPEL
BOGOTÁ
ARCHITECT Daniel Bonilla, Arquitectura y Urbanísmo
Diagonal 74A, No 2-07, OF. 201, Bogotá, Colombia
T 57 211 2296/235 9752
DESIGN TEAM Daniel Bonilla, Alejandro Borrero
COLLABORATORS Claudia Monroy, Johny Duarte
BUILDER Jaime Pizarro

CHURCH AND COMMUNITY CENTRE
URUBO
ARCHITECT Jae Cha, 1077 30th St NW, #712, Washington, DC 20007, USA
T 202 333 0166
F 202 333 0165
E j@jaecha.net
SPONSORS Kie Dong Lee, Deuk Soo Jung
COLLABORATORS Zack Hemmelgarn (CAD images)
CONSTRUCTION people of Urubo, Alex & Col, KCPC Bolivia STM 2000

ISLAMIC CULTURAL CENTRE
DUBLIN
ARCHITECT Michael Collins Associates, Newmount House, 22–24 Lower Mount Street, Dublin 2, Ireland
T 353 1 676 0916
F 353 1 661 1015
www.mca.ie
CLIENTS The Department of Endowment and Islamic affairs of Dubai and the Islamic Foundation of Ireland
STRUCTURAL ENGINEERS Arup Consulting Engineers
LANDSCAPE ARCHITECTS Brady Shipman Martin
QUANTITY SURVEYOR O'Malley Associates
SERVICES CONSULTANTS Varming Mulcahy Reilly Associates
MAIN CONTRACTOR Duggan Brothers (Contractors) Ltd

INTERFAITH SPIRITUAL CENTER
BOSTON
ARCHITECTS Office d'A, Monica Ponce de Leon and Nader Tehrani
57 East Concord St. #6, Boston, MA 02118, USA
T 617 267 7369
F 617 859 4948
E da@officeda.com
CLIENT Northeastern University Project Coordinator: Richard Lee
PROJECT TEAM Erik Egbertson, Ben Karty (computer drawings); Jill Porter, Jeffrey Asanza (working drawings); Yeong La (model); Patricia Chen (dome mock-up); Thamarit Suchart (curtain-wall mock-up); David Kunzig, Dana Manoliu, Salvatore Rafone, Philip Smith, Rusty Walker, Timothy Clark
Architect of Record: SmartArchitecture – Margaret Smart Booz, George Thrush, Nathan Bishop
LIGHTING CONSULTANTS Lam Partners, Inc.
MECHANICAL ENGINEERS Cosentini Associates LLP
ACOUSTICAL CONSULTANTS Acentech

FAITH HOUSE DORSET
ARCHITECT Tony Fretton Architects, 116–120 Golden Lane, London EC1Y OTF, England
CLIENT Holton Lee (East Holton Charity)
PRINCIPAL CONTRACTOR Unicorn Construction
DESIGN TEAM Tony Fretton, Jim McKinney, Klas Ruin, Emma Huckett (project architect during design), Matthew Barton, Matthew White (project architect during detailing and construction), Diego Ferrarri (design team artist)
STRUCTURAL ENGINEER Price and Myers
QUANTITY SURVEYOR Poynton Scrase

KOREAN PRESBYTERIAN CHURCH
NEW YORK
ARCHITECT Garofalo, Lynn, McInturf
Garofalo Architects, 3752 North Ashland Avenue, Chicago, IL 60613, USA,
T 773 975 2069, F 773 975 3005,
www.garofalo.a-node.net
Greg Lynn, FORM, T 310 821 2629
E glynn@idt.net, Los Angeles, CA, USA
Michael McInturf Architects, 1116 Race Street, Cincinnati, OH 45202, USA
T 513 639 2351, F 513 639 2353,
E go@mcinturf.com, www.mcinturf.com
CLIENT Korean Presbyterian Church of New York
ARCHITECTURAL DESIGN Garofalo Architects, Greg Lynn FORM, Michael Mcinturf Architects
DESIGN TEAM Phillip Anzalone (construction supervision), Dan Behnfeldt, Daniel Cantwell, Richard Garber, Douglas Garofalo (design principal), Chris Goode, Ellen Grimes, Donald Hearn, Kimberly Holden, Matt Jogan, Greg Lynn (design principal), Michael McInturf (design principal), Gregg Pasquarelli (construction supervision), Min Kyu Whang
STRUCTURAL ENGINEERING FTL Happold, New York
MECHANICAL ENGINEERING Lazlo Bodak Engineers
CODE CONSULTING Gerald Caliendo

STRASBOURG MOSQUE
Zaha Hadid Architects
Studio 9, 10 Bowling Green Lane, London EC1R OBQ, England
T 44 207 253 5147
F 44 207 251 8322
E press@zaha-hadid.com
www.zaha-hadid.com
DESIGN TEAM David Gerber, Ali Mangera, David Salazar, Jorge Ortega, Caroline Voet, Eddy Can, Patrik Schumacher, Woody Yao, Hon Kong Chee, Stephane Hof, Steve Power, Edgar Gonzalez, Garin O'Aivazian
STRUCTURAL ENGINEERS Adams Kara Taylor; Hanif Kara
ENVIRONMENTAL ENGINEERS Max Fordham and Partners, Henry Luker, Sam Archer
ACOUSTICS Ove Arup and Partners and Peutz et Associes S.A.R.L., Raj Patel, Richard Cowel, Yves Dehamel
LIGHTING Office for Visual Interaction, New York, Jean M. Sundin, Enrique Peiniger
DESIGN Dr. Salma Samar Damlugi
LOCAL ARCHITECT Albert Grandadam

SHINGON-SHU TEMPLE
KAGOSHIMA
DESIGN Thomas Heatherwick Studio
16 Acton Street
London WC1X 9NG, England
T 44 (0) 20 7833 8800
F 44 (0) 20 7833 8400
CLIENT Shingon-Shu Buddhists
EXECUTIVE ARCHITECT Mawatari Kogyo K.K.
STRUCTURAL ENGINEERING Packman Lucas Consulting Engineers
DESIGN AGENT Theo Theodorou
DEVELOPER Kaoru Ohsaki

JEWISH CULTURAL CENTRE
DUISBERG
ARCHITECT Zvi Hecker Architekt,
Oranienburger Str. 41, D-10117 Berlin,
Germany
T 49 30 275 82 67-0
F 49 30 275 82 67-7
E berlin@zvihecker.com
www.zvihecker.com
ASSISTANTS Petra Korff, Laurence Nash
Competition team: Eyal Weizman, Markus
Mannweiler, Magdalena Skoplak, Sönke
Christian Hutterer, Ines Bongard
CONTACT ARCHITECT Prof. Inken
Baller, Berlin
STRUCTURAL ENGINEER Prof.
Gerhard Pichler, Berlin
ASSISTANT Carsten Pammer
LANDSCAPE ARCHITECT Zvi Hecker
TECHNICAL ENGINEER Kalinowski
und Kappe, Köln

CHAPEL OF ST IGNATIUS SEATTLE
ARCHITECT Steven Holl Architects,
450 W 31st Street, 11th Floor, New York,
NY 10001, USA
T 212 629 7262
F 212 629 7312
E mail@stevenholl.com
www.stevenholl.com
CLIENT Seattle University
ASSOCIATE ARCHITECT Olson
Sundberg Architects
ENGINEERS Datum Engineers, Monte
Clark Engineering (structural); Abacus
Engineered Systems (mech., elec.,
plumbing)
GENERAL CONTRACTOR Baugh
Construction
CONSULTANTS Bill Brown, AIA P.C.
(liturgical); L'Observatoire International
(lighting), Peter George and Associates
(acoustical)

CHEMNITZ SYNAGOGUE
ARCHITECT Alfred Jacoby,
Falkensteinerstrasse 77, D 60322,
Frankfurt am Main, Germany
T 49 69 955 23316
F 49 69 555 601
E a001jacoby@aol.com
ASSOCIATE ARCHITECT Monika
Finger
LIGHTING Serien Raumleuchten, Jean-
Marc da Costa and Manfred Wolf
STAINED GLASS Prof. Johannes
Schreiter
LANDSCAPE ARCHITECT Ulrike
Stockert

KASSEL SYNAGOGUE
ARCHITECT Alfred Jacoby
(details as above)
PROJECT ARCHITECT Monika Finger
STRUCTURAL ENGINEER Schwarzbart
& Partner, Frankfurt
SERVICES ENGINEER ROM, Kassel
ACOUSTICS ENGINEER SWA, Aachen
LIGHTING DESIGNER Serien
Raumleuchten, Rodgau
STAINED GLASS WINDOW DESIGN:
Johannes Schreiter, Langen

MORTENSRUD CHURCH
ARCHITECT Jensen & Skodvin
Arkitektkontor
Kristian Augustsgt.19, 0164 Oslo, Norway
T 47 22 99 48 99
F 47 22 99 48 88
www.jsa.no
CLIENT Kirkelig Fellesråd i Oslo Terje
Oterholt
DESIGN TEAM Jan Olav Jensen (project
leader), Børre Skodvin, AnneLise Bjerkan,
Torunn Golberg, Torstein Koch, Siri
Moseng, Einar Bjarki Malmquist
ARTISTIC COORDINATOR Kirkelig
Kulturverksted
ARTIST Gunnar Torvund
INTERIOR ARCHITECT Terje Hope
STRUCTURAL ENGINEER ICG ASA
BUILDING LEADER Øivind Moen AS

**MEDITATION CENTRE AND
CEMETERY** FRÉJUS
ARCHITECT Bernard Desmoulin
Architecte
11, rue Danielle Casanova, 75001 Paris,
France
T 33 (1) 47 02 67 07
F 33 (1) 47 03 34 18
E BCD.desmoulin@wanadoo.fr
CLIENT Ministry of War Veterans
GENERAL CONTRACTOR Tassan

**SACRED HEART CHURCH AND
PARISH CENTRE** VÖLKLINGEN
ARCHITECT Lamott Architeckten BDA,
Silberburgstrasse 129a, D-70176 Stuttgart,
Germany
T 49 (0) 711-481061
F 49 (0) 711-4870291
E mail@lamott.de
www.lamott.de
CLIENT Sacred Heart Catholic Church,
Ludweiler
DESIGN TEAM Ansgar Lamott, Sonja
Schmucker, Andreas Ocker
STRUCTURAL ENGINEERS Schweitzer
GmbH
MECHANICAL ENGINEERS Manfred
Loos
CONSTRUCTION Erhardt + Hellmann
GmbH
COR-TEN FAÇADE Riehm GmBH
WOODEN CURTAIN WALL Annen KG
STEEL CURTAIN WALL Franz Hesedenz
GmbH

**CHAPEL OF ST MARY OF THE
ANGELS,** ROTTERDAM
ARCHITECT Mecanoo Architecten b.v.,
Postbus 3277-2601 DG Delft, Netherlands
T 31 (0)15 279 8100
F 31 (0)15 279 8111
E info@mecanoo.nl
www.mecanoo.nl
CLIENT St Lawrence Cemetery,
Rotterdam
DESIGN TEAM Francine Houben,
Francesco Veenstra, Ana Rocha, Huib de
Jong, Martin Stoop, Natascha Arala
Chaves, Judith Egberink, Henk Bouwer
STRUCTURAL ENGINEER ABT
adviesbureau voor bouwtechniek b.v.,
Delft
CONTRACTOR H&B Bouw b.v.
GRAPHIC DESIGN (TEXTS) Rick
Vermeulen
ARTIST Mark Deconink

JUBILEE CHURCH ROME
ARCHITECT Richard Meier & Partners, Architects
475 Tenth Avenue, 6th Floor
New York, NY 10018, USA
T 212 967 6060
F 212 967 3207
E mail@richardmeier.com
www.richardmeier.com
CLIENT Vicarate of Rome
STRUCTURAL ENGINEERS Ove Arup and Partners; Italcementi
MECHANICAL ENGINEERS Ove Arup and Partners; Luigi Dell'Aquila
LIGHTING CONSULTANTS FMRS; Erco

OUR LADY OF THE ANGELS
LOS ANGELES
ARCHITECT Rafael Moneo
Cinca 5, Madrid 28002, Spain
T 34 915 642 257
F 34 915 635 217
DESIGN TEAM Hayden Salter (project architect), David Campbell, Alberto Nicolas, Lori Bruns, Mariano Molina, Christoph
ASSOCIATE ARCHITECTS Leo A. Daly Architects, Nick Roberts, Jaime García, John Williams
LITURGICAL ART CONSULTANT Richard Vosko
LANDSCAPE ARCHITECT Campbell & Campbell
STRUCTURAL ENGINEER Nabih Youssef and Associates
MECHANICAL ENGINEER Ove Arup & Partners
CONSTRUCTION Morley Construction

NOVÝ DVUR MONASTERY PLZEN
ARCHITECT John Pawson, Unit B 70–78 York Way, London N1 9AG, England
T 44 (0) 207 837 2929
F 44 (0) 207 837 4949
E email@johnpawson.co.uk
www.johnpawson.com

CENTER OF GRAVITY HALL
NEW MEXICO
ARCHITECT Predock_Frane Architects
1819 Euclid Street, Santa Monica, CA 90404, USA
T (1) 310 399 2377
F (1) 310 399 2397
E hadrian@predockfrane.com
www.predockfrane.com
PROJECT TEAM John Frane, Hadrian Predock, Max Frixione
STRUCTURAL ENGINEER Vince Meyer, Sonalysts Inc.
MECHANICAL ENGINEER Norman Estanislao
CONTRACTOR Paul Kenderdine

CHAPEL OF RECONCILIATION
BERLIN
ARCHITECT Reitermann/Sassenroth Architekten
Roscherstrasse 4, 10629 Berlin, Germany
T 030 615 53 95
F 030 615 58 55
CLIENT Evangelische Versöhnungsgemeinde, Berlin
DESIGN TEAM Rudolf Reitermann, Peter Sassenroth
ASSISTANCE Cathrin Urbanek
STRUCTURAL CONSULTANT Pichler Igenieure GmbH, Berlin; Andreas Schulz
CLAY CONSULTANT Christoph Ziegert, Technische Universität, Berlin
COMPRESSED CLAY CONSTRUCTION Lehm Ton Erde, Schlins; Martin Rauch
FAÇADE/ROOF Merkle Holzbau GmbH
ALTAR Lehm Ton Erde, Schlins; Martin Rauch

CHURCH OF SAN GIOVANNI ROTONDO FOGGIA
ARCHITECT Renzo Piano Building Workshop
via P.P. Rubens, 29, 16158 Genoa, Italy
T 010/61711
F 010/6171350
E italy@rpbw.com
CLIENT Frati Minori Cappuccini (Province of Foggia)
PRELIMINARY DESIGN CONSULTANTS Ove Arup & Partners; Müller Bbm; G. Muciaccia; Mons. C. Valenziano, Rome; g. Grasso o.p., Genoa; STED; Studio Ambiente
DESIGN DEVELOPMENT AND CONSTRUCTION PHASE Favero & Milan, CO.RE. Ingegneria, Ove Arup & Partners; Manens Intertecnica; Müller Bbm; G. Muciaccia; Mons. C. Valenziano, Rome; Austin Italia; G. Amadeo; Tecnocons

ISMAILI CENTRE LISBON
ARCHITECT Raj Rewal Associates
S-7, Triveni, DDA Commercial Complex, Sheikh Sarai Phase-1, New Delhi-110017, India
T 26014101, 26015428
F 91-11-26015429
E rajrewal@del2.vsnl.net.in
ASSOCIATE ARCHITECT F. Vasassina
STRUCTURAL ENGINEER A2P (Lisbon)
STRUCTURAL ENGINEER FOR COMPETITION STAGE R.F.R. (Paris)

ANTIOCH BAPTIST CHURCH
PERRY COUNTY
ARCHITECT The Rural Studio, School of Architecture, 202 Dudley Commons, The College of Architecture, Design & Construction, Auburn University, AL 36849, USA
T (1) 334 844 5426
F (1) 334 844 5458
www.ruralstudio.com
STUDENT TEAM Gabe Michaud, Jared Fulton, Marion McElroy, Bill Nauck

YANCEY CHAPEL SAWYERVILLE
ARCHITECT The Rural Studio (details as above)
STUDENT TEAM Ruard Veltman, Steve Durden, Thomas Tretheway

PRIVATE CHAPEL VALLEACERÓN
ARCHITECT Sancho-Madridejos, Sol Madridejos, Juan Carlos Sancho Osinaga, C/Rios Rosas 47 B 3B, 28003 Madrid, Spain
T/F (34) 9155 36613
E soljc@sancho-madridejos.com
DESIGN TEAM Luis Renedo, Emilio Gomez-Ramos, Marta Toral, Juan Antonio Garrido, Ana Fernando Magarzo, Particia Planell, Javier Moreno
CONSTRUCTION Ignacio Diezma S.L.
PRINCIPAL CONSULTANTS Ignacio Aspe (structural engineer)

KOL AMI SYNAGOGUE
HOLLYWOOD
ARCHITECT Schweitzer BIM
5541 West Washington, Los Angeles, CA 90016, USA
T (1) 323 936 6163
E bim007@schweitzerbim.com
www.schweitzerbim.com
CLIENT Congregation Kol Ami (Rabbi Denise Eger)
DESIGN TEAM Josh Schweitzer, Tinka, Peter Strzebniok, Kelly Boston-Olvera, Robert Hsin
CONTRACTOR Howard CDM, Long Beach, California
STRUCTURAL ENGINEERS Gordon Polon
ELECTRICAL, MECHANICAL, PLUMBING Donlite and Associates
CIVIL ENGINEERS KPFF Consulting Engineers
ARTIST Laurie Gross (glass panels for the ark)

SANTO OVIDIO ESTATE CHAPEL
DOURO
ARCHITECT Álvaro Siza-Arquitecto, LDA.
Rua do Aleixo, 53 – 2º
4150–043 Porto, Portugal
T 22 6167270
F 22 6167279
E siza@mail.telepac.pt
PRINCIPAL IN CHARGE José Luís Carvalho Gomes
COLLABORATORS Ashton Richards, Rafaelle Leone, Francesca Montalto, Mitsunori Nakamura
SURCTURAL ENGINEER GOP-Eng. João Maria Sobreira
MECHANICAL ENGINEER Matos Campos
LANDSCAPE ARCHITECT João Gomes da Silva and Álvaro Siza Vieira
GENERAL CONTRACTOR João Carlos Sousa Cunha
CARPENTER José Nuno

CHRIST CHURCH DONAU CITY
ARCHITECT Heinz Tesar
Seidlgasse 41/9 A-1030 Vienna, Austria
T (43 1) 715 48 98
F (43 1) 715 48 99
E atelier.tesar@eunet.at
CLIENT Archdiocese of Vienna
PROJECT MANAGER Oliver Aschenbrenner
ASSISTANCE Achim Bilger, Urs Geiger, Heidi Schatzl, Franz Steinberger, Marc Tesar, Susanne Veit
STRUCTURAL ENGINEER ARGE Lindlbauer & Zehetner, Vienna
FAÇADE CLADDING Ing. A. Sauritschnig GesembH., St. Veit/Glan
CONTRACTOR Steiner Bau GesembH., St Paul/Lavanttal

NEW SYNAGOGUE DRESDEN
ARCHITECT Andrea Wandel, Hubertus Wandel, Dr. Rena Wandel Hoefer, Andreas Hoefer, Prof. Wolfgang Lorch, Nikolaus Hirsch,
Wandel, Hoefer Lorch + Hirsch, Dolomitenweg 19, 66119 Saarbrücken, Germany
T 0681 92655-0
F 0681 92655-95
E info@wandel-hoefer-lorch.de
CLIENT Jewish Community of Dresden
ASSISTANCE Kuno Fontaine, Christoph Kratzsch, Dirk Lang, Lukas Petrikoff, Tobias Wagner
STRUCTURAL CONSULTANT Schweitzer Ingenieure, Saarbrücken
STRUCTURAL PHYSICAL ACOUSTICS Müller BBM, Dresden
PROJECT MANAGER Fischer Projektmanagement, Leipzig

NIGHT PILGRIMAGE CHAPEL
LOCHERBODEN
ARCHITECT Gerold Wiederin
Schönbrunnerstrasse 31/19, A-1050 Vienna, Austria
T 01 586 96 76
F 01 586 81 79
E arch.wiederin@netway.at
STRUCTURAL ENGINEER Manfred Zeissel
GLASS SCULPTURE Helmut Federle
CLIENT Pfarramt Mötz, Pfarrer Cons. P. Johannes Messner O. Cist
COMPETITION ORGANIZERS Dorferneuerung Tirol

WHITE TEMPLE KYOTO
ARCHITECT Takashi Yamaguchi and Associates
7F Fusui Building 1-3-4
Ebisunishi Naniwa-ku, Osaka 556000 Japan
T (81) (0) 666333775
F (81) (0) 666335175
E ya@yamaguchi-a.jp
PRINCIPAL ARCHITECT Takashi Yamaguchi
STRUCTURE Taiki Maehara, SD Room

GLASS TEMPLE KYOTO
ARCHITECT Takashi Yamaguchi and Associates
(details as above)
PRINCIPAL ARCHITECT Takashi Yamaguchi
STRUCTURE Taiki Maehara: SD Room

INDEX

Page references in *italics* refer to illustrations

Abdelhalim, Abdelhalim I. 147, 152, *153*, *154*, *155*
alabaster 162, *167*, 169
Allmann Sattler Wappner *146*, 147, 148, *149–50*, 151
Ando, Tadao 12, *13*, 106, *107–9*, 110, *111*
Antioch Baptist Church, Alabama *186*, 187, 206, *207*, 208, *209*
Architects' Collaborative 63, 70, *71*, 72, *73*
Architecture Studio 15, 63, 64, *65*, 66, *67–8*, 69

Baig, Mirza Abdelkader 17, 22, *23–4*, 25
Ban, Shigeru 12, 187, 202, *203–4*, 205
belltowers *19*, 30, *31*, 64, *66*, 69, *99*, 100
Beth Shalom Synagogue, Pennsylvania 9, 11
Bonilla, Daniel 147, 180, *181–3*, 184, *185*
Brasilia Cathedral, Brazil 9, 11
Bryggman, Erik 162

Caltex Terminal Mosque, Karachi 17, 22, *23–4*, 25
campaniles *see* belltowers
Cathedral Church of Our Lady of the Angels, Los Angeles 147, 162, *163–8*, 169
Cathedral of Hope, Dallas 11
Center of Gravity Hall, New Mexico 12, 113, 124, *125–7*, 128, *129*
Cha, Jae 12, 15, 187, 192, *193–4*, 195
Chapel at Valleacerón, Spain 15, 38, *39–40*, 41, *42–3*
Chapel of Reconciliation, Berlin 15, 63, 78, *79*, 80, *81*
Chapel of St. Ignatius, Seattle 17, 18, *19–20*, 21
Chapel of St. Mary of the Angels, Rotterdam 17, 48, *49–50*, 51
Chemnitz Synagogue, Germany 17, 52, *53–5*, *56*, *57*
Christ Church, Vienna *62*, 63, *98*, 99–100, *101*
Christian buildings 7, 11, 63, 130, 147, 162
Church and Community Centre, Urubo, Bolivia 12, 15, 187, 192, *193–4*, 195
Church near Oslo, Norway 147, 196, *197–8*, 199–200, *201*

Church of San Giovanni Rotondo, Foggia, Italy 147, 170, *171–3*, 174, *175*
Church of the Light, Ibaraki, Japan 12, *13*, 106
Church of the Sacred Heart, Munich 15, *146*, 147, 148, *149–50*, 151
colour 17, 18, 21, 23, 48, 56, 104
computer technology 12, 17, 26–9, 90, 113, 122, 170, 174
concrete 11, 15, *19*, 21, 30, *32*, 61, 134
Crystal Cathedral, California 9, 11, 148

Dar al-Islam Foundation Mosque, New Mexico 10, 11
Deconstructionism 196
Desmoulin, Bernard 15, 113, 114, *115–16*, 117
domes 8, 22, *23*, 77, 90, 158, 174
Dresden Synagogue, Germany 63, 147, 176, *177*, 178, *179*
dry-stone walling *197*, *198*, 199, 200, *201*
Duisberg Cultural Centre & Synagogue, Germany 17, 34–5, *36*, 37
Durden, Steve 188, 191

eco-friendly buildings 12, 15, 113, 121, 124, 187, 188–209
El-Wakil, Abdel Wahed *10*, 11–12
Estudio Sancho-Madridejos 15, 17, 38, *39–40*, 41, *42–3*

Faith House, Dorset 12, 113, 118, *119–20*, 121
Fathy, Hassan *10*, 11
Federle, Helmut 134, *135*, 137
Frane, John 12, 113, 124, *125–7*, 128, *129*
Fretton, Tony 12, 113, 118, *119–20*, 121
Fulton, Jared 206
Futurism 11, 48

Garofalo, Douglas 12, 17, 26, *27*, 28, *29*
glass 15, 30, 32, 44, 47, 96, *97*, 148–51
Glass Temple, Kyoto 17, 44, *45–6*, 47

Hadid, Zaha 15, *16*, 58, *59–60*, 61
Hameed, Babar *10*, 11
Heatherwick, Thomas 15, 113, 122–3
Hecker, Zvi 12, 17, 34–5, *36*, 37
Holl, Steven 15, 17, 18, *19–20*, 21
Houben, Francine 48, 51

Imam Mohamed ibn Saud Mosque, Riyadh 147, 152, *153*, 154, *155*
International Style 38, 92
Interfaith Spiritual Centre, Boston 74, *75–6*, 77
Islamic Cultural Centre, Dublin 147, 156–7, 158, *159*, 160, *161*
Ismaili Centre, Lisbon 63, 86, *87–8*, 89–90, *91*

Jacoby, Alfred 15, 52, 102
  Chemnitz synagogue 17, 52, *53–5*, 56, *57*
  Kassel synagogue 63, 102, *103*, 104, *105*
Jamat Khana, Durban-Natal, South Africa 63, 70, *71*, 72, *73*
Jensen & Skodvin 147, 196, *197–8*, 199–200, *201*
Jesuit Retreat Chapel, Ávila, Spain 187, 210, *211–12*, 213
Johnson, Philip 9, 11, 148
Jones, E. Fay 12, *13*
Jubilee Church, Rome 30, *31*, 32, *33*

Kassel Synagogue, Germany 63, 102, *103*, 104, *105*
King Faisal Foundation Mosque, Riyadh *10*, 12
King Saud Mosque, Jeddah *10*, 12
Kol Ami Synagogue, Hollywood 63, 82, *83*, 84, *85*
Komyo-ji Temple, Japan 12, 106, *107–9*, 110, *111*
Korean Presbyterian Church, New York 12, 17, 26, *27*, 28, *29*

Lamott Architekten 15, 63, 92, *93–5*, 96, *97*
Le Corbusier *6*, 7, 11, 38, 162
Leiviskä, Juha 12, *13*
lettering 58, 61, 66, 82, 84, 96, 114
light 12, 15, 17, 18, 38, 41, 47, 77
loam 15, 80, *81*, 124, *125*
Los Nogales School Chapel, Bogotá 147, 180, *181–3*, 184, *185*
Lynn, Greg 12, 17, 26, *27*, 28, *29*

Madridejos Fernández, Sol *see* Estudio Sancho-Madridejos
Masjid-i Tooba, Karachi 10, 11
materials 12, 15, 104, 113, 117, 184 *see also* types of material
McElroy, Marion 206
McInturf, Michael 12, 17, 26, 27, 28, 29
McKinney, Jim 118
Mecanoo Architecten 17, 48, 49–50, 51
Meditation Centre & Cemetery, Fréjus, France 113, 114, 115–16, 117
Meier, Richard 11, 15, 17, 30, 31, 32, 33
metal
 brass 178, 179
 chromium-steel 98, 99
 copper 48, 50–1
 Cor-Ten (pre-rusted) steel 15, 92, 96, 114, 213
 salvaged 12, 187, 191, 206
 stainless steel 15, 63, 64, 66, 69
Michael Collins Associates 8, 147, 156–7, 158, 159, 160, 161
Michaud, Gabe 206
minimalism 44, 64, 92, 96, 106, 113, 138
Mockbee, Samuel 186, 187, 188, 189–90, 191, 208
Modernism 11, 118, 137, 148, 169
Moneo, Rafael 162, 163–8, 169
Mosque Project, Strasbourg 16, 58, 59–60, 61
mosques 7, 8, 11, 22, 63, 70, 147 *see also* individual mosques
multi-denominational buildings 8, 74–7, 114, 117
Murphy, Brian 158, 160
Myyrmäki Church, Finland 12, 13

natural setting 38, 41, 118, 121, 147, 196, 199, 200
Nauck, Bill 206
Niemeyer, Oscar 9, 11
Night Pilgrimage Chapel, Austria 113, 134, 135–6, 137
Notre-Dame-du-Haut, Ronchamp, France 6, 7, 11, 38
Nový Dvur Monastery & Chapel, Czech Republic 113, 130, 131, 132, 133

Office d'A 63, 74, 75–6, 77
orientation of buildings 8, 34, 53, 123, 160
Our Lady of the Ark of the Covenant Church, Paris 64, 65, 66, 67–8, 69

paper 12, 15, 65, 66, 187, 202–5
Paper Church, Kobe, Japan 12, 187, 202, 203–4, 205
paper tube structure (PTS) 12, 187, 202–5
Patel, Yusuf 63, 70, 72
Pawson, John 15, 113, 130, 131, 132, 133
Piano, Renzo 15, 170, 171–3, 174, 175
polycarbonate sheeting 124, 126, 128, 187, 192, 195
Ponce de Leon, Monica 77
ponds/pools 19, 32, 52, 88, 89, 96, 107, 184
Postmodernism 196
Predock, Hadrian 12, 113, 124, 125–7, 128, 129

rammed earth *see* loam
Rauch, Martin 80
recycled materials 12, 15, 65, 66, 80, 187, 188–91, 206
Reitermann, Rudolf 78
Reitermann Sassenroth Architekten 15, 63, 78, 79, 80, 81
Rewal, Raj 63, 86, 87–8, 89–90, 91
Ruíz Barbarín Arquitectos 187, 210, 211–12, 213
Rural Studio
 Antioch Baptist Church 12, 186, 187, 206, 207, 208, 209
 Yancey Chapel 12, 187, 188, 189–90, 191

Sacred Heart Church & Parish Centre, Völklingen, Germany 63, 92, 93–5, 96, 97
Saint-Pierre, Firminy, France 11
Sancho Osinago, Juan Carlos *see* Estudio Sancho-Madridejos
Santo Ovidio Estate Chapel, Portugal 113, 142, 143, 144, 145
Sassenroth, Peter 78
Schweitzer, Josh 63, 82, 83, 84, 85
separation in buildings 7, 8, 22, 61, 72, 117
Shingon-Shu Buddhist Temple & Ossuary, Japan 15, 113, 122–3

Siza, Álvaro 113, 142, 143, 144, 145
slate 34, 104, 210, 213
Sogn Benedetg chapel, Switzerland 12, 14
spirituality 7, 15, 17, 21, 22, 41, 106, 113
St. Peter's, Rome 7
stained glass 38, 56, 66, 102, 104, 137
stone 37, 116, 144, 170, 174
symbolism 17, 34–5, 37, 56, 64, 69, 84
synagogues 7, 147 *see also* individual synagogues

Tange, Kenzo 10, 12
Tehrani, Nader 77
temples 8, 44, 47, 106, 124, 147 *see also* individual temples
Tesar, Heinz 15, 62, 63, 98, 99–100, 101
Thorncrown Chapel, Arkansas 12, 13
Tretheway, Thomas 188, 191

urban environments 15, 17, 58, 62–111, 163, 164, 169

Veltman, Ruard 188, 191

Wandel, Hoefer, Lorch & Hirsch 15, 176, 177, 178, 179
water 58, 61, 110 *see also* ponds/pools
White Temple, Kyoto 44, 112, 113, 138, 139–40, 141
Wiederin, Gerold 113, 134, 135–6, 137
wood
 in building structure 106, 110, 122–3, 206, 208
 cladding 15, 100, 102, 104, 105, 118, 121
 in eco-friendly buildings 12, 128
 polished 76, 77
 salvaged 188, 191, 206
Wright, Frank Lloyd 9, 11

Yamaguchi, Takashi
 Glass Temple 17, 44, 45–6, 47
 White Temple 112, 113, 138, 139–40, 141
Yancey Chapel, Alabama 12, 187, 188, 189–90, 191

Zumthor, Peter 12, 14

PICTURE CREDITS

6 Paul M.R. Maeyaert/©FLC/ADAGP, Paris and DACS, London, 2004
9 no. 2, Alan Weintraub/Arcaid; no. 3, John Edward Linden/Arcaid; no.4, Reto Guntli/Arcaid;
10 nos 5,7,8, courtesy of the Aga Khan Trust for Culture; no. 6, courtesy Gary Otte
13 no. 9, Mitsuo Matsuoka; no. 10, Arno de La Chapelle; no 11, Timothy Hursley
14 Hélène Binet
16 courtesy Zaha Hadid
18 no.1, Hisao Suzuki
19 no. 4, courtesy Steven Holl Architects; no.5, Paul Warchol; no. 6, Hisao Suzuki
20 no. 8, Paul Warchol
21 no. 9, Paul Warchol
22–25 The Aga Khan Trust for Culture
26–29 Michael McInturf Architects
30–33 all hand sketches © Richard Meier; computer renderings, photos and drawings © Richard Meier & Partners
34–37 Michael Kruger
38–43 Hisao Suzuki
44–47 Yamaguchi Associates
48–51 Christian Richters
52–57 Werner Huthmacher, Berlin
58–61 Zaha Hadid
62 Christian Richters
64–69 Architecture-Studio
70–77 The Aga Khan Trust for Culture
78–81 Bruno Klomfar
82–85 Douglas Hill
86–91 Manu Rewal and Architectural Research Cell
92–97 Werner Huthmacher, Berlin
98–101 Christian Richters
102–105 Werner Huthmacher, Berlin
106 no.1, Shigeo Ogawa; no. 2, Tadao Ando Architect & Associates
107–111 Mitsuo Matsuoka
112 Yamaguchi Associates
114–117 Bernard Desmoulin
118–121 Hélène Binet
123 Steve Speller/Thomas Heatherwick Studio
124–129 Jason Predock/Courtesy Predock_Frane Architects
130–133 John Pawson
134–137 Christian Kerez/Gerold Wiederin
138–141 Yamaguchi Associates
142–145 Duccio Malagamba
146 Christian Richters
148 Christian Richters
149 no. 2, Florian Holzherr; no. 3, Christian Richters
150–151 Christian Richters
152–161 The Aga Khan Trust for Culture
162–169 Duccio Malagamba
170–172 Gianni Berengo Gardin/©Renzo Piano Building Workshop
173 Michel Denancé/©Renzo Piano Building Workshop
174–175 Gianni Berengo Gardin/©Renzo Piano Building Workshop
176–179 Norbert Miguletz
180–185 Jorge Gamboa/Daniel Bonilla Arquitectos
186 Timothy Hursley
188–191 Timothy Hursley
192–195 Daniel Lama/Jae Cha
196–197 Jiri Havran
198 no. 5, Jiri Havran; no. 6, Jan Olav Jensen
199 Jiri Havran
200–201 Jan Olav Jensen
202–205 Shigeru Ban
206–209 Timothy Hursley
210–212 Hisao Suzuki

ACKNOWLEDGEMENTS

The author wishes to thank all of the architects included in the book for their participation and assistance. In many cases they have supplied their own photography which has been invaluable to the project. Though architects and staff for each project have provided help with questions and material for which I am grateful, I would thank some by name, such as Monika Finger, in the office of Alfred Jacoby, Kirsten Martin at Thomas Heatherwick, Lisetta Koe at Richard Meier, Alison Morris at John Pawson, Sandra Dominguez at Rafael Moneo and Sonke Christian Hutterer at Zvi Hecker for dealing with extra queries, details, photos, drawings, etc. Thanks to Yusuf Patel of Architects' Collaborative for answering questions about mosques in general and many details of his design in particular. Thanks to Tony Fretton for a lengthy talk about Faith House and energy-saving architecture and to Thomas Heatherwick for a fascinating tour around the studio. Thanks also to Peggy Kelly for an early preview of the Los Angeles Cathedral and to the Ismaili Council Management Board, one of whose members provided an enlightening impromptu guided tour of the London Ismaili Centre. Grateful acknowledgement to Farrokh Derakhshani of the Aga Khan Trust for Culture for taking me through the archives in Geneva and William O'Reilly for searching out and providing numerous images – we thank the Trust itself for allowing us to reprint them all here. I am grateful to those architects who sent me images of their work that I wasn't able to include but which provided inspiration nonetheless. I must express my appreciation for the enthusiasm and support of Liz Faber, Philip Cooper, Kim Sinclair and all at Laurence King who made the book happen. Special thanks to Sue Walters for invaluable care and attention during this project and others.